WHITE HORIZON

SUNY series, Studies in the Long Nineteenth Century
Pamela K. Gilbert, editor

WHITE HORIZON

THE ARCTIC IN THE NINETEENTH-CENTURY BRITISH IMAGINATION

Jen Hill

STATE UNIVERSITY OF NEW YORK PRESS

Published by
State University of New York Press, Albany

© 2008 State University of New York

Printed in the United States of America

Cover: Ice floes in the Arctic, c1913. Courtesy of the Library of Congress Prints and Photographs Division, Washington, D.C. 20540. Reproduction no. LC-USZ62-101009

A portion of Chapter 2 appeared in *Nineteenth-Century Studies* and is used with permission of the University of California Press and the Regents of the University of California. "National Bodies: Robert Southey's *Life of Nelson* and John Franklin's *Narrative of a Journey to the Shores of the Polar Sea*." *Nineteenth-Century Studies* Vol. 61, no. 4, pp. 417–448. Copyright © 2007 by the Regents of the University of California.

For information, contact State University of New York Press, Albany, NY
www.sunypress.edu

Production by Kelli Williams-Leroux
Marketing by Fran Keneston

Library of Congress Cataloging in Publication Data

Hill, Jen.
  White horizon : the Arctic in the nineteenth-century British
imagination / Jen Hill.
     p. cm. — (SUNY series, studies in the long nineteenth century)
  Includes bibliographical references (p.   ) and index.
  ISBN 978-0-7914-7229-3 (alk. paper)
  1. English fiction—19th century—History and criticism. 2. Arctic
regions—In literature. 3. Geography in literature. 4. Explorers in
literature. 5. Adventure and adventurers in literature. 6. Imperialism
in literature. I. Title.

PR868.A72H56 2007
823'.80932113—dc22

                                        2007008098

              10 9 8 7 6 5 4 3 2 1

CONTENTS

ACKNOWLEDGMENTS

Support for this project came from many sources. At Cornell University I received generous travel, study, and research support from the English Department, The Graduate School, The Mellon Foundation, The School for Criticism and Theory, and the Shin family. A Junior Faculty Research Grant from the University of Nevada, Reno, and appointment as Lincoln and Meta Fitzgerald Distinguished Professor of the Humanities made completion of the manuscript possible.

I am also indebted to the faculty, staff, and resources of Cornell University Libraries, the Scott Polar Research Institute, the John Johnson Collection of Printed Ephemera at the Bodleian Library, the Derbyshire County Council Archives, the British Library, and Getchell Library at the University of Nevada, Reno.

My thinking continues to be shaped by many individuals whom I encountered at Cornell. I especially thank Dorothy Mermin, who as director of my dissertation helped me become a scholar. Harry Shaw, Paul Sawyer, and Mark Seltzer encouraged my work in its earliest incarnations. The generosity of Michael Koch and Stephanie Vaughn is evidenced on every page. Thanks are due also to Benedict Anderson, A. R. Ammons, Laura Brown, Walter Cohen, Mark Dimunation, Lamar Herrin, Timothy Murray, Reeve Parker, Katherine Reagan, Neil Saccamano, and Shelley Wong.

At the University of Nevada, Reno, I have been encouraged by members of the Consortium for British Isles and Empire Studies, including Stacy Burton, Dennis Dworkin, Louis Niebur, Aaron Santesso, and Tom Nickles. I would also like to thank Kathy and Phil Boardman,

Dennis Cronan, Jane Detweiler, Ann Keniston, Susan Palwick, and Ann Ronald, as well as deans Bob Mead and Heather Hardy. Gwynne Middleton, Sarah Hillenbrandt, and Jack Caughey helped prepare the manuscript. I cannot calculate my debt to the Center for Child and Family Development, in particular to Mary Schuster and Geri Thweatt.

This book is better for the careful considerations and encouragement that many people gave the manuscript. My reading of *Jane Eyre* arrived in conversation with Bethany Schneider, and it is unclear where her ideas end and mine commence. David Agruss, David Alvarez, Leah Rosenberg, and Kate Thomas also helped shape my arguments. Nancy Henry and Noah Heringman provided excellent and clarifying comments, as did a few anonymous readers, and Philip Rogers supplied thoughtful and generous connections with his own work. Mark Quigley helped me talk through and realize final versions of the argument.

My parents Frances and David Hill have always supported my endeavors, as have my sister Ali Hill and her cheerful family, Chris, Will, and Nick Ford.

Finally, I wish to thank Larry and Ella Cantera, who have encouraged, supported, persevered, and laughed with me in times both charmed and challenging.

I dedicate this book to the memory of John D. Hill: brother, friend, teacher.

CHAPTER ONE

HEART OF WHITENESS

In the opening pages of *Heart of Darkness*, the narrator names two of the great "knights" of British exploration, Sir Francis Drake and Sir John Franklin.[1] Readers can still place Drake, but most modern editions describe Franklin in a brief footnote as a nineteenth-century explorer who commanded an ill-fated expedition in search of the Northwest Passage. Joseph Conrad's contemporaries needed no such note: for them, the reference to Franklin and his ships the *Erebus* and *Terror* evoked both nineteenth-century geography at the height of its promise and, more importantly, the eclipse of that promise, and the recognition of the limits of British exploration that was the legacy of Franklin's spectacular failure. While the invocation of a doomed polar explorer at the outset of Conrad's great critique of imperialism serves to foreshadow Marlow's own horrific voyage up the Congo, the reference maps Arctic geography onto the national imagination, enfolding a literally white space into the heart of darkness. Thus, when Marlow speaks of white spaces on the map, a meditation on Arctic exploration and the limits of the European imperial project lingers behind Conrad's image.

In 1844, Sir John Franklin was awarded command of the Arctic exploration ships *Erebus* and *Terror* and given an Admiralty mandate to find the Northwest Passage. The expedition's departure was a kind of mass spectacle, with newspaper articles detailing its preparations and the public thronging to see the ships before they embarked in the spring of 1845. Franklin and his 130 men departed and, after calling in at Greenland on their way to the frozen seas, were never heard from again, despite numerous and concerted efforts to find them. The mystery of

1

what happened to these British seamen and the effort to discover and interpret the expedition's traces captured Britain's—and much of the world's—attention for years. A historian's description of the ships' provisions reads like the introduction to the greatest Arctic narrative never written by its participants:

> Enormous quantities of provisions and fuel were carried; china, cut glass, and heavy Victorian silver encumbered the wardrooms; each ship had a library of twelve hundred volumes ranging from treatises on steam engines to the works of Dickens and Lever and volumes of *Punch*. . . . Slates and arithmetic books, pens, ink and paper were provided for classes during the winter; testaments and prayer-books were available for all; and a hand-organ, playing fifty tunes, ten of which were psalms or hymns, was purchased for each ship. Of special Polar equipment, except for scientific research, there was none apart from large supplies of warm underclothing and a few wolf-skin blankets.[2]

It is easy to read a distinctly "Victorian" narrative into the Franklin expedition's failure, one of men done in by knickknacks: taking silver tea services instead of lightweight sledges; wearing the blue cotton and wool of the British Navy in place of sealskin anoraks; reading novels and plays by Shakespeare in lieu of survival manuals. Under this rubric, Franklin's disappearance is a product of what we think of as Victorian hubris; the confidence that led Franklin to scoff at provisions for his rescue in planning his mission is a direct extension of the same self-confident assumption of privilege with which the British Empire claimed the globe. No wonder mid-century Britons so desperately wanted to find Franklin and his crew that over the next ten years dozens of Admiralty-affiliated and privately sponsored voyages embarked in search of the *Erebus* and *Terror*. Not surprisingly, the mystery of the ships' disappearance fuelled intense public interest: while editorials speculated about the missing men, families who visited the Arctic panorama at Vauxhall shivered to imagine the expedition's fate. For twenty-first-century readers, it seems as if the avidity with which the Victorians sought to retrieve Franklin was part of some prescient effort to arrest (or at least delay) the collapse of the British Empire and Great Britain's twentieth-century decline.

But of course that is an argument of hindsight, a narrative with Robert Scott's 1912 quest for the South Pole (and his Franklin-like failure) as its telos. The mid-nineteenth-century cultural preoccupation with the fate of the Franklin expedition can be more fully understood in context of the wider and more long-term function of Arctic space in the British national-cultural imaginary. Even before Samuel Taylor Coleridge's *The Rime of the Ancient Mariner* and Mary Shelley's *Frankenstein*, polar space had come to represent the limit of both empire and human experience. Exploring and mapping the Arctic was a self-conscious exercise in national masculine identity building perceived to take place in "empty" space, documented in best-selling expedition accounts that marketed a heroic masculinity that found its origin in representations of Trafalgar hero Horatio Nelson's early voyage to the Arctic seas, the Antarctic voyages of Cook, and a romanticized recollection of Henry Hudson. Framed in this heroic context, Franklin's disappearance reads as a form of cultural aporia, an incident of literal "lost passage" that revealed the important symbolic role of the Arctic in imagining national and imperial masculinity, and forced on Victorians a reluctant recognition that these models were much less stable than had been understood. In Franklin's failure to negotiate it, Arctic space was revealed—perhaps as unexpectedly for contemporary Britons as it is to us—to be central to the ways Britons imagined, justified, and even critiqued their nation and empire.

Building on rich archival investigations and fine analyses by Eric Wilson and Francis Spufford,[3] I argue in the pages that follow that the Arctic was a test limit for ideas the Romantics and Victorians had about themselves, a place in which they experimented with and made legible forms of identity and their attendant anxieties. In other words, the Arctic was as much ideological as physical terrain, one on which Britons could stage debates about domestic and imperial identities, far from British and colonial shores. Ian Baucom has argued in his investigation of English identity that Englishness "has consistently been defined through appeals to the identity-endowing properties of place," and that debates about identity are thus frequently spatialized, both in discussions that are framed with spatial metaphorics and in military and other imperial actions that seek to define national and imperial spaces.[4] The Arctic in the nineteenth century was one such space, one that even as it was mapped by British explorers, remained out of the physical reach of ordinary people, and was thus paradoxically perceived to be accessible to all as a representational space, a blank page on which to draft different national and imperial narratives that either embraced or critiqued Britain's increased investments in imperial and colonial projects.

In that regard, the shifting representations of Arctic exploration and geography in nineteenth-century discourse provide a remarkably rich corpus of material to trace larger cultural discussions relating to gender, nation, race, and empire. In the chapters that follow, I examine widely read early polar exploration accounts and, in turn, the literary texts they influenced. I am not arguing for a hidden polar subtext that, when brought to our attention, reveals heretofore inaccessible meaning. Rather, I seek to include Arctic space in the complex cultural imaginary that critics such as Edward Said and Gayatri Spivak have encouraged us to read for its unexamined articulations and justifications of imperial practices. Certainly, for nineteenth-century readers, the Arctic was not in any way a "hidden" subtext nor limited to the paratextual polar engravings from Bewick's *History of British Birds* that Charlotte Brontë describes in her opening chapter of *Jane Eyre*. Popular depictions of Arctic endeavor and its relationship to a metropolitan populace ranged widely, from George Cruikshank's satirical skepticism of the scientific value of the much-lauded 1819 Arctic expeditions in his engraving "Landing the Treasures" to Arctic-themed dinner parties to sheet music celebrating ice floes, such as Frost's "Arctic Expeditions Galop." In this context, it shouldn't surprise us that when accusations of cannibalism were leveled at the missing crew members of the *Erebus* and *Terror*, Charles Dickens's popular journalism documented an Arctic obsession he later displaced into melodrama in his production of and performances in the play *The Frozen Deep*, written with the sensation novelist Wilkie Collins.

As I examine in the following pages, there is a genealogy of polar narrative in the nineteenth century, one that starts with masculinist exploration accounts, embraces domestic and sensation fictions of mid-century, and ends with the overtly imperial genre of boy's adventure fiction of George MacDonald and R. M. Ballantyne. British Arctic narrative is traceable through three distinct phases that correspond with different periods of British colonial encounter and expansion: an early phase during which Britain's main imperial focus is on the West Indies and fears of miscegenation and disease, a second phase in which the disappearance of Franklin coincides with unrest and resistance to British rule in India, and a third phase, following the discovery of the Northwest Passage, that accompanies Britain's expansion into Africa and its recognition that its imperial preeminence would not last.[5] In each of these periods, Arctic space was a literal and metaphorical terrain on which Britons seeking to navigate between and integrate national and imperial identities mapped British values, a "pure" space conceived as being separate from not only from the problematic political, racial, and economic relations of empire, but from potential class conflict at home. In articles, novels, plays, and poetry, the Arctic was a landscape on which assertions and critiques of nation and empire could unroll at a literal "safe distance."

FRANKLIN'S DISAPPEARANCE

What is known of Franklin's 1845 expedition is a fragmented tale, assembled over an expanse of space and time: hundreds of thousands of square miles of territory were covered in more than 150 years of searching and speculation. The *Erebus* and *Terror* left England in the spring of 1845, laid up in western Greenland for a transfer of supplies, and then departed in search of the Northwest Passage. At the end of July, two passing whalers noted them. Afterward, silence.

With no word from the expedition by spring of 1847, the Admiralty shipped extra supplies of pemmican to Canada's northern trading posts, but stopped short of launching a rescue mission. When William Parry's 1819 mission had not been heard from for three years, a search expedition had been discussed, but in the end he had turned up. Why shouldn't Franklin? The official search for the *Erebus* and *Terror* started in 1848. Franklin's companion from his first Arctic expedition, Sir John Richardson, joined Hudson's Bay employee Dr. John Rae on an overland expedition designed to intersect with Franklin's likely coordinates; from the Bering Strait, the crew of the H.M.S. *Plover* worked eastward, while Sir James Clark Ross and the men of the *Enterprise* and the *Investigator* made their way west from Greenland. In the most active searching period of the next ten years, nearly forty expeditions, both Admiralty-sponsored and privately funded, worked over the same geography. Franklin's first winter quarters were discovered on Beechey Island in August 1850, but they revealed nothing of the fate of the expedition. In 1854, John Rae learned from native sources that Franklin and his men had perished of starvation, and reported to England that "[f]rom the mutilated state of many of the corpses, and the contents of the kettles, it is evident that our wretched countrymen had been driven to the last resource—cannibalism—as a means of prolonging existence,"[6] a discovery the public was reluctant to accept. Finally, in the spring of 1859, the men of the *Fox* expedition commanded by Sir Francis Leopold McClintock discovered a cairn that cached a document from Franklin's expedition signaling that all was well with the expedition in spring of 1847, but altered in April

1848 to indicate that the *Erebus* and *Terror* had been deserted, Sir John
Franklin had died in June 1847, and twenty-three others had perished.
McClintock continued his search and in May 1859 found abandoned
longboats and three corpses of British sailors. The rest of the bodies were
assumed dispersed in Arctic space.

The Arctic into which Franklin disappeared had a history as a proving ground of a heroic British masculinity associated with national and
imperial identities. Admiralty-sponsored Arctic exploration expeditions
participated in what Gary Kelly has identified as "the remasculinization
of culture" in the second decade of the century,[7] and the rigor of male-
only Arctic expeditions discovered and articulated a masculinity positioned in opposition not only to women at home and to upper-class
male dandies in the metropole, but to colonial threats as well. In the
exploration accounts generated by the first wave of Arctic missions, the
Arctic was understood to be an arid and cold space that stood in masculine opposition to the torrid humidity of the tropics. Numerous widely
read polar exploration accounts, such as John Franklin's own 1821
Narrative of a Journey to the Shores of the Polar Seas, examined in detail in
chapter 2, manufactured both swashbuckling heroes and a familiar
"Arctic," one in which a narrative of exploration often became a narrative of survival that foregrounded the explorer's embattled body while
providing evidence of the resilience, ingenuity, and staunchness associated with British national character.[8] The resulting irrefutable, "hard"
masculinity answered threats of effeminacy, miscegenation, and vulnerability to physical, psychological, and moral weakness associated with
Britain's tropical colonies.[9] In the early century, the Arctic was thus a
space that could provide a counter to the troubling moral questions
raised by domestic economic reliance on slavery and other forms of
colonial exploitation, an ultimate space of white masculine self-reliance.

Yet perhaps because the Arctic of the early century was a male-only
space of physical exploration, it was a fertile imaginary location for
female writers in the early century. Lady Mary Wortley Montagu, Mary
Wollstonecraft, and others had shown that English women could travel
the world but, as Admiral Croft's wife in Jane Austen's *Persuasion* (1816)
laments, explorations of the North Seas were off-limits to women. The
companionate marriage of the admiral and his wife is disrupted only by
the admiral's Arctic duty, a disruption that Mrs. Croft recounts precipitated her only illness. In this small detail, Austen may be seen to gesture
at the disruptive potential of a national identity that privileges males—
the admiral is identified only by his naval affiliation throughout the

text—as well as trying to make visible national demands on women that remain largely invisible in a culture that glorifies and allegorizes male participation in war and exploration. The separation the Arctic literally and symbolically demands between males "away" and females "at home" in the early part of the century anticipates the gendering of separate public and private spheres that both coalesced and gained ideological force as the century progressed. It should not be surprising, then, that in 1818 both Mary Wollstonecraft Shelley's *Frankenstein* and Eleanor Anne Porden's *The Arctic Expeditions* use the polar world as a space in which to imagine and critique women's position in narratives of scientific and national progress.

In providing her critique of masculinist knowledge projects with Arctic bookends, Mary Shelley not only underlines women's exclusion from such projects but also draws our attention once again to how Arctic space, although geographically peripheral, was understood as a place for British self-realization. Robert Walton's appetite for discovery is set in motion when as a youth he reads exploration accounts in his uncle's library. As a result he believes that the Arctic will be a place where, if he "put[s] some trust in preceding navigators," "snow and frost are banished" and he will be wafted to "a land surpassing in wonders and in beauty every region hitherto discovered on the habitable globe."[10] Work by Mary-Louise Pratt and others has made visible the way travel writing "*produced* 'the rest of the world' for European reader-ships," and in turn how the resulting narratives produced the origin and originators of the journey by expressing and perpetuating the cultural mores, biases, and behaviors of the explorers.[11] Yet authors and readers of exploration accounts understood this early on as well; in 1710 the Earl of Shaftesbury observed of voyage narratives that they were "in our present days what books of chivalry were in those of our forefathers."[12] Voyage narratives, like earlier books of chivalry, outlined and historicized codes of gendered heroic behavior that then performed local functions. When Walton's discovery of Victor Frankenstein and the monster in a frozen, hostile Arctic coincides with the mutiny of Walton's crew and the failure of his mission, the texts Walton trusts are shown to be faulty. Shelley suggests that their lie encompasses both polar geography and the "heroic" males who produce and document that geography in exploration accounts.

In similar fashion, when Franklin failed to reappear a few years after his 1845 departure, not only did he fail to produce an account of Arctic travel, he failed to produce the legible heroic masculinity on which larger national and imperial projects relied. The ensuing rescue fever and public debate—including Rae's famous assertions of possible cannibalism among the party—developed in Franklin's absence and the multiple volumes of Arctic expedition accounts generated by the parties sent in search of the lost expedition make up the second phase of Arctic obsession in the nineteenth century.

Empty Arctic space, despite or because of its removal from colonial spaces, had helped to define a form of British masculinity that enabled and naturalized British rule of colonial spaces. Coinciding with Britain's increasingly complicated relationship with India and larger public debate on the relations between Britain and its empire, this mid-century era of polar discourse draws comparison between Arctic purity and racial whiteness. In this period, even more ideological pressure was put on polar endeavor, with Arctic exploration paradoxically understood as an imperial project that took place in a "pure" space outside of empire. As the journalist Henry Morley documented in Charles Dickens's *Household Words* at the height of popular concern with the disappearance of the Franklin expedition in 1853, the remote Arctic was not a colonial or imperial space in any ordinary sense:

> Typhoons, hurricanes, and tropical heats, Inner Africa, Central America, China, Japan, and all such topics interest us; but there are not tales of risk and enterprise in which we English, men, women, and children, old and young, rich and poor, become interested so completely, as in the tales that come from the North Pole. We would rather hear of travellers among the snowflakes and ice floes than among cypress and myrtle; and we have good reasons for our preference. Snow and ice are emblems of the deeds done in their clime. . . . The history of Arctic enterprise is stainless as the Arctic snows, clean to the core as an ice mountain.[13]

Morley makes clear the place of the Arctic in the binary constructions that justified empire when he contrasts the "clean" space of the Arctic with the "dark" continents of Africa, Asia, and South America. By the nineteenth century, hope of any fast route to China via an as-yet-undiscovered Northwest Passage was gone, and thus the Arctic stood outside of the economic relations that defined Great Britain's relationships with colonial spaces. Linked to "pure" scientific and geographic curiosity instead, polar space was understood to be free of the exploitative economic relations condemned in abolitionist rhetoric of the early century and by mid-century Britons anxious about incipient and unchecked imperial expansion. For those such as Benjamin Disraeli who argued that imperial expansion was important primarily as an expression of Britain's destiny and greatness on the world stage, successful navigation of the Northwest Passage would be a symbolic achievement that articulated and naturalized Great Britain's imperial destiny.

Essential to a "stainless" Arctic in these formulations is its un-peopled emptiness—Morley ignores the native presence, perhaps because their nomadic traditions made them invisible[14]—which enables Arctic exploration to be morally stainless as well, in contrast to Morley's list of "Inner Africa, Central America, China, [and] Japan," names that metonymically represent the "dark" populations against which Britons defined themselves. If Arctic exploration was "stainless" because it lacked economic motive, it also seemed pure because British mapping of and imperial claims on the Arctic were not threatened by the moral and racial threats of slavery and miscegenation present in traditional colonial and imperial encounter. In addition to participating in the discourse of racial hygiene that imperial and nationalist discourses would come to rely on later in the century, Morley's rhetoric of purity and "whiteness" makes abundantly clear to his contemporary readership that the history of Arctic exploration is important *because* it is a "white" history about white Englishmen in a white space. Peopling his Arctic with white explorers and their deeds only, Morley not only makes a distinction between expansion into polar lands and other colonial spaces, but reveals that British investment (literal and psychological) in the Arctic is as a symbolic space, a blank space on which to map white deeds that in turn produced a legible national identity, one that could be transported back to the metropole.

The national identity embodied by Franklin and his men was represented in tales of Arctic exploration, which, as Morley describes, do important national work: "For three hundred years the Arctic seas have now been visited by European sailors; their narratives supply some of the finest modern instances of human energy and daring bent on a noble undertaking, and associated constantly with kindness, generosity, and simple piety"(245). The static, ahistorical Arctic landscape in which specific "instances of human energy and daring . . . and . . . kindness, generosity, and simple piety" occur, enables readers of Arctic accounts to dehistoricize, generalize, and transform those qualities into "emblems" of behavior at "the core" not of Morley's ice mountain, but of the British subject (245, 241). In "Unspotted Snow" the three-hundred-year history of Arctic exploration coincides with England's own written history since Elizabeth I, and becomes then part of the shared, mythic national past that Ernest Renan identified as essential to national identity. By hitching Arctic exploration to Britain's history, Morley's article concisely reveals the place of the Arctic in what Lauren Berlant has called the "national symbolic," the "shared spatial and temporal experiences [that] reflect, perform and/or affirm" a national subjectivity.[15] In this symbolic system, efforts at mapping Arctic space did not only produce scientific knowledge in the form of temperature and magnetic readings, but were to their nineteenth-century audience expressions both of the cartographic project of empire and of national identity.

In addition to enabling us to further connections between national and imperial identities, looking at the Arctic's role in nineteenth-century Britain helps us to understand how Britons perceived and accounted for their newly expanding empire and to consider more widely the role of space and geography in nation and empire. Certainly nations and empires have borders, but as Benedict Anderson famously writes in his study of national identity, nations are "imagined communities" that are not coextensive with geographical borders, nation-states, or ethnic identities.[16] Yet geography remains part of that imagining, with people inhabiting or populating spaces that are clearly defined as national, extra-national, and other—spaces that in turn may define who can be a national subject. Anderson's influential theory makes visible the force of the "idea" or imaginary component of nation, an abstraction that transcends the geographical outline of the state. Yet even for scholars who follow Anderson, the spatial component of nation (and empire) is still assumed somehow to correspond to that mapped "real" geography on an atlas. This spatial component of national identity increasingly has been shown to be more complex.[17] As David Harvey has pointed out, spaces are discursively constructed, and "the imaginary of spatiality is of crucial significance in the search for alternative mappings of the social process and of its outcome"; it follows that understanding the imaginary of spatiality is also important to mapping both history and identity.[18] In other words, how Britons perceived and structured the geography both of their nation and of their expanding empire necessarily influenced the many social processes by which individuals became Britons.

The dominant models of nineteenth-century British identity consider geography, but primarily as the representative boundary of cultural difference. For example, Linda Colley's important model of British national identity understands it as coalescing in opposition to Others (particularly the French) in the eighteenth and early nineteenth centuries, but is concerned primarily with cultural, political, and linguistic difference.[19] Yet it was Napoleon's imperial agenda, as expressed in France's geographical expansion, that contributed to the long conflict between Great Britain and France in the early century in which Colley locates the oppositional strategies of national identity-formation. Not coincidentally, the first wave of polar exploration followed closely on the heels of war's end: if conflict with France strengthened British identity, what would take its place? The departure of three different Northwest Passage discovery missions in 1818, including Franklin's first voyage, occurred in answer to this question. Championed by John Barrow, long-time Secretary to the Admiralty and himself an Arctic veteran, as a way to provide economic support to naval officers now out of work after the Napoleonic wars, the simultaneous expeditions of John Ross, John Franklin, and William Parry were conceived of as a military assault on the secret of the Northwest Passage. Barrow well understood that peace with France had negative implications for England's sense of itself as a nation, and invoked nationalism as a rationale in his championing of Arctic exploration throughout his forty-year tenure in Admiralty administration. In his letter supporting funding for Franklin's ill-fated 1845 mission, Barrow links Arctic geography to a British domestic interior, picturing the Arctic as an empty room, just waiting for an English presence: "If [exploration of the Northwest Passage is] left to be performed by some other power, England by her neglect of it, having opened the East and West doors, would be laughed at by all the world for having hesitated to cross the threshold."[20] Thus, for Barrow, Arctic space is already British, and imperial expansion is a form of national security.

Anticipating Thomas Carlyle, Barrow understood that the effects of industrialization and mechanization—the very processes that for Benedict Anderson enable the spread of print capitalism and culture responsible for national identity—posed a threat to British character, one answerable for Barrow by further polar exploration. He also understood the metonymic relationship between England's seamen and England itself, and if the end of the naval-intensive conflict with France threatened the British Navy, so too did increasing mechanization. "It is admitted," Barrow continues in his proposal in support of Franklin's 1845 expedition, "that the arctic expeditions have produced a finer set of Officers and Seamen perhaps than any other branch of the Service. . . . We have much need of increasing such men, now that Steamers are supplanting our best Seamen" (158). The "purity," to use Morley's word, of a national identity produced, refined, and tested in Arctic space, existed for Barrow in some sort of eternal space, a space not simply outside of socioeconomic practices, but outside of modernity itself. In this way, the Arctic as proving ground for Britishness removed from that identity traces of its historical roots in Four Nations conflict or conflict with Europe. In a geography pared to its essentials, a geography that was neither colonial nor national space in any traditional sense, one could discover or reveal an essential identity.

The geographical remove of the proving ground of British identity to an Arctic periphery conveniently removed it from colonial locations. Following Edward Said, Simon Gikandi argues that colonial spaces were "indispensable spaces of self-reflection" for Britons, and that "Englishness" was "a cultural and literary phenomenon produced in the ambivalent space that separated, but also conjoined, metropole and colony."[21] Colonial spaces are therefore essential to British identity, and the ubiquity of the imperial in nineteenth-century discourse pointed out by Patrick Brantlinger and others only emphasizes yet more insistently the usefulness of the Arctic in debates with implications for national and imperial identity.[22] For Britons, the empty white Arctic was a concrete space that could function as abstraction where other forms of abstraction failed.[23] In other words, its geographical distance from both colonies and metropole literalized its perceived disengagement from the economic, social, and political debates about colonial and imperial projects and as such, as Lisa Bloom has argued in her discussion of polar space and American imperialism, the Arctic "literalized the colonial fantasy of a tabula rasa where people, history, and culture vanish," an emptiness in which to celebrate "empire without the mediating disfigurations associated with the actualities of a colonial state."[24]

While abstract economic and statistical representations might enable some politicians and intellectuals to sidestep larger ethical and moral questions of colonial encounter and exploitation, racial difference was an insistent and material reminder and disruption of those abstractions. The Arctic once again provided a convenient solution: although Arctic exploration accounts made native populations and traditions known to their readers, native migratory traditions ensured their evacuation from the Arctic in the popular imagination, an erasure enabled by the representation of polar space in two hundred years of exploration accounts as uninhabitable. As Henry Morley's insistence on Arctic purity as a synecdochic expression of Englishness revealed, the national identity established there was understood to be racially pure, and thus an examination of its construction and representation complicates discussions of British identity that understand it as coalescing in opposition to a racial Other in a hegemonic system wherein the metropole dominates the periphery. Indeed, Britain's investment, both representational and economic, in Arctic exploration throughout the nineteenth century would seem to suggest that writers and politicians were altogether cognizant of what we now understand were often more complex or "rhizomatic" relations between metropole and periphery. The Arctic relation of white man and white landscape, one in which the British explorer and his tale took on allegorical significance, provided refuge from such complications in a legible plot of national behavior and geographical triumph, one that could resolve or at least ameliorate uncomfortable questions about nation and character raised by imperial excesses and foreign policy debacles abroad, as well as national unrest, poverty, and speculation at home.

The Arctic's literal geographic separation from quotidian issues was furthered by the participation of Arctic exploration in scientific and geographic knowledge projects, which helped to establish the perception that both the Arctic and the identity reified there were apolitical and ahistorical. Yet Arctic exploration affirms the link between geography and political projects.[25] The career of the Arctic veteran Clements Markham, for example, instances geographical and imperial connection in a particularly vivid way. Born in 1830, Markham was important in the development of the Royal Geographic Society first as secretary (1863–1888) and then as president from 1893–1905. His early years were spent in the Navy and as a young officer, he found himself on an Arctic exploration ship in search of the Franklin expedition, documented in his 1852 account, *In Franklin's Footsteps*, the first of more than twenty-seven volumes produced by his travels. After leaving the Navy, Markham pursued geography, literally traveling the globe in the latter half of the century to produce accounts as various as *A Quichua Dictionary and Grammar* (1863), *Missions to Thibet* (1877), and a history of Peru (1880). His most memorable achievement, however, underlines the link between geographical science and empire: in 1860 Markham was responsible for the importation of cinchona—the source of quinine— from South America to India for cultivation, resulting in fewer malarial infections for both the British in India and the native plantation labor forces on which the economy relied. This imperial contribution by Markham alone affirms John Barrow's sense of the Arctic as a proving ground for imperial males.

The title of Markham's first book, *In Franklin's Footsteps*, indicates his sense of his own genealogy and trajectory as a heroic explorer, citizen, and author. Later, as president of the Royal Geographic Society, Markham was responsible for sponsoring Robert Scott's Antarctic expedition of 1901; that Scott, like Franklin, would die on a polar mission closes the circuit. The chronological torch-passing from Barrow to Franklin to Markham to Scott reveals polar genealogy to be entirely male, and not surprisingly the narratives of national identity produced there privilege male national participation. Building on gendering of Arctic experience explored by Southey, Franklin, Mary Shelley, Eleanor Porden, and Jane Austen in the early century, mid-century discussions of the Franklin expedition and the homosocial nature of Arctic exploration addressed fears of female contamination associated with both colonial spaces and British domesticity.[26] The Arctic itself was gendered male: unforgiving, but constant, a geography that corresponded to an ideal and thus would bring out the best in the men who mapped it. As a result, the Arctic could produce a British male separate from the moral space of British domesticity so clearly associated with female authority. When Sarah Stickney Ellis famously claimed moral primacy for women in *The Women of England* (1839), she situated the civilizing forces of religion, education, and gentle manners in middle-class women. While early century exploration had participated in the re-masculinization of public culture, the masculinist fantasy of mid-century Arctic exploration promised to reappropriate domestic and private authority to males and the public sphere.

But as Morley's hyperbole and Franklin's own experience on his first mission indicate, there are dangers in locating authority in an overly embodied national masculinity: any failure of Franklin and the men of the *Erebus* and *Terror* was a failure of British character. Perhaps the Arctic, rather than being proving ground to and evidence of a British male uniquely suited to dominating the natural world and other countries, instead points out his limit. It follows that the national obsession with discovering the bodies of Franklin and his men was as much driven by a desire to find the heroic masculinity understood to have been forged by polar exploration as it was by curiosity about the men's fates. As such, the human bodies—first thought to be living, later widely accepted as dead—that were the object of almost thirty years of search expeditions had a metonymic relation to Britain's imperial endeavors, part of a metonymic chain that extended to Britons at home. Not only did

Franklin himself embody a national masculinity that was then deployed at home, but the libraries of sermons, working pipe organs, and fine crystal listed on the expedition manifest were the same material possessions found in middle-class sitting rooms.

The trail of detritus from the Franklin expedition—parts of uniforms, tin canisters, cloth, rope, and wood fragments, images of which were reproduced in the *Illustrated London News*—that search expeditions came across and brought back to England resisted oracular efforts made to read it. The persistence of the "stuff" of the Franklin expedition in light of the seemingly complete disappearance of the sailors, and the resistance of the fragmented material to interpretation, were articulations of the larger tension between crass materialism and human values that underlay the arguments of so many Victorian intellectuals, among them Thomas Carlyle, whose 1841 *On Heroes, Hero-Worship, and the Heroic in History* exhorts Britons to embrace and perpetuate heroism and hero worship as an antidote to the commercialism and moral erosion of the modern era. The pieces of silverware and officers' buttons the search parties turned up in place of the missing sailors' bodies formed a grim proposition that "things" might have staying power while humans did not, a proposition in the face of which the entire idea of a resistant, reproducible, or "hard" British masculinity collapsed.

In the end, if the Arctic was for Britons a place to reify, stabilize, and naturalize a definition of Britishness that could provide an antidote to increasingly unstable and multiple versions of Britishness that existed at home and in the colonies, the metonymic chain broken by the missing bodies of the Franklin expedition had far-reaching implications for the stability of Britain's sense of itself not only as a nation, but as a colonial and imperial power. The identification of metropolitan readers with successful narrators of earlier expeditions had affirmed their own un-self-conscious placement at the authoritative center of an empire. Franklin's absence and the failure of the search missions that sought him forced upon these readers a recognition of the possible bankruptcy not only of the national masculinity embodied in Franklin, but of the sense of an empire controlled from the metropole. The great blank Arctic expanse on which Franklin had promised to write an imperial narrative revealed itself to be a potent, life-taking force that turned on and absorbed the British explorer. As a result, Great Britain might be compelled to envision itself as an icebound Arctic exploration ship: immobile, surrounded by hostile, uncaring forces, and shockingly vulnerable.

GOING AFTER FRANKLIN

I hope to demonstrate in this contextualization of Franklin's disappearance in the first two phases of nineteenth-century Arctic narrative that paying attention to how nineteenth-century Britons approached, represented, and used extraterritorial polar space can nuance our broader understanding of national, colonial, and imperial identities and practices in the nineteenth century. The Arctic that this project is concerned with is not the "real" Arctic, for as the following chapters will show, Britons had no use for the complex material realities of Arctic environment or well-established native cultures and traditions. As Henry Morley so clearly articulates, the Arctic is important as a geography that is not a geography (because perceived as blank), as an imperial space that is not part of empire (because there are no economic and colonial goals in its exploration), and as a place that is everywhere (on Arctic-themed menus, in panoramas, in paintings) because it is nowhere.

In accounts from the earlier part of the century, the Arctic was a space perceived to make distinct the difference between human and "nature" even as it defined and naturalized a heroic British masculinity. This led to a mid-century investment in Arctic navigation as a triumphant nationalist narrative, captured by Henry Morley's characteristic excess:

> Unfading be the laurels of our northern navigators thus won by exercises of all the finest qualities of manhood! Let us be glad, too, that we have one unspotted place upon this globe of ours; a Pole that, as it fetches truth out of a needle, so surely also gets all that is right-headed and right-hearted from the sailor whom the needle guides. (245)

Yet Morley's hyperbolic assertions in 1853, as well as the multiple, speculative accounts of the voyage that circulated in place of the anticipated authoritative Admiralty-authorized account that would have been authored by Franklin, betray uneasiness about Franklin's disappearance. What if Arctic whiteness did not produce a distinct, readable, and reproducible masculinity? What if the bleak desolation of polar terrain absorbed British males rather than making them stand out in sharp relief? If white Arctic space was indistinct and horizon-less, might white British male identity be the same? Franklin's disappearance disrupted "right-headed" and "right-hearted" certainties about gender, race, nation, and empire that Arctic expeditions and their accounts were counted upon to deliver. The third phase of representing the Arctic in the nineteenth century grappled with these rents in the Arctic canvas.

While rescue missions read the polar landscape for traces of the crew of the *Erebus* and *Terror*, Britons read published expedition accounts—from earlier missions as well as those generated by search missions—for reassurances about the British masculinity that the loss of Franklin imperiled. Read through the lens of possible failure, these accounts reveal the active disconnect between the "idea" or symbolic function of Arctic exploration and its actuality as experienced by the British explorer. One standard trope of polar accounts, for instance, is the experience of overwintering in pack ice. The originary tale of a shipboard winter in the ice was written by William Parry, who, locked in the ice with his men during an 1819 expedition, waited for the thaw, an explorer who couldn't explore, patiently measuring the distance away from his goal that the ice inexorably dragged him.[27] Passively enduring—like the women waiting for them at home—Parry's men and the others who followed them turned to domestic pursuits, including Bible study and needlecraft, as well as diverting theatre evenings. This shipboard routine became the oft-repeated staple of Arctic accounts generated by the Franklin rescue missions, and in its repetition we see that increasingly the Arctic the British male is thought to dominate instead effeminizes him.[28] Certainly overwintering in pack ice returns the domestic sphere and its attendant moral authority to British males, but it does so at the cost of making them women—quite literally in the case of the sailors who cross-dress as women in shipboard theatricals. Far from clarifying or delivering a heroic masculinity dependent on gender divisions practiced at home, the Arctic suggested that gendered behaviors were situational.

If in the Arctic men could behave as women, at home the mobilization of search missions for Franklin gave women a national public venue in which to redefine and assert their otherwise private role of moral influence. Lady Jane Franklin was a paradoxically public widow, a figure who, while grieving, still managed to influence politics, travel the world, meet foreign heads of state, and maintain a grueling social schedule. In her letter to Lord Palmerston asking for reversal of the declaration and for new funds from Parliament to continue the search, one sees Lady Jane's negotiation of widowhood in both her supplicant tone and her self-portrait as a suffering woman. She expresses her disbelief and

disappointment that her government should abandon not only her husband and the men under his command, but the woman who must wait
for him, resourceless: "Though it is my humble hope and prayer that the
Government of my country will themselves complete the work they
have begun, and not leave it to a weak and helpless woman to attempt
the doing that imperfectly which they themselves can do so easily and
well, yet, if need be, such is my painful resolve, God helping me."[29]
Alternately exploiting the morbid economy of sentimentality that surrounded the death of a beloved spouse and asserting that her husband's
disappearance did not automatically equate to his death, Lady Jane challenged and changed Admiralty policies and parliamentary budgets, raised
a private navy by soliciting wealthy, influential donors to support Arctic
missions, and helped shape Britain's foreign policy with the United
States. In contrast to Victoria's careful gendering of her withdrawal as a
womanly reaction to grief ten years later, Franklin's active public presence navigated a careful line between appropriate female behavior and
unseemly assertiveness that gained her the following observation by an
Orkney boatman: "If the wife is such a man, what can the husband
be?"[30] These were questions of identity the Arctic was supposed to safely
resolve at a distance, not raise insistently at home.

When the Admiralty finally removed Franklin and his men from the
roster of crews in the Navy List, Lady Jane promptly changed out of
mourning and started to dress in bright colors. Intended as a vibrant testament to her belief that her husband still lived, her clothing was in stark
contrast to the indistinct whiteness of the landscape that had absorbed
him, a landscape that by mid-century seemed to have an endless ability
to absorb money, ships, and men with barely a trace. The Arctic was now
a place of erasure rather than of the promised clarity, its emptiness inter-
rupted by British dead; in effect a literally whited sepulchre.

In place of the bodies it absorbed, however, Arctic space volunteered
only a reflection and mystification of British desires. If in winter there
was no day, in summer there was no night. Minds benumbed by mal-
nourishment and exposure had to comprehend phenomena such as
"paraheliae," a ring of false suns created by the atmospheric refraction.
The "blink"—light reflected from snowfields or pack ice onto the
undersurface of clouds—caused halos around the sun, as well as mirages
resembling mountain ranges and even exploration ships. In *Franklin's
Footsteps*, Markham writes of the shifting, unstable environment he
encountered, one that called into question all perception:

Sometimes an iceberg is raised up into the shape of a lofty pillar, at another a whole chain of them will assume the appearance of an enormous bridge or aqueduct, and as quickly change into a succession of beautiful temples or cathedrals of dazzling whiteness, metamorphosed by the fantastic wand of nature. Ships too would in appearance rise up and stand on their heads, with the main trucks of the real and imaginary one touching. The grandeur of the scenery was rendered tenfold more beautiful and strange by these wonderful effects, and during the hard work of pressing through the ice, our weariness was relieved by beholding this magnificent panorama, constantly changing and presenting new and more beautiful shapes, like the varying configurations of a kaleidoscope.[31]

The kaleidoscopic, shifting nature of Arctic space resisted standard interpretive models, both scientific and aesthetic, and brought into question the explorer's strategies for making sense of the world, an uncertainty that extended to perceptions of the larger work of Arctic narrative in culture. By mimicking man-made objects such as aqueducts and cathedrals, the polar landscape reflected a distorted Englishness back at the explorers, a distortion that in turn revealed the protean, constructed nature of civilization itself.

The uncertainty about landscape and natural phenomena Markham voices extended to British identity and the "civilizing" project of the empire. On the one hand, recognition that British bodies and Arctic landscape were conjoined conflated the search for Franklin with mapping Arctic geography for the British Empire, and answered critics who wondered about squandering resources in search of corpses. On the other hand Franklin's literal joining of Arctic landscape in death erased the difference between human and "thing" on which definitions of civilization rested and called not only the search for Franklin but all of Arctic exploration into question as logical practice.

If earlier Arctic accounts were valuable for their insistence that national identity was not dependent on cultural or racial Others, then post-Franklin accounts were less certain of this. The men of the Franklin search vessel *Investigator* for example, iced in for months and starving, had resigned themselves to a long and improbably successful walk out of the Arctic to the south when Captain McClure and his lieutenant were baffled by the approach of a human figure:

On getting within a hundred yards they could see from his pro-
portions that he was not one of them. [He] began to screech
and throw up his hands, his face as black as your hat. This
brought the captain and lieutenant to a stand, as they could not
hear sufficiently to make out his language. He was a considerable way ahead of his sledge—a solitary man, and that man as
black as Old Nick. McClure says he would have turned and run
if he had seen a tail, or a cloven foot. . . . He at length found that
the solitary stranger was a true Englishman; an angel of light he
says. (39)

The promised clarity of Arctic space somehow does not enable
McClure and his men to recognize another Englishman. On the empty
snow, the Briton is "black" (perhaps darkened by frostbite), his language
an incomprehensible "screech"; he is not only racially different, but
perhaps supernatural. McClure's account has him mistaking the figure
not for a devil, but for an Inuit, proof that the Arctic erases difference.
When the figure replies to McClure's hails, "I'm Lieutenant Pim, late of
the *Herald*, now of the *Resolute*. Captain Kellett is with her at Dealy
Island," the Arctic "Dr.-Livingstone-I-presume?" moment reveals the
workings of national identity in a place largely empty of the usual
markers of identity and difference.[32] The movement of Pim from devil
to native to dark stranger to, finally, Englishman, echoes the instability
of the landscape itself as described by Markham, and undermines the
stability and legibility of national identity Arctic narratives so forcefully
sought to assert.

In addition to forcing them to reflect on the rather slippery nature
of national identity, the McClure-Pim encounter also revealed to readers
that Arctic space was not, in fact, empty or indeed blank: it was filled
with white British and American explorers. McClure's misrecognition
of Pim completed the Northwest Passage: McClure's ship had started
from the west, Kellett's from the east. That the moment of uniting the
coasts through a Northwest Passage is anticlimactic seems an expression
of a sense of Arctic exhaustion by the explorers themselves, one shared at
least in part by the British public. This exhaustion is a hallmark of the
late phase of Arctic narrative. By 1876, one reviewer could comment
that recent polar exploration narratives "could be characterised in the
Stud-Book of literature as 'Sire, Scissors, out of Dam, Paste-Pot'" and
speak distastefully of a "wilderness of rechaufée print."[33] For readers,
Arctic purity had become Arctic sterility when once-potent tropes

exhausted themselves; worn narratives equated with worn models of identity that, while useful for justifying imperial projects, were no longer infallible, much less "new." Yet paradoxically, the nostalgia for the power and promise of Arctic narrative persisted, with one writer advocating further exploration of the Arctic even as he envisioned the Arctic as a destination for bored academics:

> Are other nations to outstrip us? Have we done all that has to be done in this frozen world? Have we no further difficulties to solve, no more heroism to display? Do we shrink back daunted, and are others to win the trump? We think not. It is not in the nature of a Briton to be second when risk has to be run or a triumph is to be achieved. Already there are fishing and hunting visitors in the North Seas—dons tired of ascending Mont Blanc, and bent on Adventures in the ice.[34]

Here, the Arctic has become a space in which a specifically historicized British masculinity based on heroic actions and daring endeavors can be re-performed and realized anew by an educated upper class whose social and political dominance in the domestic sphere had been fortified by the foundational narratives of masculinity of the earlier polar explorers. These academic explorers sought to garb themselves in the heroic mantle of the earlier British explorers who had voyaged into what was (for them at least) the complete unknown. At the same time, however, these later explorers asserted a sense of familiarity and ease with Arctic space. The Arctic to some degree had been made known, with the result that the new scientific knowledge gained there could confirm a national genius. The atavistic desire expressed in this logic attaches persistent British exploration of the Arctic in the late nineteenth century to the logic of imperial expansion, in which geographical dominance affirms a sense of cultural superiority and progress.

In his late essay, "Geography and Explorers," Joseph Conrad explicitly links his own lifelong interest in geography, travel, and imperialism to John Franklin, whom he names "the dominating figure among the seamen explorers of the first half of the nineteenth century," and "the last great explorer," who "served geography even in his death."[35] When, early in *Heart of Darkness*, the narrator describes the geographical reach of the Thames as "leading to the uttermost ends of the earth" (104), he quickly links the river to Sir Francis Drake and Sir John Franklin, as well as to the "conquests" of the *Erebus* and *Terror* and the East India fleets.

Hunters for gold or pursuers of fame, they had all gone out on
that stream, bearing the sword, and often the torch, messengers
of the might within the land, bearers of a spark from the sacred
fire. What greatness had not floated on the ebb of that river into
the mystery of the unknown earth! . . . The dreams of men, the
seed of commonwealths, the germs of empires. (104–105)

Franklin's presence at the outset of the passage enables us to read the list
that follows the ellipsis after the narrator's exclamation about "greatness"
if not ironically, then with suspicion, for Franklin's dreams were not realized—and by extension, the imperial "seed" and "germs" his enterprise
carried were lost, their potential scattered and frozen on an anonymous
icefield. Indeed, the speculations about cannibalism that followed his
disappearance link him explicitly to Kurtz.[36]

When a few pages later Marlow begins his tale, he situates himself in
terms of a boyhood "passion" for maps in which he would "lose" himself
in "all the glories of exploration":

At that time there were many blank spaces on the earth, and
when I saw one that looked particularly inviting on a map (but
they all look that) I would put my finger on it and say, When I
grow up I will go there. The North Pole was one of these places,
I remember. Well, I haven't been there yet, and shall not try now.
The glamour's off. . . . But there was one yet—the biggest, the
most blank, so to speak—that I had a hankering after.

True, by this time it was not a blank space any more. It had
got filled since my boyhood with rivers and lakes and names. It
had ceased to be a blank space of delightful mystery—a white
patch for a boy to dream gloriously over. It had become a place
of darkness. (108)

Marlow's horrifying experience in the Congo is the post-Franklin
world of exploration and empire, one in which Franklin—who to
Conrad the child was a "good man" "of high personal character"
("Geography," 10)—no longer can exist. As a boy, Conrad had imagined the North Pole as "mere imaginary ends of the imaginary axis
upon which the earth turns" before reading and rereading the "stern
romance" of Sir Leopold McClintock's 1869 account of his search for
Franklin, *The Voyage of the Fox in the Arctic Seas* (11). The appeal of the
North Pole for Marlow is its abstraction and unattainability, a blankness

corresponding with the purity of "the idea at the back of it" (107) that he offers as an explanation of the appeal of imperialism. For the aging Marlow, product of the grown Conrad's imagination, as blank spaces become known and their details filled in as geographical detail on maps, the purity associated with imaginary or discursive spaces vanishes. Even the ultimate place-as-idea, the North Pole, as yet "undiscovered" at the 1902 publication of Conrad's novel, loses its appeal for Marlow. The "idea" of the North Pole in this case is darkened not by the act of inking its exact location on a page, but by the end of an era that Conrad terms "geography militant,"[37] an era of masculine exploration, promise, and moral clarity that he explicitly identifies as coming to a close with Franklin's death ("Geography," 6, 12). The framing of the Arctic as a once-inspirational "white" space whose "glamour had gone off" underscores the extent to which the changing perceptions of extraterritorial British space and imperial expansion in the late Victorian era were as much a sense of a national masculinity and ambition whose day had passed, as they were a result of colonial saturation and revulsion at its brutality.

Conrad's recognition of the many resonances of imperialism and its effects on the imagination, as well as on people and concrete geopolitical spaces, is enacted in Marlow's tale.[38] The narrator describes Marlow's narrative as carrying its meaning "not inside like a kernel, but outside, enveloping the tale which brought it out only as a glow brings out a haze, in the likeness of one of these misty halos that sometimes are made visible by the spectral illumination of moonshine" (105).[39] Not only does Conrad's description capture the mechanics by which understanding Arctic exploration can illuminate the larger national and imperial practices of which it is part, but the instability and opacity of his compounded optical metaphor evokes the logic of the "blink," that light reflected from snow and ice responsible for disorienting visions in the Arctic. Appropriately, if surprisingly, the metaphor Conrad uses to express a modernist aesthetic here extends his overt polar textual references to the *Erebus* and *Terror* and the North Pole, while embedding the Arctic as an invisible strand both in Marlow's tale and in the novel's larger argument about empire. Like Marlow's experience of imperialism, far from delivering the vaunted experience of clarity to its explorers, Arctic space disorients them, vexing their project of national self-realization and even, as it did in Franklin's case, killing them. Thus, the opaque and elliptical nature of Marlow's narrative that seems at once to lull and infuriate his shipboard audience is for Conrad the only way to speak the "truth" about imperial excess, with its enveloping, convincing, and linear logic, and its far-reaching moral costs.

In this context, Marlow's journey up the Congo River reads as a rewriting of McClintock's *Voyage of the Fox*, the text that had sent Conrad as a boy "off on the romantic explorations of [his] inner self; to the discovery of the taste of poring over maps; and revealed to [him] the existence of a latent devotion to geography" ("Geography," 12).[40] Conrad's conclusions in *Heart of Darkness*—that the darkness associated with empire's periphery originates in and surrounds London, that every product arriving in the Thames is a kind of cannibal consumption of Others, and that women, while seeming to be peripheral and disengaged from imperial projects, are central to them[41]—are assertions about the far-reaching implications of imperialism, but also an attempt to map the "real" geography of empire, a geography not captured on maps that reveals networks of connection between representations and actions, as well as circuits of relation between physically separate spaces.

Captured in Marlow's deadpan descriptions of everyday violence on the river, Conrad's comprehension of how quotidian experience has larger sociopolitical significance effectively supports the larger claim and methodology of this book. That is, that Arctic space, overlooked due to our sense of its peripheral connection to the larger questions that inter-est us about the nineteenth century—perceived by us as transparent or unimportant due to the persistence and persuasiveness of a centuries-old rhetoric of purity attached to polar exploration, and understood as being somehow outside the boundaries of "civilized" discourse due to its rugged natural environment and sparse population—might *for these very reasons* be useful to us in our attempts to comprehend not just how the Arctic functions in the nineteenth-century imaginary, but how to understand that imaginary itself. The Arctic's runic quality, its shifting, multiple nature as an imagined place that nonetheless has a material presence, its resistance to singular interpretation, and its resistance even to "logical" reading and thus to containment, uncannily reflects the very qualities we associate with national and imperial identities. In this regard, Conrad's insistence on meaning cohering in the nimbus sur-rounding the "kernel" of materiality perfectly expresses the evolving role of Arctic space in the nineteenth-century British imagination and shows why polar exploration was such a perfect starting point for the transition into a modernist aesthetic that *Heart of Darkness* articulates.

In order to chart the Arctic's participation in these larger processes, the following study begins with an investigation of the vast literature of

Arctic exploration from the late eighteenth century through the Romantic period in order to examine more closely how exploration accounts construct one form of a foundational, nationalistic heroic masculinity. Starting with the unlikely Arctic narrative in Robert Southey's 1813 *Life of Nelson*, a text that establishes the hero of Trafalgar's national masculinity as being Arctic in origin, I trace the centrality of the male body to British Arctic experience in best-selling exploration accounts of the early century. I focus on John Franklin's bestselling 1823 *Narrative of a Journey to the Shores of the Polar Sea*, in which imperiled bodies, uncertain geographies, near-death, and cannibalism lead to the paradoxical conclusion that the Arctic is a proving ground for a British masculinity uniquely suited to imperial projects. Franklin's own history following the publication of his account, however, details the difficulty of an explorer's return: codes of honor and behavior not only appropriate to the edges of empire, but mapped as "British," do not in fact translate into workable identities either at home or in colonial administration.

The national masculinity born in Arctic endeavor was not, however, hegemonic, as two Arctic narratives published by young women in 1818 indicate. In the subsequent chapter, I argue that Mary Shelley and Eleanor Porden perceived and used the Arctic as a phantasmic space where science and myth coexist, a space in which to rewrite gendered knowledges and, conversely, knowledges of gender. Eleanor Porden, for example, in her first published poem *The Veils*, envisions an imagined geography that places Britain's women at the center not only of the globe, but of the cosmos. Porden, who would later be John Franklin's first wife, explores similar themes in poems including *The Arctic Expeditions* written in praise of departing exploration ships and the 1822 *Coeur de Lion*. Porden shares her sense of Britain's destiny as an imperial power with her contemporary, Anna Seward. In contrast to the Arctic of *The Veils*, Shelley's Arctic is a place where science and humans find their limits. The novel's dominant narrative of Victor Frankenstein's misguided attempt to create life seems only tangentially engaged with issues of British nationhood and empire, but Shelley's narrative frame of letters written by an explorer back to his English sister draws our attention to gendered spatial practices of geographic and scientific exploration, while the domestic ideology articulated in Walton's, Victor's, and the creature's stories encourages readers to look at how Britons conceived of and perpetuated a collective national identity in the Arctic and at home.

Thirty years later, the Arctic remained a forceful, if unlikely location for women to situate narratives critiquing gendered participation in national projects. Published two years after the embarkation of the Franklin expedition and coinciding with public questions about the status of the *Erebus* and *Terror*, Charlotte Brontë's *Jane Eyre* uses the Arctic to critique England's domestic and imperial policies. I examine in the fourth chapter how Brontë's frequent invocation of ice and cold, too often dismissed as a simple metaphorics of passion, can be understood as an attempt to use Arctic imagery and polar space as nationalist antidote to the perceived "taint" of tropical colonial spaces. Brontë's rendering of female, domestic participation in discourses of Arctic exploration— Jane's "Arctic" sufferings and her eventual rescue of Rochester—reveals the centrality of women to the spatial practices of empire. In Brontë then, we see a reversal of gender roles that indicates a resistance not to ideas of heroism or nationalism, but specifically to the heroic national masculinity in ascendance at the beginning of the century.

From the outset, Sir John Franklin haunts this project, and he is the absent center of the fifth chapter, in which I discuss the status of evidence and racial and national identities in the evolution of sensation fiction, particularly in the work of Charles Dickens and Wilkie Collins. In 1854, Hudson's Bay Company employee John Rae returned from the Arctic with information and evidence that the Franklin expedition had ended in anarchy and cannibalism. In the periodical debate that followed, Rae and his detractors defined and redefined English character, with Dickens asserting a stable national character while Rae countered that human actions and identities were situational and uncertain. I argue that Dickens's and Collins's interest in the (im)possibility of cannibalism by the Franklin expedition contributed directly to the development of the sensation genre of the late '50s and early '60s, to which reassertion of the stability of identity (racial, national, gendered) and the status of evidence was central. Dickens and Collins co-authored *The Frozen Deep*, an Arctic drama that drew from the Rae debate in which their portraits of the Inuit reflect developing discourses of ethnology and anthropology. Collins later wrote *Poor Miss Finch*, a novel that reprises the questions of nation, citizenship, and skin color investigated in the play. While other critics have discussed Dickens and Collins's play and its relation to Rae's revelations about the Franklin mission, introducing Arctic space to larger discussions of the sensation genre complicates existing critical discussions of sensation and its relation to domestic space, nationalism, and colonialism.

My final chapter considers the participation in empire by boys' adventure novels that rewrite Arctic exploration narratives. Although by the late nineteenth century the Arctic was no longer empty space and the Northwest Passage had been safely "discovered" and mapped, authors including R. M. Ballantyne and George MacDonald would return to polar space as a setting for novels that resurrect the plots of heroic masculinity associated with the early years of the century. In *Giant of the North* and *The World of Ice*, Ballantyne detailed Arctic hardship to reveal how qualities of English boyhood like pluck and courage, when developed through the rigors of exploration, could be enlisted in the expansion and maintenance of empire. Yet his efforts reveal that the impenetrable geography of the polar Arctic disrupts the easy erasure of geographical difference on which the adventure genre relies. In his repeated attempts to write a triumphant Arctic adventure, Ballantyne instead foreshadows the exhaustion of Arctic space in imperial narrative and questions the very logic of boys' adventure and empire itself.

THEN, NOW

The prominence of Arctic space in nineteenth-century Britain may also explain the recent popularity of accounts of extreme travel both historical and contemporary, evidenced by resurgent interest in the Antarctic exploration of Sir Ernest Shackleton, the recent reprinting of Apsley Cherry-Garrard's account of the Scott expedition, *The Worst Journey in the World*, and the popularity of Jon Krakauer's *Into Thin Air* (1997) and other accounts of extreme exploration. I would propose that the recent public appetite for first-person accounts of harrowing encounters with extreme conditions—what John Tierney has termed "explornography"[42]—has everything to do with contemporary articulations of the very concerns this study explores. Like our nineteenth-century counterparts, we have access to new technologies, not to mention larger enabling structures including economic prosperity and subsequent leisure, that enable us to explore and "conquer" territories that were once off-limits. Indeed, although more women participate in these endeavors than did in the nineteenth century, they remain largely the domain of (white) men. Following the lines of the argument set forth in this introduction and examined in the following pages, it may be possible to see that our fascination with these accounts and the pursuit of ever-more-extreme experiences in forbidding climates is a response to anxieties about contemporary articulations of imperialism and/or globalization. The very global positioning systems, Goretex, neoprene, and satellite phones that enable adventures make it yet more impossible to have the unmediated relationship with nature that the explorer seeks. And while the complex politics of a new global order make it imperative that Western powers listen to multiple points of view articulated in different languages by culturally diverse populations, where better to go for silence than an isolated mountaintop or a barren icefield?

Although my argument complicates our perceptions of the Arctic as empty, pure, and undeveloped, its claim for the importance of that perception of the Arctic to nineteenth-century society may lead to recognition of the importance of an undeveloped, empty space to the present. The recent push in the United States to open the Arctic National Wildlife Reserve to oil and gas exploration, for example, endangers not only an ecosystem that supports animal and plant life and the native populations that have traditionally relied on those resources, but also endangers a landscape that has shaped the way the metropole has thought about itself for centuries. Paradoxically, the Arctic's rhetorical and symbolic importance to projects of capital and empire in the nineteenth century may help those who seek to arrest global warming and to protect Arctic landscapes from industrialization in our own time.

CHAPTER TWO

======

NATIONAL BODIES

Robert Southey's *Life of Nelson* and John Franklin's *Narrative of a Journey to the Shores of the Polar Sea*

Richard Westall's 1809 painting "Nelson and the Bear" shows a determined young midshipman attempting to bludgeon a menacing polar bear with the stock of his gun. In the center of the painting, the slight, teen-aged Horatio Nelson stands in his naval uniform, barehanded, arms and weaponry upraised and outlined in a halo of white smoke that issues from his ship's guns. The sailor and the bear, locked in struggle, are the only animate things in an unarticulated and uniformly grey Arctic ice field. The ruddy pink of Nelson's cheeks matches the interior of the bear's open mouth, suggesting that the blood circulating under Nelson's skin could easily be coating the animal's teeth. Here, in his representation of a moment identified as Nelson's earliest heroic act, Westall reveals the utility of the Arctic landscape to a British audience: it is a blank canvas on which to paint the dramatic endangerment of a male body, a landscape that exists as a background for British actions that in turn make national character legible.

Like Westall's painting, Robert Southey's *The Life of Nelson* (1813) made Nelson's early voyage to the polar seas central to character formation of the young man who would later become the hero of the nation. Through Southey's account of Nelson's rash behavior on the ice, readers learned that heroic leadership originated in the kinds of challenges

Nelson found in the frozen north: the pluck demonstrated by the young midshipman seeking a way out of the threatening polar ice pack remained a part of the admiral who outmaneuvered Napoleon's fleet. What endows this with greater significance and pushes it from the secular myth making of Southey to constitute an important instance of a broader social phenomenon is the way in which Southey's *Life* contributed to a larger discourse of nineteenth-century British masculinity and its casual reliance on distant foreign spaces for its discussion and realization. Accusations of British susceptibility to foreign influences in the debate surrounding Warren Hastings's impeachment, as well as widespread popular fear of epidemic and contagion thought to originate in the colonies made clear that colonial practices in populated, tropical areas, once believed to both establish and perpetuate British superiority and stability of character, often destabilized it, inviting a critique of colonial practices that extended to a critique of British identity.[1] In contrast, in the Arctic wastes, rugged, even reckless individualism served national goals without threatening social order at home.

In this way, the Arctic serves as a surprising and important site for the coalescence of an imperial British masculinity, a space starkly opposite to the more troubled space of the hot and humid tropical and subtropical lands compassing most of the British empire. Following the *Life*, numerous Arctic exploration accounts published in the early century contributed to a perception of the Arctic as a bleak space that challenged the bodily limits of its British explorers, and thus defined a specific, corporeal British masculinity that the nation then called upon in fighting its wars and administering its colonies. Participating in voyages of exploration, Southey argued, shifted individual allegiances and interests to national foci and made national heroes out of unthinking individual bodies. The sense that in the Arctic relationships between the geographic and the corporeal existed in stark relief and thus made legible and articulate invisible spaces of ideology and national subjectivity, as we shall see, both separated Arctic space from other colonial spaces and gave the Arctic a unique place in the national and imperial imaginary.

Southey's emplotment of Nelson's character development, with its quick conflation of heroic masculinity and Arctic space, belies the experience of explorers such as John Franklin, whose account of his 1818–21 Arctic mapping expedition told quite another story about British male bodies in the Arctic. In Franklin's account, the "unpeopled" Arctic is shown to be populated by diverse groups of self-sufficient—and to Franklin, surprisingly sophisticated—native men and women. It is also a

place where disciplined, resourceful British naval men almost succumb
to starvation and madness, a place in which the resistant, intact male
body so central to imperial heroic masculinity meets its limits. Though
his narrative depicts the fragility of the human body and, in turn, the
possible shortcomings of a national identity or character so dependent
on male embodiment,[2] the acceptance of Franklin as a hero in the
metropole on his return points to the intense and persistent ideological
investment attached to male bodies by a nation concerned in the early
nineteenth century with a sense of itself both as Union and on the
larger stage of world politics as a colonial power. Contrary to the apparent failures, or near failure, of male bodies depicted in Franklin's text, the
British reading public received his bestselling *Narrative of a Journey to the
Shores of the Polar Seas* (1823) as an account of British resourcefulness
and geographical triumph, and as further evidence of the British male as
uniquely suited to exploration and colonizing.

The accounts of national masculinity by Southey and Franklin
examined in this chapter serve to claim new geographies for national
space and to privilege male citizenship in the era of British imperial
expansion. As Tim Fulford has argued, the heroic figures central in tales
like these embodied British "virtues . . . such as patriotism, self-reliance,
courage, paternalism, and above all, attentiveness to detail" in order to
"renew" and promote a "myth of national character" ("Romanticizing
the Empire," 162). Thus, works as different as *The Life of Nelson* and
Franklin's *Journey* engage the pedagogic function of biography and autobiography. If, as Benedict Anderson has famously argued, nations are
conceived of and consolidated in the imaginations of a reading public,[3]
the representation of the nation by means of the male body imperiled in
alien space defines the nation at once as geographical space and as an
identifying set of character traits. Complicating claims by Linda Colley
and others that British identity in the early nineteenth century was consolidated against European or colonial "Others,"[4] these accounts affirm
national identity in an alien geography perceived as being (even if not literally) empty of other humans.[5] Far from "home," the British sailor-
explorer as national subject or "homo nationalis," discovers his own limits
and paradoxically consolidates and naturalizes a stable national identity.[6]

Taking place as they do far from Britain and equally far from viable
colonies, these Arctic narratives reinforce a national identity that conveniently is neither conservative nor radical. "Patriotism" was a much-
contested word in the early century, with loyalists and radicals alike
laying claim to it.[7] In comparison to domestic politics, colonial

concerns, and ongoing European geopolitics, Arctic space was perceived as uncomplicated and "pure." Of course, these perceptions of Arctic space as "pure" and "white" erased the area's geographical complexity. That its "blankness" lent itself to such an erasure of complexity made the Arctic a useful geographical space for articulating a racialized, gendered subjectivity in elemental, almost hagiographical terms. As a result, Arctic accounts smoothed over local political and class divisions and made citizenship and patriotism available to all readers. At the same time, however, the otherworldliness of the Arctic as the source of that identity ultimately points to the limits of the model of citizenship inculcated in the British explorer there. Arctic exploration identified and developed qualities unique to the British male in empty polar space, but the question remained as to how those qualities translated to the geopolitical space of Great Britain and its colonies. In Southey's account, the skills learned and character qualities discovered in the Arctic by Nelson lay essential groundwork for the admiral's later heroism in the service of the nation. Yet the Arctic location of Nelson's innate or latent heroism also threatens to destabilize that character. Like earlier, more successful accounts of Captain James Cook's voyages and Samuel Hearne's early Canadian exploration, Franklin's narrative of his expedition's near-disaster documents an investment in and preoccupation with imperiled male bodies. As the discussion that follows will document, however, Franklin's narrative reveals the male body—so essential to the public portrayal, comprehension, and consolidation of British identity as demonstrated by Southey to be enormously fragile, and, as a result, it imperils the national character that that body was believed to house.

I

Southey's *Life of Nelson* is overtly pedagogic, invested in what Tim Fulford has called "training in imperial duty," a text "by which Romanticism educated the British in an ideology of empire" ("Romanticism and Colonialism," 37). As David Eastwood has argued, Southey was invested in "affirm[ing] a more broadly based national politics that found expression not in narrowly political figures but in national heroes."[8] That *The Life of Nelson* is concerned with national questions is evident from its first pages. The account opens as one might expect with the birth of Nelson in 1758. By the end of the first page, however, the motherless twelve year old has joined the Royal Navy, where familial relations are replaced with naval structures of command, a dislocation Southey identifies as painful and literally uprooting:

> The pain which is felt when we are first transplanted from our
> native soil, when the living branch is cut from the parent tree, is
> one of the most poignant which we have to endure through
> life. There are after-griefs which wound more deeply, which
> leave behind them scars never to be effaced, which bruise the
> spirit, and sometimes break the heart: but never do we feel so
> keenly the want of love, the necessity of being loved, and the
> sense of utter desertion, as when we first leave the haven of
> home, and are, as it were, pushed off upon the stream of life.[9]

The demands the nation makes on young Nelson are expressed as
bodily: pains, bruises, and a broken heart. Young Nelson is "cut" from his
family tree only to be absorbed by the national tree, the British oak long
associated with naval service.[10] Southey's conflation of family tree and
British oak makes explicit that Nelson's body is a British body from
birth, one already called upon by its nation, although the miserable
young midshipman cannot recognize it until naval discipline makes it
clear to him.

In exchange for their bodies, the Royal Navy promised to provide
careers, money, and opportunities for heroism and glory to its sailors.
When he learns of the young boy's desire to serve, Nelson's uncle, Captain Suckling, writes to the family, "What has Horatio done, who is so
weak that he, above all the rest, should be sent to rough it out at sea?—
But let him come, and the first time we go into action a cannon-ball
may knock off his head and provide for him at once" (14). Suckling's
darkly humorous vision of the headless body literalizes the country's
demand for the unthinking bodies of its serving men. While the challenge to all naval subjects was to keep their heads attached to their
bodies, the challenge to Southey's Nelson—and by extension to readers
of *The Life* at home—was how to be a citizen subject without being
absorbed completely into the larger body politic. *The Life* seeks to provide a model of heroic national masculinity based on the cultivation of
something within the (unthinking) body, something unique to the
nation. Unlike intellect, which differed across a population, character
was understood to possess uniquely British components: accessible,
identifiable, and even quantifiable. In his portrait of Nelson, Southey
sought to describe qualities at once unique and replicable, discovered in

a distant place and yet latent in all British men. In this sense, Nelson becomes quite literally the embodiment of British national identity

We see this quite clearly in Southey's representation of Nelson as a commander. When Nelson advises a midshipman in *The Life*, "There are three things, young gentleman, which you are constantly to bear in mind. First, you must always implicitly obey orders, without attempting to form any opinion of your own respecting their propriety; secondly, you must consider every man your enemy who speaks ill of your king; and, thirdly, you must hate a Frenchman as you do the devil" (59), his words are prescriptive of a kind of national behavior. The "gentleman" addressed may be, like Nelson, middle-class young men pursuing social advancement in the Navy, but Nelson's advice also addresses Southey's audience of readers, transforming them into agents of nation as proxy midshipmen. To be such citizen-agents, Southey's Nelson suggests, sailors and readers must always and consistently locate themselves in relation to the sociopolitical order, both "vertically" within British society by understanding one's duty and obedience to superior officers (or classes) and the King, but also "horizontally" or geographically, by identifying as "anti-French" (a recommendation commensurate with Colley's assertions about the role of the French in the evolving British nationalist sentiment in the eighteenth and nineteenth centuries). This horizontal axis plays a crucial metonymical role in this process of identity formation by enlisting a more "democratic" geographic orientation that at once reinforces a sense of the physicality of nation while legitimizing the vertical axis of class identity.

Yet it is Nelson's suggestion about obeying orders that bears closer examination, coming as it does from someone who famously and literally turned a blind eye to orders at the Battle of Copenhagen. To reconcile the complex and sometimes contradictory demands of following orders, behaving as gentlemen, and acting heroically in Nelson's advice to the midshipman, Southey's narrative puts forward a model of duty and heroism not as simply *performed by*, and as a result embodied in the British sailor, but also as naturally *contained in*—and thus inevitably performed by—the male national body. The circular logic of national subject formation here posits national character as at once incipient in the sailor's body to be revealed in heroic adventure, and also produced by the very heroic adventure that simultaneously reveals it. Tim Fulford describes eulogizers of Nelson portraying a man who, "[b]y adherence to his duty, by self-command and courage in the face of danger, and by chivalric concern for his men [. . .] had maintained discipline and won"

("Romanticizing the Empire," 165). But, while Nelson's heroism was linked forever with his naval victories against the French at Copenhagen, the Nile, and Trafalgar, Southey locates Nelson's national masculinity, his heroism, and his reconciliation to duty much earlier, in Nelson's boyhood voyage to the Arctic.

Just a few pages into the *Life*, the teenaged Nelson embarks on a "voyage of discovery" to the North Pole as crew member of the eerily (and aptly) named polar exploration ship, *The Carcass*. As the first instance of Nelson's biography to which Southey attends thoroughly, the voyage to the pole is remarkable for several reasons. It makes concrete the "pains" required by Nelson's duty to navy and country due to the demands of polar navigation and the specific privations of the Arctic environment. Above all, the Arctic is the place where Nelson matures from boy to man, a transition that completes his break from his blood family and the realm of private citizenship and marks his allegiance to naval and national communities. By linking Nelson's national citizenship and heroic masculinity to qualities of physical hardiness and mental toughness cultivated and articulated in the alien landscape of the Arctic, Southey reasserts his earlier claim that Britishness is an embodied quality, and that character is thus concrete and quantifiable. At the same time, Southey's use of the sailor's body as site of both physical trial and national character formation analogizes bodily struggle (experienced on Arctic exploration voyages) as national struggle, and as a result shows national character to be something that needs to be cultivated in extremis.

That Southey should identify one source of Nelson's character to be Arctic in origin follows a British tradition of perceiving Arctic exploration as a kind of military engagement, due in part to the resistance of the polar climate and geography to English mercantilist expansion. Like so much of British imperial expansion, the history of British Arctic exploration is a confusion of private and governmental efforts. The quasi-military status of private expeditions was evident as early as Henry Hudson's 1610 voyage,[11] which as related by the seventeenth-century geographer Hakluyt, became part of a greater British national mythology of self-sacrifice and discipline.[12] Hakluyt's account reveals what soon became a recognizable trope and a strange logic associated with Arctic exploration: the misapprehension of Arctic experience in the metropole. Far from being successful, Henry Hudson's last mission resulted not in the discovery of the Northwest Passage, but in his death. Hudson's crew mutinied, and put Hudson, his son, and five others to sea in a small boat without provisions.

While Hudson is remembered for his heroic leadership, it is the *mutineers*—those disrupters of naval order—who bring back the certainty (later debated) of a Northwest Passage, escaping prosecution only by volunteering their geographical knowledge of previously uncharted space in return for amnesty on their return to England. The foundational texts in the British history of Arctic exploration—Hudson's logs and charts—can therefore be traced to the unpunished transgression of naval discipline and revolt against authority. Yet the Arctic persisted in being a site where discipline and authority, though tested, always emerged triumphant. The nation remembered a heroic Hudson, and the loyal shipmates who followed him to certain death rather than participate in the mutiny entered the national mythos for their self-sacrificing loyalty to their commander and became models of exemplary naval discipline. This willed misremembrance underlines British investment in the symbolic function of Arctic exploration as an investigation and articulation of British character. In the case of Hudson—and *The Life of Nelson,* and later, as we will see, in response to Franklin's first voyage—the reading public could read failed geographical discovery as successful national endeavor because the expedition produced a necessary and legible British masculinity, one that was self-sacrificing, loyal, resilient, and duty-bound. The Northwest Passage was important, but the model of British masculinity revealed in the search was perhaps even more so.

Since Southey actively drew from eighteenth-century polar exploration accounts in order to create a polar origin for the admiral's heroic masculinity, the *Life* taps into a powerful national investment in the Arctic as a space of national identity formation and discipline already well established by Hakluyt, Cook, Hearne, and others. At the same time, Southey reinforced and extended the popular perception of the Arctic as a desolate, empty space in which to discover British qualities. The chapter subtitle for the polar section of the *Life* reads, "He sails in Captain Phipps' Voyage of Discovery." Although Nelson's early mission for a northeast passage to the Pacific took place under Captain Constantine Phipps,[13] it was the account of exploration resulting from the mission, *A Voyage Toward the North Pole: Undertaken by His Majesty's Command, 1773* (1774), that commenced with the subtitle *Captain Phipps' Voyage of Discovery,* and Nelson, as warrants an unimportant teenaged junior officer, is nowhere to be found in that text. Yet Nelson becomes, through Southey's inclusive title and narrative, a retrospective part of the official record of exploration. By positioning Nelson's Arctic experience in a previous textual representation that is also the official document of the expedition, Southey establishes links between scientific travel and Nelson's later role as British hero of empire, an early recognition of the imbricated relation between scientific imperative, geographical knowledge, and the workings of empire.[14] In effect, what Nelson will learn in the Arctic—what he is taught about himself by it and what, in turn, Southey's readers learn about Nelson and national subjectivity—is as much the "Discovery" of *Phipps' Voyage* as the published scientific data and new maps generated by the expedition. Southey's substitution of Nelson's subjectivity for Phipps's "discovery" metonymically makes British masculinity and national character material fact, as concrete, quantifiable, reproduce-able, and organic as scientific and geographical measurements.

By constituting the British character in contrast to the empty landscape, the barren Arctic environment brings the materiality—and thus in early-nineteenth-century minds, the inarguable stability—of British character into stark relief in a way that the metropole and the colonies did not. Southey borrows freely from the published account of Phipps's voyage[15] in his descriptions of polar landscape as desolate, empty, and defined by negatives. In Southey's reiteration of Phipps's account, the Arctic's "dreariness" is indicated by absences, both of animate life and familiar weather:

> There was no thunder nor lightning during the whole time [the sailors] were in these latitudes. No insect was to be seen in this dreary country, nor any species of reptile—not even the common earth-worm. Large bodies of ice, called ice-bergs, filled up the valleys between high mountains, so dark, as, when contrasted with the snow, to appear black. The colour of the ice was a lively light green. Opposite to the place where [Phipps's men] fixed their observatory was one of these ice-bergs, above three hundred feet high: its side towards the sea was nearly perpendicular, and a stream of water issued from it. Large pieces frequently broke off, and rolled down into the sea. (10)

Thunder and lightning, like "the common earth-worm," are references to the familiar, to home. Not only is the Arctic unhomely, its very materiality is unstable: the sea quickly congeals into pack ice; seemingly solid icebergs calve into smaller bits that threaten passing vessels.[16] Southey's borrowed description of the chaotic landscape employs a vocabulary associated with the sublime, one that foregrounds the text's preoccupation with human fragility and hints at an almost otherwordly ecstasy of strange sensation.[17] Yet in this passage of rather clinical description, the sublime's dual promise of exhilaration and erasure ultimately resolves into the looming threat of extinction, a reminder of the precarious nature of self-preservation on Arctic voyages and a return of narrative attention from a large, unbounded landscape to the British body, and to the need to sustain a threatened national identity.

For Southey, it is in the unstable and unpopulated northern land-scape—as opposed to the various "unstable" colonial landscapes of numerous contemporary British texts—that Nelson's stable national identity coalesces. The moment of Nelson's maturity, of his transition from boy to man, from private subject to national citizen, is for Southey the same moment that the painter Westall depicted. Having stolen from the ship one night with a friend, Nelson encounters a polar bear. Southey's account of this incident contains what will become familiar plot points of Arctic narrative: bodies at risk and the danger of indiscipline.

> The fog thickened and Captain Lutwidge and his officers became exceedingly alarmed for [Nelson and his companion's] safety. Between three and four in the morning the weather cleared, and the two adventurers were seen at a considerable distance from the ship, attacking a huge bear. The signal to them to return was immediately made. . . . "Never mind," [Nelson] cried; "do but let me get a blow at this devil with the but-end of my musket and we shall have him." Capt. Lutwidge, however, seeing his danger, fired a gun, which had the desired effect of frightening the beast; and the boy then returned, somewhat afraid of the consequences of his trespass. The captain repri-manded him sternly for conduct so unworthy of the office which he filled, and desired to know what motive he could have for hunting a bear. "Sir," said he, pouting his lip, as he was wont to do when agitated, "I wished to kill the bear, that I might carry the skin to my father." (9)

The captain's reprimand forces "Young Nelson" to replace his desire to prove himself to his father with loyalty to his commander and country. Given the pedagogic nature and intent of national biography, Nelson's encounter with the polar bear teaches readers of Southey's text that the Royal Navy makes disciplined British men out of headstrong boys[18] while making visible the embodied nature of citizenship. Impetuous behavior is punished not because it puts an individual at risk, but because it puts a British body at risk. The sailor—that headless body Nelson's Uncle Suckling writes about—must be unthinking and selfless, but he must be unthinking and selfless in the right way, having substituted the nation's interests for his own.[19] Once Nelson became a midshipman, his body is no longer his own, and his will must accordingly be redirected from his desires to national ends, a redirection that results in a legible performance of national character.

The polar bear incident makes Nelson's newly discovered (although always there to be discovered) character visible, both to the young Nelson and to Southey's readers. Just as the individual gives way to the nation, and just as personal desires give way to national demands, so too does individual intransigence give way to national discipline. The young Nelson does not yet possess a dedication to the shipboard disciplinary structure with which he would become so familiar later in his career, since he has yet to learn to whom his allegiance is owed: in going after the bear for his father, Nelson chooses family tree over British oak.

Nelson's ample strength of will is demonstrated early in the Arctic section of *The Life*, when he commands the crew of a four-oared cutter across ice-filled open water to help save the expedition's ships from being caught in the pack ice. Yet without discipline, strength of will is simply willfulness. Thus, even as Nelson bravely marshals the resources of self for the good of nation in his efforts to save the ships, his actions are only part of the process of being reconciled to national identity. More than simply courage or will, that process ultimately requires recognition of and insertion in the vertical axis of rank and hierarchy: naval discipline served to condense and refine British character; the clarity of the Arctic canvas reified it, and in the process, made the components of heroic masculinity clearly legible.[20] That Southey has Nelson learn his "duty" to his captain and king in the threatening arctic wastes is no small thing for the man whose last words were, "Thank God, I have done my duty."[21]

Nelson's sense of duty, according to Southey, is cultivated by bodily risk in the shape of menacing walruses, marauding polar bears, and incapacitating ice. As such, Nelson's body becomes the fetishized center of the narrative early in the text. Since a standard trope of Arctic narratives is the disappearing body—the fewer the pages to the end, the less of the frostbitten body remains—Nelson's later career both extends and concentrates the narrative investment in embodied masculinity born in the polar north. Indeed, the admiral's physical body acts as what Anne

McClintock has identified as a national fetish,[22] an overinvestment that remains in circulation to this day. Although his Uncle Suckling's vision of a head shot off by cannon fire is never realized, as Nelson's character becomes more mythic his physical body diminishes: first the eye, then the arm, until ultimately only the bloodstained uniform in the National Maritime Museum remains. Southey's focus on Nelson's body thus reinforces the embodied and particularized nature of national masculinity, while strangely insisting on or even entailing the disappearance of that very patriotic body in order to bring national character to the fore.[23] The myth of Nelson, fabricated by writers such as Southey, occludes or surpasses Nelson himself; his hardy character and his national body— available, replicable—replace his diminished and disappearing physical body.

If Arctic narratives such as Southey's were not entirely unique in enabling individual bodies to be read as and replaced by national bodies, they differed from other imperial narratives in their persistence—necessary perhaps due to the very nature of Arctic exploration—of reading imperial "failures" to be read as national/ideological successes. Although Phipps's voyage fails in locating the North Pole, it produces a resistant British male body in which it locates national character, and in turn produces a model for heroism to be deployed in the cause of a national subjectivity accessible and legible to a politically diverse reading public. Later Arctic narratives, as we shall see, structured the experience of the British explorer on Southey's model, turning failures of stated expedition objectives into narrations of the successful negotiation of desolate, dangerous landscapes by strong British bodies having equally tenacious national characters. Indeed, the reaffirmation of British faith in male British bodies and in their usefulness and appropriateness to imperial and colonial projects would remain an important function of Arctic exploration throughout the nineteenth century as Arctic narratives shaped a widely circulated and just as widely misunderstood model of national heroic masculinity.

II

One of the first people to see Admiral Nelson's famous signal at Trafalgar—"ENGLAND EXPECTS THAT EVERY MAN WILL DO HIS DUTY"—was a young signal officer on board the *Bellerophon*, John Franklin.[24] In 1844,

Franklin would respond to the Admiralty's request that he direct his third and famously disastrous Arctic expedition with, "The highest object of my desire is faithfully to perform my duty," and become, as a result, the most famous Arctic explorer of the nineteenth century due to his unexplained disappearance in the vast polar north.[25] But while Nelson's Arctic genealogy was manufactured by Robert Southey, Franklin wrote his own when he documented his first Arctic expedition in the bestselling *Narrative of a Journey to the Shores of the Polar Sea*, a ripping page-turner of danger, disorientation, and near starvation that established Franklin as the most recognizable British naval hero since Nelson. Franklin's account of his four-year exploration of northern Canada developed and perpetuated the polar origins of national subjectivity set out by Southey while further establishing that Arctic exploration was as preoccupied with "Britishness" and masculinity as it was with mapping a baffling new imperial landscape.

Like Southey's *Life of Nelson*, Franklin's *Journey to the Shores of the Polar Sea* charts new imperial territory through the unrelenting demands the Arctic places on the human body, and as such the *Journey* maps national character and the boundaries of duty onto the cartographies of geographical space. While affirming the centrality of the imperiled British male body to Arctic narrative, Franklin ultimately underlines the precariousness of such a model, depending as it does on an ultimately fragile human body to house national character. The perils Franklin and his men encounter in the Arctic environment nearly kill them, and certainly smudge what for Franklin is a clear-cut line between British and other, civilized and savage. Only a fortuitous encounter with sympathetic and generous members of the Copper nation saved Franklin and his English companions, John Richardson and George Back, from death by starvation, but that intervention does not come soon enough, however, to save the expedition from a descent into murder and cannibalism that results in the death of an Englishman. Although the sensational conclusion of the *Journey* would seem to emphasize the perils of both the narrative's and the nation's over-investment in an embodied British masculinity, in the end that same overinvestment obscures the narrative's chronicle of the dispersal, disintegration, and even ingestion of British bodies.

Franklin participated in Britain's formal expansionist foreign policy when, as a young lieutenant in the Royal Navy in 1819, he set out to determine what his Admiralty orders called "the latitudes and longitudes of the Northern Coast of North America, and the trending of that Coast from the Mouth of the Coppermine River to the eastern extremity of that Continent"(xv) in an attempt to map the coast of the Northwest Passage. His "voyage" was primarily a land expedition, one that mapped the rugged landscape of the Canadian Shield. Although this landscape would certainly have been challenging both to traverse and to represent for Franklin and his men, it is by no means blank, unpeopled, and undifferentiated in the way that Britons both perceived and represented the truly "polar" Arctic space of sea exploration and northern whaling voyages. In a companion expedition to Franklin's, one that also covered the years of 1819–21, Captains John Ross and William E. Parry attempted to chart a sea route through the Northwest Passage through a landscape much more similar to that experienced by Nelson and Phipps than to the sub-arctic forests and rocky coasts encountered by Franklin. Yet such is the power of the Arctic exploration genre and of the nation's investment in it that Franklin's experiences were understood to take place in the empty space of Phipps's Arctic Ocean, even as facts insisted otherwise.[26] This misapprehension of the geography in which Franklin's narrative takes place was in part due to Franklin's rather sketchy representation of his surroundings, but also a testament to the power of representations such as Southey's of the Arctic as a blank space in which to map the character of British explorers.

Like others including Phipps before him, Franklin sought to supplement his naval income with the publication of his expedition memoirs, memoirs that are at once a personal account and a national production. A revision of his expedition summary submitted to the Admiralty, *The Journey* reproduced and refined the official account of the expedition while maintaining its general structure: its plot is chronological, with its parameters defined by Admiralty orders. Time is indicated throughout by both calendar dates and the documentation of physical movement, with Franklin's frequent and assiduous measurements of latitude and longitude recorded in his section headings and appendices. As early as mid-eighteenth century, sea narratives, according to Tobias Smollett, were "so stuffed with dry descriptions of bearings and distance, tides and current, variations of the compass, leeway, wind and weather, sounding, anchoring, and other terms of navigation, that no one but mere pilots or seafaring people can read them without disgust."[27] Yet Smollett's dismissal aside, measurements of "bearing" and "distance" do not function impersonally, as they locate the writer/explorer, reminding readers of the specific source of the narrative. In Franklin's case, latitude and longitude serve to remind both explorer and his readers of where, within a fraction of a degree, he is in relation to Greenwich and the Thames, paradoxically and insistently linking explorer and reader, voyager and home, by measuring the distance between them. It is precisely this distance, evoked as it is in listed compass and temperature readings, that sharpens the focus of the narrative onto the body of the explorer, making his a prosthetic national body that stands in for the citizen/ reader at home.

While measurements of compass points and temperature recorded in the narrative precisely located the explorer in terms of home, the reading public, and his political agenda, the Canadian landscape profoundly dislocated the explorer and also, by extension, his readers. Compass and clock, certainties in an uncertain landscape, helped Franklin map his location on his journey, but also reinforce the alien nature of his experience and force attention back on the body of the explorer as isolated subject. The problem was not one of location (defined as a fixed coordinate determined by compass readings), but one of *position*, which as Neil Smith and Cindi Katz observe, "incorporates a sense of perspective on other places."[28] It is just that perspective that the Arctic landscape, and the hardships associated with it, denies the explorer. Although Franklin, traversing the rocky wastes of the Canadian Shield, encounters a more differentiated landscape than the ice pack encountered by Nelson and Phipps, he still perceives that environment as a barren, inhospitable wasteland, one that he rarely even describes. For much of Franklin's narrative, the landscape he traverses could just as well be the utter white blankness his readers already associated with the Arctic, a blankness that, for lack of descriptive detail, his readers happily supplied.

Uncharacteristically attempting to capture the "rude and characteristic wildness" of the Hill Gates—a series of waterfalls—Franklin describes "rocks piled on rocks [that] hung in rude and shapeless masses over the agitated torrents which swept their bases, whilst the bright and variegated tints of the mosses and lichens, that covered the face of the cliffs, contrasting with the dark green of the pines, which crowned their summits added both beauty and grandeur to the general effect of the scene."[29] The old-world framing device of "romantic defile"—the language of the picturesque—ultimately fails to describe and contain Arctic space when a page later Franklin nearly drowns after slipping into the river between two sets of falls. Thereafter, Franklin largely abandons lengthy descriptive passages to resume narrating the movement of bodies through an un- or under-described landscape for much of the

rest of the text, a kind of surrender to the subgenre that Southey established in which the explorer's body eclipses landscape and geography as
the focus of the text and what is being mapped is British masculinity
and character over and above Arctic space.

Franklin's plunge into Hill Gates and his subsequent life-threatening
immersions in freezing rivers and bays coincide with a retreat from the
sublime in the narrative. The sublime—that merging of subject with
object that Coleridge described as the "sense of self-annihilation" that
occurs when "the beholder . . . becomes as it were a part of the work
contemplated"[30]—is exactly what Arctic exploration both promises and
threatens. For Arctic explorers, the fear is that Coleridge's "self-annihilation" might be realized in a breach of the limits of the sturdy, resistant
bodies of Franklin and his men, necessarily revealing the end of British
character.[31] Since survival for Franklin depends on moving through and
across landscape, to stop or to be overwhelmed by his surroundings by
opening himself up to the experience of the sublime is to risk a literal
joining with the landscape by the explorer being frozen in his tracks.

Paradoxically, however, the sublime that Franklin carefully avoids in
his narrative is still at work in the text in a way that Franklin's avoidance
of it makes all the more intense. The textual inexpression of the landscape's danger and beauty only amplifies the experience of the sublime
for the reader. Reading the *Journey*, fearful, invested readers wonder
what the explorers will encounter next, and who will survive and who
will not. Even more awful, however, is the tension and uncertainty created by a landscape that Franklin does not or cannot describe to his
readers. Safe on the other side of the Atlantic, readers' encounters with
the sublime, mediated first by Franklin's body standing in for their
bodies and second by his prose as evidence of his survival, enabled them
to participate in the expedition's overcoming of Arctic threat, and thus
to read Franklin's text as evidence of a British male national character
uniquely suited to imperial mapping projects, rather than as evidence of
human fragility.

As the text's investment in threatened bodies and, in turn, national
character mounts—and as those bodies become increasingly imperiled
in the course of the book—Franklin employs a narrative strategy of displacement and impersonalization in order to contain and control his
experience. His focus on the explorer's body is not on the body as individual, feeling, and sensate, or even *his* body, but rather on the body as a
generalized vessel or "thing," and his resulting "personal" narration of

Arctic hardship is strangely impersonal and remote. Franklin's narrative distance is in part a result of his speaking as a naval officer and thus as a scientific representative of his nation, but it is also a method of mediating the pressure of a hostile Arctic environment on the human body. In order to illustrate the difficulties of Arctic travel, Franklin incorporates into his account a journal entry by Midshipman Hood:

> The surface of the snow, thawing in the sun, and freezing at night, had become a strong crust, which sometimes gave way in a circle round our feet, immerging [sic] us in the soft snow beneath. The people were afflicted with snow blindness; a kind of ophthalmia occasioned by the reflection of the sun's rays in the spring. The miseries endured during the first journey of this nature, are so great, that nothing could induce the sufferer to undertake a second, while under the influence of present pain. He feels his frame crushed by unaccountable pressure, he drags a galling and stubborn weight at his feet, and his track is marked with blood. The dazzling scenearound him affords no rest to his eye, no object to divert his attention from his own agonizing sensations. When he rises from sleep, half his body seems dead, till quickened into feeling by the irritation of his sores. (173–74)

Hood's journal makes clear that Arctic exploration is first defined by the experience of bodily hardship. Progress, for him, is literally marked by blood on the landscape, the trail of a leaky human vessel. But Hood distances that hardship by employing a third person "he" in place of "I," in order to remove himself from the bodily pain that defines him and thus to contain the experience and to disavow his corporeal dissolution.

Yet the move to contain via the third person also generalizes Hood's experience, and as a result extends it to Franklin. This logic enables Franklin to remove himself from the bodily hardship entailed by northern exploration by letting Hood and his generic "he" do that work instead, a strategy of doubled containment that distances Franklin's resistant, intact body from the blood on the trail. The paradoxical result of this narrative strategy is to underline the body's centrality to Arctic exploration while depersonalizing and generalizing that same bodily experience. At the same time, however, Franklin's narrative distance also produces an ideological, mythic, national body that replaces his physical, individual body: as Hood's body stands in for Franklin's, so does

Franklin's body stand in for the national male body. Franklin's ultimate success in his endeavor—his return from the Arctic with scientific measurements, his negotiation of miles of open landscape without bleeding, freezing, or starving to death—relies on this ever more elongated metonymical chain and is thus attributed not to unique individual qualities but rather to his possession of a replicable, resilient body housing an equally replicable, resilient character, one that Franklin and his readers identify as British.

Franklin's body is both uniformly British and clothed in a British uniform, a fact brought to our attention when he and his men prepare to meet some natives "by decorating ourselves in uniform, and suspending a medal round each of our necks," gathering around their tents, over one of which "a silken union flag [is] hoisted" (201). That the success of this imperial mission relies on specifically British bodies is further emphasized by Franklin's insistent assertion of national difference in relation to the expedition's British participants (four officers, one seaman, and an employee of the NorthWest Company, a competitor of the Hudson's Bay Company), its sixteen French Canadian and Métis voyageurs, and its occasional native guides. Franklin can appreciate the hardiness of the voyageurs—who, even at the expedition's grimmest moments, outpace their British companions while carrying the bulk of the expedition's supplies—but the comprehension and navigation of Arctic landscape, conducted as it was in a space empty of the usual markers of identity and difference, demand of Franklin an exploration of and attention to "Britishness," those values and ideas about nation, behavior, and virtue housed in the British body.

As the expedition grows short of supplies, Franklin and the officers ration food and struggle with voyageurs who would "incur the hazard of absolute starvation, at a future period, for the present gratification of their appetites" (362). An internal sense of discipline paired with physical hardiness is identified as a British quality and thus, when the expedition threatens to descend into anarchy in September 1821—when running low on provisions, and caught farther north than they might like, the travelers headed south toward a NorthWest Company trading post—and the more physically fit voyageurs break rank and leave, the slower British participants are able to overtake them due to what Franklin identifies as superior intellect and discipline (431). Yet Franklin's insistence on the stability of Britishness in the face of near-starvation and death is a tension that eventually points to problems with an overly embodied model of national character. For human bodies that are conceived of as things even as they are understood to be incorporations of national identity are vulnerable to becoming no more than their materiality.

On September 13th, 1821, having turned south from the northern coast, the group faced imminent starvation, and Franklin orders the abandonment of all but the most basic of the scientific equipment, including the "dipping needle, azimuth, magnet, [and] a larger thermometer" (408). In addition to threatening the expedition's mandate, the abandonment of these instruments with which they map their relationship to the metropole brings into question and contest the categories that the British explorers use to define themselves. Out of supplies, the party finds itself scraping and boiling buffalo hides, and making soup out of abandoned and rotted wolf carcasses. As categories of civilized and savage, animate and inanimate, destabilize in the face of a hunger so extreme that the men are reduced to eating "their old shoes and a few scraps of leather," so too does national identity recede in the face of a universal and weak human body. When Dr. Richardson, the expedition doctor, almost drowns while crossing a river and is stripped to prevent hypothermia, the expedition members recognize themselves, with "the Canadians simultaneously exclaim[ing], 'Ah que nous sommes maigres' at seeing the skeletal officer" (424). In recognizing Richardson's skeletal thinness as their own ("Ah, we are thin"), the Canadians refuse to recognize national difference and Franklin underlines this lapse in national self-assertion by recording it in French. As this process continues in the days before the expedition's rescue by generous Copper natives, a group of survivors, including Franklin and two voyageurs, embrace as aphasic near-cadavers who pay no attention to rank or nationality as they await death. The distance between Franklin's account and what we see in Southey's *Life of Nelson* is quite striking. One can only imagine what Nelson (at least the Nelson presented by Southey) would say about such merging with the hated francophone. Yet in this moment of metonymy's collapse, we see an effect, similar to that of the "absent" sublime in the text, where the very threat of lapsing into savagery or Frenchness becomes a reassertion of national identity.

The tension between Arctic navigation requiring a body that resisted absorption in that alien geography and Franklin's strategy for negotiating that desolate and unfriendly environment by objectifying the human body in order to distance and contain his suffering results in what was for Franklin's contemporary readership a startling and sensational account of cannibalism. That the cannibal moment, so heavily associated with encounters with tropical and colonial Others,[32] encroaches on Arctic narrative again points to the difference between the Arctic associated with Nelson—white, pure, a landscape of stark relief—and the darker, messier, scree-filled sub-Arctic space Franklin navigates. Yet as the strangely logical result of a narrative invested in the objectification of the body, cannibalism in the *Journey* is yet one more narrative by which the diminution of the physical body is staged so that the national or ideological body—and in turn the character housed in that body—can come to the fore.

Richardson's account of the incident, included near the end of Franklin's text, establishes just how removed from England the Arctic really was by bringing home the effective "ends" of Arctic hunger, of an embrace gone too far, as well as the Arctic's ability to turn the human into a "thing." Split off from Franklin and the main party in order to search for food, Richardson's party grows increasingly desperate. The Canadian Métis voyageur Michel launches into antiWhite invective, accusing earlier voyageurs of eating his ancestors. After first urging the others to kill him and eat him, he kills the British sailor Hood while the others are out foraging for food. Hood's murder forces the expedition's survivors to confront the fact of their own unknowing cannibalism. Earlier, Michel had returned from a supposed hunting expedition with "wolf meat" that the other expedition members had partaken of, and Franklin concludes on Hood's death that the "wolf meat" had been the human flesh of others in their party whom Michel had killed while ostensibly hunting.

Unlike Nelson's polar bear, an external danger that retreats in the face of British derring-do, Franklin's cannibalism reveals that the Arctic threat, like Arctic landscape, is more indefinite. Like the Canadian landscape that threatens to consume the British bodies that traverse it, the explorers consume one another. The Arctic landscape, which for Southey functions as an empty stage on which to perform British identity, for Franklin becomes a place frighteningly capable of erasing difference. Franklin's possible ingestion of human flesh and his uncertainty about whether or not he has done so forces him and his readers to recognize that seemingly stable categories of British and Other, human and inanimate, are not at all reliable.

In face of this revelation and of the physical evidence of the expedition's cannibalism, however, the narrative energetically asserts that while

Englishmen might eat anything—their shoes, the hair off the dead seaman Hood's buffalo robe—they don't eat each other. Richardson kills Michel and the uneaten corpse of Hood is buried. "Had my own life alone been threatened, I would not have purchased it by such a measure," Richardson writes, justifying his restoration of British values to the expedition. "I considered myself as entrusted also with the protection of [the English sailor] Hepburn's [life], a man, who, by his humane attentions and devotedness, had so endeared himself to me, that I felt more anxiety for his safety than for my own" (458). A resurfacing of the now-sublimated logic of "selflessness" seen in the sacrifice of Hudson's loyal crew and Nelson's Arctic lesson, Richardson's justification for killing Michel is also a reassertion that conscious cannibalism is limited to the practice of the uncivilized, of those inhabitants of Africa and Central America whom the Arctic, at least the Arctic as imagined by British readers, is supposed to be *beyond*. At the moment where the Arctic reveals itself to be just like other spaces of colonial encounter, Franklin and Richardson emphatically reassert its difference.

That physical peril recruits and solidifies one's identity (learned via texts such as Southey's *Life of Nelson*) reassures Franklin's readers, but the disquieting truth of Franklin's *Journey*, one understood and articulated by the explorers themselves, is that the men risk losing not only their lives in the Arctic, but their "civilized-ness" as a direct result of demands on the physical body. Once the citizen of the wasteland, how might one return? Despite his reassuring quotations of scripture and his moral justification, Richardson is still a killer. The anxiety about the lasting effects of the voyage and the party's capacity to resume its place in British society are best expressed by Franklin's junior officer, Hepburn, as they slowly starve and wait in desperation for deliverance: "Dear me, if we are spared to return to England, I wonder if we shall recover our understandings" (466).

Whether or not the explorers were ever to recover their understandings, readers of the *Journey* certainly understood the text as a triumphant narrative of British masculinity. Fittingly, the mechanism of reifying the national body with its accessible, replicable character is itself cannibalistic: Nelson's national body replaces the awful, unthinking object, the physical body of the (even inadvertent) British cannibal Franklin. British readers supplied the interiority and introspection missing from Franklin's narrative with what they had learned from earlier accounts such as Southey's, and embraced Franklin as a "new Nelson" upon his return to the metropole and publication of the Admiralty reports that served as the first draft of his published account. Welcomed to society balls and literary salons, a popular guest of the cultured class who was able to move from staterooms of Arctic ships to sitting rooms in Belgravia, Franklin was a literal embodiment of British heroism. In his attempt to map real space, he was perceived to have mapped the interior resources of an individual, and that space in turn was generalized into a map of national character, one learned not from Franklin himself, but from a tradition of understanding British character—resilient, hardy, and courageous—as emerging through Arctic tests. These legible, even quantifiable qualities were recruited to justify colonial expansion and to naturalize the claims Britain made during mapping projects subsequent to the one Franklin commanded, thus solidifying the symbolic role of Arctic exploration in the larger imperial project throughout the nineteenth century.

III

Franklin's account and his subsequent career, however, not only reveal how powerful the link between the male body and national character was, but also the limits of it. Developed in isolation and in extremis, the heroic masculinity of Romantic-era Arctic explorers did not in the end translate well to the metropole where the symbolic functions of that identity were embraced at the expense of the men. The reception of the *Journey* and the public's interpretation of the explorer as an embodiment of British character led to Franklin's 1836 appointment as governor of Van Diemen's Land. Qualities of character revealed in Arctic trial, apparently, made one an ideal colonial administrator.[33]

But Franklin's six-year tenure in Hobart revealed that the special talents of that paragon of Britishness, the Arctic explorer, did not, in fact, translate into extraordinary administrative qualities. The full tale of Franklin's self-destruction as colonial administrator is a complicated one that includes self-promoting and self-serving assistants cooperating with an unfriendly press,[34] but it unfolds to indicate a protagonist with little or no political savvy or social awareness. Franklin's Tasmanian debacle is an unwritten epilogue to the *Journey*, one that might affirm Midshipman Hepburn's doubt that survivors of the journey could function in society on their return, and one which reveals the limits of the circulated model of masculinity perpetuated by Arctic exploration accounts.

The last nail in the coffin of Franklin's governorship was an incident that eerily echoed his triumphant return from the Arctic. In 1842, Franklin, his second wife Lady Jane,[35] and a small party of friends, supported by twenty convicts, took a trip on horseback to Lake St. Clair in the interior of Tasmania. The plan was to camp for a while, cross a river, and then continue on foot to nearby Macquarie Harbor where they would meet a ship to return them to Hobart. Poor weather and floods first delayed them at the lake and later made the river impassable. The group had insufficient provisions and were weakened by food shortages when, finally, two of the party managed to make it to the ship to bring help. But the saga continued: poor weather held the ship up in harbor for another three weeks, during which they once again ran out of food. By the time they returned, the governor and his party were thought dead and a party of convicts had been dispatched to rescue them. These convicts, in turn, required rescue from starvation. It was the Arctic narrative all over again, but played out on a different, colonial landscape, with different (civilian and female) participants. No matter that Tasmania's interior was not tame—it was *mapped* after all, and thus known.

The press had a field day: imagine, the great Arctic navigator being lost in an island's interior! Franklin's pardoning of the prisoners who had searched for his party makes perfect sense using the rationale of polar expedition: their willingness for self-sacrifice in attempting a rescue— even if it turned out to be gestural—was behavior an Arctic veteran recognized and valued. Franklin himself had gone without food and restricted the diets of others in his party at Lake St. Clair so the escort of prisoners could maintain their strength; a command decision based on their usefulness as porters and the possibility of a long-term stay while waiting out the floods. When his actions became known, they, like the pardon, were (mis)interpreted by the free citizens of Hobart as Franklin's inability to understand how social divisions in the new colony worked. Techniques developed and refined in the Arctic did not, in fact, translate to civilization, even at the edges of empire. Franklin rather ignominiously learned of the appointment of his gubernatorial replacement while reading the newspaper, and returned "home" to England, condemned to being misunderstood.

Lady Jane knew that her husband's reputation depended on his Arctic actions. To restore him not only to his former glory, but to himself, she lobbied for his appointment as commander of the Admiralty's 1845 Arctic expedition, writing a member of the Arctic Council, "I dread exceedingly the effect on his mind of being without honourable and immediate employment."[36] Both Franklin and Lady Jane understood that the Arctic could restore Franklin to what he had been, because it could restore him to the place and situation where he had *become* it. His effectual disintegration in colonial territories could only be reconstituted or halted in a space of utterly symbolic colonialism.

CHAPTER THREE

A Propitious Hard Frost

The Arctic of Mary Shelley
and Eleanor Anne Porden

... voyages to the Poles,
Are ways to benefit mankind, as true,
Perhaps, as shooting them at Waterloo.
—Byron, *Don Juan*, Canto I, stanza cxxxii

How much happier that man is who believes his native town
to be the world, than he who aspires to become greater than
his nature will allow.
—Victor Frankenstein

I hope this fine cold weather suits both you and the book. I
used always to find a hard frost propitious to my writing, and
certainly it ought to be peculiarly congenial to the subject of
your narrative.
—Eleanor Anne Porden, letter to John Franklin,
December 28, 1822

As the Arctic expeditions of Sir John Ross and John Franklin
prepared for departure, two very different young women wrote
and published popular literary works on Arctic themes. Mary
Shelley had started *Frankenstein* in Switzerland in the summer of 1816,
but only added its Arctic framework later that autumn or in the winter
of 1817, before finally publishing the novel in 1818.[1] Meanwhile, in

53

London, the eighteen-year-old poet Eleanor Anne Porden commemorated the impending polar missions with her poem *The Arctic Expeditions*. Other than their interests in writing and the Arctic, the two young women had little in common. Daughter of the architect William Porden, Eleanor grew up in a circle that included the Disraelis and the Flaxmans. Like his friend John Flaxman, the sculptor who famously voiced the conservative side of the Romantic aesthetic debate, William Porden's politics sided with those of his aristocratic clients, and although his daughter presided over a monthly salon, her notebooks and journals reveal her to be fully invested in middle-class propriety.[2] In contrast, Mary Godwin Shelley, whose radical mother Mary Wollstonecraft had died as a result of Mary's birth, famously had eloped with Percy Bysshe Shelley, and retreated with her half-sister Claire to Europe, where they spent the summer of 1816 living near Byron in Switzerland.

Despite their different backgrounds and politics, in 1818 Shelley and Porden both published works that employ Arctic space in order to critique masculinist geographical projects that—due to their importance in the national imagination—limit female participation not only in voyages of exploration themselves, but more widely in culture. The shared assertions and confidence of Shelley's and Porden's very different works further reveal the public perception of Arctic space in Britain as an extraterritorial space in which to constitute a masculinity that was then deployed at home and abroad as the basis and justification for nation and empire. As women who addressed national subjects in their writing, Shelley and Porden were not alone, and joined others including Maria Edgeworth, Mary Mitford, Felicia Hemans, and Anna Seward. Gary Kelly has argued that in the 1800s through 1810s, the nation became an especial focus of women writers and that as a result "national history and culture were made to seem a particularly feminine domain," due to the widely-read work of women novelists in particular. Yet, Kelly continues, the feminization of these topics was "resisted and eventually appropriated by the remasculinization of culture," of which, as noted in the first chapter, the resurgence of interest in polar exploration with its emphasis on male hardiness and derring-do in the name of national endeavor could be considered part.[3] Certainly *Frankenstein* and *The Arctic Expeditions* both assert that traditionally male topics and domains are appropriate subjects for women writers and, although Shelley and Porden conceive of very different roles for women in the national project and disagree on the larger issue of imperialism, each text in the end argues for female authorship as a form of national participation.

Patricia Meyer Spacks identifies the strategies open to women writing in the early nineteenth century as taking two forms: women could either write about what they knew from experience, or they could employ fantasy to escape the constrained realities of their lives.[4] Obviously, Porden and Shelley could not rely on their own physical experiences and observations of polar space in their accounts. Yet having defeated male attempts at mastery, the Arctic might have seemed equally available to them as an imagined space on which to map a response to the gendered narrative that saturated polar exploration accounts. In any case, the geographical distance of the Arctic from Britain made it a safe place on which to stage a discussion of issues that were perceived as domestic because they had to do with women and local or national concerns. George Levine asserts in his influential reading of *Frankenstein* that the Arctic was "distant from the centers of realistic drama [where] illicit and uncivilized extremes are played out," and as a result was a space in which and against which to define realism.[5] I propose substituting nation and the national subject in Levine's equation: as a place of extremes distant from the center of nation, the Arctic was for Shelley and Porden—like male explorers and writers of Arctic exploration accounts—a space in which and against which to define a national subject.[6]

While both women produced texts in reaction to a prevailing masculinity expressed in the exploration of polar space, Shelley's and Porden's engagements with national issues and their writing of national projects are very different. For both authors, representations of the distant place of the Arctic north work to redefine a space appropriated as all-male, and each asserts for women and their texts a role in the nation previously reserved for men. Shelley uses polar narrative in *Frankenstein* to rewrite masculinist projects of scientific exploration—as well as to critique the related aesthetics of male Romantic poets—by pushing the limits of Walton's narrative to collapse. Her novel's condemnation of homosocial order as the basis of a national identity that favors male imperial appetite over domesticity and community indicts the imperial project, and by extension the society that both underpins and is constituted by it. In contrast, in *The Arctic Expeditions*, Porden claims for women those qualities made manifest in men's exploration of vast, unfriendly spaces, and in so doing asserts women's equal participation in and importance to national and imperial projects that, although she would rewrite their specifics, she embraces as a whole. Perhaps as a result of their political differences, different aesthetics emerge in these pieces as well: Shelley claims literary writing for women by dismissing male forms in her ventriloquism of them, while Porden inscribes herself into male discourse and borrows her literary authority from them.

Long celebrated as one of the most important literary treatments of the legacy and the limits of the age of reason, *Frankenstein* is literally an outlandish tale: the novel famously takes the form of letters and an expedition journal sent back to England by an English polar explorer, Robert Walton, to his sister Margaret Saville. Though the Arctic frame of *Frankenstein* has been noted by a number of commentators, critical attention tends to focus on the novel's explorer-narrator, his travels, and his encounter with Victor Frankenstein, rather than on the figure to whom the text is addressed, Walton's sister at home.[7] As a result, for critics such as Peter Brooks, Walton's sister "has no more existence in the novel than a postal address."[8] However, given that the opening line of Frankenstein is "To Mrs. Saville, England," it would seem unwise to dismiss her so easily. It may make more sense to read *Frankenstein* as an Arctic narrative about the limits of men addressed to a female British audience. If we do so, we can see it more concretely as a response to the well-documented preparations of the 1818 Arctic expeditions as the material conjunction of national and imperial endeavor to heroic masculinity. For, as documented in the previous chapter, polar exploration, although carried out under the aegis of science, was also—and perhaps primarily—a project of masculine imperial and national identity building. As expressed by John Barrow, who as Secretary to the Admiralty vocally and energetically advocated polar exploration, the quest for "a north-west passage to India and China has always been considered as an object peculiarly British."[9] Yet in his history of voyages of Arctic exploration, Barrow's use of a recognizably imperial rhetoric that seeks to enfold polar geography and scientific knowledge into a British domain only highlights the exclusion of women from the project. For women, then, polar exploration not only physically excluded them but indicated larger ways in which women's participation in national and imperial projects either was already limited or in danger of being eroded.

As Jessica Richard's reading of *Frankenstein* as a "polar romance" argues, Shelley's use of contemporary arguments advocating polar exploration in Walton's fantasy of a warm polar sea augment and strengthen the novel's critique of Romantic enthusiasm.[10] I would like to extend Richard's claim for Shelley's novel as critique of both the "romantic quest" narrative of polar exploration (such as those endorsed by polar enthusiasts Daines Barrington and John Barrow) and Romantic imaginings more generally, to include the easy coalescence and naturalization of imperial masculinity that underpins both projects.

If the premises and promise of polar exploration reveal and constitute flawed romance, as Richard has argued, the model of identity produced by that flawed romance has larger aesthetic and political repercussions. Arctic narratives discussed in the introduction and the previous chapter—in their consumption by readers, at least—shared with male Romantic writers a tendency toward universalizing and transcendental aspirations. Where in polar narrative the experiences and qualities of a few explorers were exported and applied to the British male, the Romantic lyric form as practiced by Percy Bysshe Shelley and others universalized the sensations and experience of the poet. By establishing a parallel between Arctic exploration and a specific male Romantic aesthetic, Mary Shelley enables us to read the "extradomestic" focus of Romantic poetry—articulated as an escape from the domestic into nature by Wordsworth, from England into Orientalist fantasy by Coleridge and Byron, or, in the case of Percy Shelley, into continental European landscape and classical myth[11]—not as a retreat from imperial or national questions, but as an articulation of the same impulse that early-nineteenth-century Arctic narrative both enacted and made legible: the importance of an extranational space to naturalize and make legible a masculinity that could then be enlisted for the larger political project of imperial expansion while at the same time shoring up a newly assured masculinity at home.

The seemingly dissimilar endeavors of polar exploration and poetic expression are united in *Frankenstein* by means of their exclusion of women. Walton's letters home to his sister from the Arctic literalize the exclusion of women from larger national and cultural projects, since for Britons in the early nineteenth century travel to the Arctic was uniquely limited to men. As a result, the identity developed and disseminated through polar exploration accounts was only available to males. By narrating the novel to a female audience in the metropole from a male polar geography, Shelley reveals not only women's exclusion from the imbricated aesthetic, scientific, and national-imperial projects with which the novel so rigorously engages, but also that her skepticism of such projects rests on their emphasis on the homosocial, extradomestic, and extranational as the source of their authority and knowledge, be it political or scientific. Such a focus or trajectory, the novel indicates, is also suspect in that it is an imperial logic, one that would constitute the national via the imperial at the cost of more local values.

Shelley offers competing solutions to these layered problems in *Frankenstein*. On the one hand, she argues for persistent female participation in these processes of national identity formation, both in her own writing of *Frankenstein* and in her sense that her primary audience is those who, like Mrs. Saville, are left behind by brothers, husbands, and sons. On the other hand, the excess of the novel, its careening narrative shot through with the Gothic—so often "blamed" on Mary Shelley's lack of writerly control—seems in itself a critique of male narratives, be they by Arctic explorers, Swiss scientists, or Romantic poets. While female authorship and, by extension, participation in what are national projects, is important to Shelley, simply inserting or reinserting women into these projects will not address what for her are larger problems with them, that is, their paradoxical reliance on extradomestic spaces and their restless rejection of feminized local or domestic spaces. The overwrought nature of the different narratives in *Frankenstein* serves to indict the linked projects of geographical expansion, scientific exploration, and Romantic representation by pushing them to their extremes in order to sap them of the very masculinity they are deemed to construct, one used in turn to justify and perpetuate further projects. In this sense, we might extend Richard's point about reading *Frankenstein* as romance to suggest that Shelley's use of what by then had become a feminized genre as the vehicle of her critique deflates the masculine pretensions of the Romantics both by inserting them within a broader narrative of impotent and unsuccessful questing and by embroidering that narrative with the excesses of sentiment and drama for which the novel is by now almost infamous. By pushing romance close to the bounds of parody, Shelley ironically encloses the "questing" masculinity of the early-nineteenth-century polar explorers and Romantic poets in the very femininity they are so desperately trying to escape.

That Shelley locates the source of her critique in the Arctic makes clear her understanding of how Arctic exploration is itself a kind of romance and thus, although a scientific and geographic project, linked to imaginative projects such as those of Romantic poets. Walton's "favourite dream" of his "early years" is exploration, dating from a childhood spent reading "accounts of various voyages" found in his uncle's library, and to pursue it he must leave England.[12] Walton's conception of a North Pole surrounded by a warm ocean is one he has found in books, including those by the English naturalist-lawyer Daines Barrington, an ardent supporter of the Constantine Phipps voyage that changed Horatio Nelson from boy to man in his first act of national heroism. Thus, Walton's journey—including its yearning for romance and its source in the imagination—while it seeks to discover the pole is also a journey toward what he hopes will be working model of mature masculinity.

In imagining the Arctic as a tropical paradise even as "a cold northern breeze play[s] upon [his] cheeks" (26), Walton privileges the imagination over fact and experience. We might read *Frankenstein* as an impossible bildungsroman; the real discovery that Walton (and for that matter Victor) pursues is the discovery of himself as a man. The Arctic's appeal to Walton lies in it being "never before visited" a place of imagination that, through his exploration, may be transformed into a space of authorship. Walton wants to "tread a land never before imprinted by the foot of man" (26) both to inscribe his own footprints and write his own narrative, and thus the act of exploration is itself a kind of writing and the Arctic a blank page on which to inscribe a narrative.[13] The idea of an empty Arctic and by extension of a *sui generis* masculinity for Walton, however, is as much a fiction as the open, tropical Polar Sea envisioned by Barrington: Walton encounters other beings—Frankenstein and the creature—and an impenetrable ice field. His link between writing and self-making and indeed the very genre of bildungsroman itself are problematized when Walton's tale is replaced by Victor Frankenstein's story at the same time as his physical progress toward the North Pole halts.

If in stalling Walton in his conjoined quests for geographic and self-knowledge, Shelley points to the impossibility of self-generation (a point also made by Frankenstein's haunting by his creature), she extends this critique to larger issues of British expansion and exploration. Crucially, the unmapped Arctic of *Frankenstein* is already recruited into the mythos of British expansion and exploration. Not only did Arctic veteran John Croker review the novel in the *Quarterly Review*, but his piece on *Frankenstein* was wedged between reviews of an account of a recent Congo Expedition and a history of the rise of the Bengal Native Infantry. This juxtaposition suggests that Arctic space was considered a space of British expansion, and Walton himself employs a rhetoric of imperial expansion that links his knowledge project with power and domination when he relates his ambitions to Frankenstein:

How gladly I would sacrifice my fortune, my existence, my
every hope, to the furtherance of my enterprise. One man's life
or death were but a small price to pay for the acquirement of
the knowledge which I sought; for the dominion I should
acquire and transmit over the elemental foes of our race. (35)

While Walton's voyage is one of demystification and domination of "elemental foes" rather than human enemies, his language of domination
conflates scientific knowledge and geopolitical domination.[14] It is not so
difficult to imagine almost identical language being used to legitimate
dominance over colonized "primitives." Conjecturing that the Arctic's
"productions and features may be without example, as the phenomena
of the heavenly bodies undoubtedly are in those undiscovered soli-
tudes," Walton hopes to "there discover the wondrous power which
attracts the needle; and may regulate a thousand celestial observations,
that require only this voyage to render their seeming eccentricities consistent forever" (26). The erasure of "eccentricities" frames Walton's project in a science that hopes to subjugate nature to human use. In Walton's
case, this use is imperial: by mapping natural and geographical phenomena, he links his voyage to England's expanding empire, since at least
part of his purpose is to find and "confer on all mankind" (26) the "ines-
timable benefit" (26) of a passage between the Atlantic and the Pacific.

Walton's transition to maturity is thus conjoined to his understanding of himself as British, an identity that paradoxically requires him to
leave England and his sister behind. Yet his letters to his sister and his
hope for eventual publicity for his achievements reveal that, unlike
Victor, in his quest Walton sees himself in terms of community: brothers
require sisters, national heroes require a public to adore them, Walton's
discovery must be conveyed back to England. His opinions of shipboard
life and relations with his crew reflect the trajectory of Walton's own
comprehension of the demands of male citizenship. At first uneasy as a
member of the ship's crew, he attributes his "intense distaste to the usual
brutality exercised on board ship" (29) to the years spent under his
sister's "gentle and feminine fosterage" (29) instead of in the environment of all-male education. Walton is surprised to find "some feelings"
"in these rugged bosoms," although it is not surprising that of the two
seamen he singles out for praise, one is an Englishman, "a man of wonderful courage and enterprise," "madly desirous of glory: or rather, to
word my phrase more characteristically, of advancement in his profession" (29). Although Walton misses his "gentle" sister and by extension

the society that she represents, the centrality of the homosocial to his layered project is itself enough to condemn it for Shelley.[15] The explorer's wish for "the company of a man who could sympathise with" him, a friend "to participate [in his] joy" and "sustain [him] in his dejection," reflects his desire to connect with others, but also reflects his ambivalence toward abstracted, anonymous citizenship. Writing, he admits to his sister, is "a poor medium for the communication of feeling" (28), because it is not reciprocal. When Walton writes, "I have no friend, Margaret: when I am glowing with the enthusiasm of success, there will be no one to participate my joy" (28), he expresses how even his "beloved" reader Margaret cannot supply him with "eyes that would reply to mine" (28). Yet when Walton uses the "language of [his] heart" to share his ambition with Frankenstein, he is met simultaneously with the recognition of their similitude and the incompleteness and failure arising from the traits on which their sympathy is based. Shelley underscores the necessary failure of both questers when Frankenstein responds to Walton, "Unhappy man! Do you share my madness?" (35).

If, for Robert Southey, Nelson's capacity for national heroism was the "discovery" of Constantine Phipps's journey in search of the North Pole, Victor Frankenstein's narrative is Walton's discovery. In place of an open polar sea, Walton encounters Victor's fantastical tale and ultimately the monster himself. Walton's belief that in Frankenstein he has found "a brother of [his] heart" (29) is at once true and erroneous. For while the two men share ambition and an interest in science, for Walton the "vast and irregular plains of ice" are simultaneously an uncharted space of imaginative potentiality and a source of as-yet-undiscovered scientific laws and certitude. In contrast, Victor's Arctic is a bleak landscape across which he chases his rejected, embittered creation, the sterility of which is symbolic of the price his commitment to overreaching "Promethean" science exacts.[16]

Yet Walton and Victor share the radical, disinterested individuality Shelley associates with Victor's quest for scientific knowledge, one that requires his repudiation of family and community and puts them at risk. Victor's famous circumvention of heterosexual reproduction results in the destruction of community when the creature goes on his murderous rampage. The death of Victor's family is at once the personal cost of his overarching ambitions, and a method by which Shelley discusses the impact on the nation of the model of masculinity and knowledge that Victor and Walton represent. The monster's haunting of Victor, his extermination of Victor's family, and the scientist's ultimate defeat and death indict both solipsistic masculine endeavors and the belief, so central to Arctic accounts and other imperial writing, that nation formation happens "elsewhere," in the cultivation of heroic men and the extension of geographical domination in distant places.

Shelley invites a reading of family domesticity as a representation of nation by portraying the Frankensteins as an assembled family, rather than an organic one. Anca Vlasopolos links the family's annexations of single women—of Victor's "more than sister" Elizabeth and of the elevated domestic Justine—to the Frankensteins status as aristocracy, and certainly the family's class position enables these quasi-adoptions to occur.[17] But Elizabeth's adoption can also be read through the lens of nationalism: her stateless and property-less existence previous to her adoption is linked directly to questions of nation and national identity by her biological father's imprisonment in Austria for political activities linked to Italian nationalism. Joining the Frankenstein family gives the stateless Elizabeth two kinds of citizenship, familial and national. She becomes sister, cousin, mother (when Victor's own mother dies), and future wife; in short, Elizabeth inhabits an array of figurations of women on which both domestic ideology and national discourses depend. At the same time, the assembled nature of Frankenstein's family reflects the ethnic and linguistic composition of Switzerland, a unified and stable state despite its many languages, religions, and perceived ethnicities. If the composition of Frankenstein's family reflects Switzerland, it also echoes the composite nature of Great Britain. Thus, while Victor's tale conveys the cost of his ambition and solipsism on his family/nation, Walton's polar navigation on behalf of Great Britain—as well as the national masculinity and character understood to be produced by it—can be understood as threatening to the very nation it seeks to define.

Shelley solidifies the connection between Victor's story and British identity not only in her transnational pairing of Victor and Walton, but in Victor's account of his travel to Great Britain. Traveling with his friend Clerval, the restless Victor tours England's historic sites, but driven by his desire to track the creature, he ignores their deeper significance for national allegory.[18] Clerval on the other hand, whose early interest in chivalric romances and "masquerades" reveals his understanding of links between domestic and public/national interests, and who is effeminized by his selfless love of Victor, is attentive to Britain and so taken with it that he declares he could spend his life there. Shelley, who identifies Clerval's "sensibility" (133) with "ardent affections" (133) and devotion, recognizes in him a masculinity in distinct contrast to Walton/Victor's.

For Shelley's British readers, the journey allows for a greater understanding of the entwined spatial and social components of England and
its distinctiveness from Great Britain; landscape and national history are
mutually constitutive in Victor's travel narrative: "Almost every town was
marked by the remembrance of some story" (134). Victor says of
Oxford, "As we entered this city, our minds were filled with the remembrance of the events that had transacted there more than a century and a
half before. . . . The spirit of elder days found a dwelling here, and we
delighted to trace its footsteps" (136). The history that fascinates Victor
and Henry is political; Oxford is experienced as a place where Charles I
"collected his forces. This city had remained faithful to him, after the
whole nation had forsaken his cause to join the standard of parliament
and liberty" (136). Victor's identification with Charles I may be in his
own failed effort to be monarch of a race, and in his subsequent embattled exile. Yet while Shelley's invocation of Charles I makes Victor's
predicament universal—failed ambition and exile are not new to him—
his interest in the failed monarch reveals Victor's goals as being opposed
to "liberty" and sociability. In the importation of the monstrous into
Britain, both in Victor's goal of creating a new monster there and by his
creature's vow to shadow Victor wherever he goes, the abstract threat of
Victor's scientific endeavors becomes concretized in a threat to popular
liberty and the nation, specifically Great Britain.

    Victor's retreat to the literal physical end of Great Britain, the
Orkney Islands, in order to construct a female companion for his creature signals Shelley's understanding that energies expended in imperial
expansion should be redirected in order to solidify British national identity as British, rather than English. "Hardly more than a rock" and
"barren," supporting a minimal complement of male inhabitants, the
Orkneys prefigure Victor's eventual exile to the Arctic. Shelley's rewriting of Arctic landscape into British space—her representation of British
space *as* Arctic space—anticipates a strategy that Charlotte Brontë uses
in *Jane Eyre* (discussed in the following chapter), in which the merging
of Arctic and British geographies acknowledges the power of the
national masculinity made legible in Arctic spaces via polar exploration
narratives, while at the same time pointing to that model's shortcomings. As Walton's proxy, Victor experiences defeat in this British-yet-
Arctic space, and his inability to construct a female creature not only
anticipates his final defeat—the creature's eluding him on the ice—but
expresses Shelley's larger sense that one need not look elsewhere for
national identity formation.

It is striking how much the novel's description of this landscape dif-
fers from a similarly bleak one Shelley describes in her 1831 preface:

> I lived principally in the country as a girl, and passed a consider-
> able time in Scotland. I made occasional visits to the more pic-
> turesque parts; but my habitual residence was on the blank and
> dreary northern shores of the Tay, near Dundee. Blank and
> dreary on retrospection I call them, but they were not so to me
> then. They were the eyry of freedom, and the pleasant region
> where unheeded I could commune with the creatures of my
> fancy. . . . I did not make myself the heroine of my tales. (20)

Here, the quasi–Arctic of Scotland's shores is, for Mary Shelley, a fertile
blankness for developing a female imagination, and central to her narrative of becoming a writer. Read in the context of Shelley's own
authorial birth, Victor's efforts to construct a female monster can be
seen as a misguided attempt to create and animate a female imagination. Such an effort, a "filthy process" based in Victor's masculinist
ambition, must be monstrous, and Victor is right to destroy his half-fin-
ished creation. The implication, however, is that projects such as Victor's
(and by extension Walton's), which place the creator as the hero of his
own story at the expense of community, destroy the possibility of
female imagination and authorship, as much or more than the demands
of domesticity do, while also making the men who embark on those
projects monstrous themselves. Instead of a place in which to "com-
mune" with his fancy in an "eyry of freedom," the island's blankness
reflects Victor's miserable condition back to him. It is here that Victor
finally realizes that he himself has become a monster, remarking, "I
walked about the isle like a restless spectre, separated from all it loved,
and miserable in the separation" (143).

Because of the importance of imperial narrative produced by
adventuring males both to national masculinity and to a larger national
identity, Shelley's critique of how masculine knowledge projects exclude
women is also an assertion of how women are thus limited in their participation in nation. Shelley literalizes the threat such a model of
national and imperial masculinity poses to women in Victor's vampiric
predation on British female remains. The monster's vision of a female
companion is of a creature with whom he can live "in communion with
an equal" (127) and through whom he can "feel the affections of a sensi-
tive being, and become linked to the chain of existence and events, from

which I am now excluded" (127). In short, the monster craves the entrance into sympathy and community that domestic affiliation brings. In parallel fashion, Victor's inability to complete the "filthy process" of building the female monster can be attributed to his own ambivalence toward domesticity. His fear is of a monstrous, uncontainable female, a synergy of British female parts resulting in a being "ten thousand times more malignant than her mate, and [who would] delight, for its own sake in murder and wretchedness" (140). He imagines the creatures multiplying in South America into "a race of devils" (140) that "might make the very existence of the species of man a condition precarious and full of terror" (140). In this way, we once again see the rehearsal of a universal imperial fantasy projected onto far-flung territories and inflected by a misogynist terror of the "true" horrific nature of feminine domesticity. Here, Shelley lays bare the nightmare underpinning national masculine anxiety in the early nineteenth century and fueling the expansionist energies of its preeminent explorers and poets. Victor's terror of a "race of devils" who, propagating, will menace "the species of man" at once makes it apparent why women must be kept under control at home and why a bold imperial masculinity is necessary to maintain order over restive natives abroad.

Shelley reinforces this dominant vision of separate gender and geographic spheres through her depiction of Walton and his correspondence. The Arctic provides a space for Walton to clarify his place in the nation as a public figure in the discourse of empire and as a masculine subject. When Walton asks of his sister on the death of Victor, "What can I say, that will enable you to understand the depth of my sorrow?" (181), his question underlines the distance between the siblings. He is in the Arctic, writing and experiencing; she is in England, reading and imagining: how *can* she understand him? Of Margaret, readers only know that she is married and has children—and this information Walton provides in his Arctic correspondence. Margaret writes letters to Walton in Russia—he asks for more—but we never read them, presumably because domestic news is always familiar. But Margaret's silence is a telling one; for women's retreat into domesticity as effected by the ascension of a model of national subjectivity that values the Waltons of the world excludes women from actively participating in public discourse, that is, in writing that matters.

Margaret's essential role in Walton's project as an audience echoes one way in which the domestic ideology of "separate spheres" functions in the nineteenth century; invisible women in the private sphere enabled men to partake in a public sphere of politics, commerce, and sociability. This is not to argue that separate spheres ideology was hegemonic or even dominant in the early century, but rather that projects such as Arctic exploration systematically and definitionally excluded women from active participation in larger projects, including nation. As a result, while a middle or upper-class woman's experience in the early nineteenth century might include political letter writing, philanthropy, scientific study, and authorship, her most legible contributions to and participation in nation included biological motherhood, conveying and producing national culture by perpetuating her values in her children, and acting as symbol of the nation.[19] With the ascension of a national heroic masculinity profiled in biographies of war heroes such as Wellington and Nelson and accounts of imperial voyagers, women might feel newly relegated to a complementary role in—if not excluded entirely from—the national project.

In Mrs. Saville's silence, Mary Shelley implicates women's insular remove to the domestic as participating in their own destruction. As Johanna Smith and Kate Ellis suggest, there can be such a thing as a surfeit of domesticity, to the detriment of both men and women in the novel.[20] The Frankensteins are self-contained, withdrawn from the world of politics and community relations in the "considerable seclusion" of their home at Belrive (42). In a union that will perpetuate the self-contained nature of the family, Victor and Elizabeth are expected to marry. Alphonse is a "feminized patriarch" (278), retired from public life and inattentive to Victor's education. As a result, Victor grows up disregarding society outside of his immediate family, interested in "neither the structure of languages, nor the code of governments, nor the politics of various states" (43). Domestic insularity is not only responsible for Victor's development into an impassioned egotist, but is itself an analogous form of solipsism in its closed circuitry of containment. Elizabeth's "reward" for her "trifling occupations" is "seeing none but happy, kind faces around me" (63).

The pursuit of individual interests at the expense of "domestic affections," however, remains a greater evil than domesticity in *Frankenstein*. Shelley clearly identifies ambition with imperial expansion and threats to social order. If Victor's ignorance of "the code of government" and "the politics of various states" is engendered by a surfeit of domesticity, his own single-minded ambition perpetuates rather than addresses that ignorance. We see this with a particular starkness in Victor's caution to Walton about the importance of limiting ambition:

If the study to which you apply yourself has a tendency to weaken your affections, and to destroy your taste for those simple pleasures in which no alloy can possibly mix, then that study is certainly unlawful, that is to say, not befitting the human mind. If this rule were always observed; if no man allowed any pursuit whatsoever to interfere with the tranquility of his domestic affections, Greece would not have been enslaved; Caesar would have spared his country; America would have been discovered more gradually; and the empires of Mexico and Peru would not have been destroyed. (57)

Yet in the juxtaposition of local "affections" and "simple pleasures" with global expansion and empire building, Shelley reveals the centrality of the domestic to larger geopolitical concerns. Tyranny has its source in the "unlawful" ignoring of moral codes present in and learned through social interactions that are the staple of a healthy domesticity. Counter-poised and yet central to Victor's Arctic ordeal and eventual demise is Shelley's vision of a community based on sympathy and the integration of difference, one that neither the masculinist expansion of nation nor suffocating domesticity allows. True, Walton becomes a man and a citizen in the course of his Arctic voyage, but significantly it is not through performed heroic acts, but in his recognition of the claims of community, claims that take the form of affiliations to family and the familiar landscapes of home.

The collapse of the imperial project and the flight from domesticity signaled by Victor's death in the Arctic is accompanied by his subsumption once again into domesticity by means of the somewhat unlikely figure of the creature. In a curious echo of the much-disputed Hindu practice of suttee or widow sacrifice, the creature conveys to Walton his plan to self-immolate on a funeral pyre at the North Pole.[21] Domesticity thus finally overtakes Victor and the more taut bonds of homosocial affection that have previously been in ascendance in the novel. The creature's assertion of the importance of a familial tie with Victor, as strangely convoluted as it is, suggests the ultimate primacy of the domestic circle even in the far-flung extraterritorial space of the Arctic. The simultaneous destruction of the creature through this assertion of filial connection conflates the defeat of Victor's project with the failure of a new overarching model of imperial British masculinity. Shelley's substitution of the funeral pyre for the domestic hearth amplifies this defeat through its subtle reminder of the pyre's significance for British colonial

masculinity in India. There, suttee similarly underscored the ultimate triumph of the domestic sphere over that of British imperial maleness. As
Gayatri Spivak famously argues in "Can the Subaltern Speak?" the
emergence of suttee can be seen as a means of contesting British dominance especially as it extended to the Indian domestic sphere. Spivak's
memorable description of British efforts to ban the ritual as "White
men saving brown women from brown men"[22] concisely articulates the
project of an imperial British masculinity seeking to contain and order
domesticity by presenting itself as the guardian of an enfeebled femininity at home and abroad. Just as Spivak shows this project to be imperiled
by the very idea of suttee, we can read the creature's proposal of his own
death by fire as a repudiation of a nineteenth-century British imperial
masculinity that unites its Arctic origins with its broader deployment in
the "torrid" zones of British colonial rule.

In the end, the Arctic narrative Walton brings home is a story of neither heroic survival nor scientific exploration. Walton's "failed" journey
ultimately is one that reasserts the importance of the address with which
the novel begins and to which all of Walton's thoughts and aspirations
are ultimately directed. Walton's "citizenship" is tested at the end of the
novel when he must decide whether to pursue his goal of the North
Pole or to turn back in time to save the mission and his men. Urged
onward by Frankenstein who, despite the cautionary words at the outset
of his tale, exhorts the men with the rhetoric of individual glory, Walton
is torn between continuing and turning back, and indeed "had rather
die than return shamefully—[his] purpose unfulfilled" (179). The men's
threat of a Hudson-like mutiny confronts him with the fact that a "glorious" death in the service of individualistic goals is a solitary death, one
opposed to the sympathy of others that he craves.

Walton's decision is unheroic—at least in the terms set by the Nelsons of the world. Sympathy and community win, not in an active decision by Walton, but when he lets the men decide their fate. Saved from
making a decision that would actively repudiate his deeply felt ambitions, Walton, in his acquiescence, nonetheless admits his responsibility
and allegiance, both toward the men under his command and to the
nation-building project of bringing his hard-won narrative back to England. Returning to his "native country" is Walton's undesired acknowledgment of one of the primary, irrational demands of citizenship, the
suppression of individual goals for the restitution and continuation of
nation. By contrast, Victor is steady in his purpose and uncomprehend-
ing of community to the end, and needs Walton to explain the happiness

of the crew. "They shout," Walton explains to Frankenstein, "because they will soon return to England" (179). That it is Walton who survives and who carries forward Victor's tale makes clear where Shelley sees the future of Britishness and British writing. In the end, the Arctic can be fully experienced only as a place of imagination, not as a place of experience. Arctic narrative is one of the limits of men, but in those limits a different kind of knowledge comes back, the recognition that women's imagination transcends domesticity, and women's authorship has an essential role in the national imaginary.

THE ARCTIC EXPEDITIONS

If Eleanor Anne Porden is known at all today, it is as the first wife of John Franklin, whom she married in 1823 after his return from his difficult first Arctic expedition and the publication of his bestselling *Narrative of a Journey to the Shores of the Polar Seas*. But Porden was herself a published poet whose work was reviewed in the *Quarterly Review* and the *London Literary Review*. Indeed, it may have been Porden's poetry that led family friends to introduce her to Franklin, for in 1818, as an eighteen-year-old, Porden had published *The Arctic Expeditions*, a triumphal paean to Franklin's own departing mission and, more largely, to what she understood as Britain's imperial destiny.[23] Like *Frankenstein*, Porden's two hundred line poem makes clear that the act of making Arctic geography legible is male, but for Porden, even if women are physically excluded from legible nation-making projects, they are essential to them. She suggests that the British male identity that coalesces in those projects is an expression of domestic values and female virtues. Thus, British femininity is necessary to an imperialism that justifies itself as extending those values and virtues to wild or uncivilized places. If the well-documented Admiralty-sponsored polar expeditions of 1818 invited a kind of national participation-by-proxy by civilians who followed their preparations in the newspapers, Porden used their departure as an opportunity to write women into male-only heroic narratives of Arctic exploration not only by revealing their centrality to it, but by claiming women's authorship for the production of Arctic narrative and thus in its larger project of national identity building.

The Arctic Expeditions opens with an address to the ships that illuminates the national and geographical agendas behind the pursuit of scientific knowledge:

Sail, sail, adventurous Barks! go fearless forth,
Storm on his glacier-seat the misty North,
Give to mankind the inhospitable zone,
And Britain's trident plant in seas unknown.
Go! sure, wherever Science fills the mind.[24]

In her exhortations to "brave seamen" and "heroic bands," Porden depicts polar exploration as a male martial effort, a gendering that she augments in a footnote that contrasts the Arctic to Capua, which she describes as "long proverbial as destructive of the courage and virtue of the Roman legions," and Tahiti, which was "almost as fatal" in its sexual temptations of seamen (footnote 8). The triumphal tone and the valorization of male achievement in a womanless space that opens the poem predicts a description to follow of uninterrogated conquest, of "sure" and certain success. Yet Porden complicates the ode's generic pull toward such an unproblematic narrative by conveying her investment in women's participation in knowledge projects in the very next lines, in which she draws attention to the national resonances of individual acts by the "heroic seamen" (1.7). The exploration ships, having left "native land," are an extension of the "nation's hopes," dependent on "prayers and blessings" to "swell [their] flagging sails" (1.8). If the sailors perform an essential service to the nation, they are only able to do it with the nation's support. In her seemingly conventional but deft link between home and away, between prayers and acts—female and male—Porden disrupts the hierarchization of national participation that privileges a visible, active male over a female contribution deemed passive—are certainly less easily quantifiable—but one that Porden recognizes as containing an agency of its own nonetheless.

In writing *The Arctic Expeditions*, Porden is aware of how her authorship is itself a form of active participation in larger, public projects—one not somehow ancillary or subsidiary to male physical participation in polar exploration or to the "real" productions of such voyages, be they narratives by men or the identities constructed in and conveyed by those narratives. That authorship provides a method by which women participate in nation is a recurring theme in Porden's writing, traceable from her early published poem *The Veils* through *The Arctic Expeditions* and into her premarital negotiations with John Franklin in 1823. Looking at her explicit insertion of women into traditional romance in *The Veils* and her later comparisons of authorship to exploration in her correspondence with her Arctic explorer fiancé enables us to further complicate and contextualize Porden's claims for women and nation as well as her specific interest in polar spaces in *The Arctic Expeditions*.

The Veils or, The Triumph of Constancy appeared in 1816. The unlikely result of an incident in which her friend Maria Denman's veil was carried away in the wind at the seaside, the scope of the 285-page poem is panoramic, covering geography, geology, botany, and chemistry in an ambitious and odd mix of scientific fantasy and romance. Its mixed scientific, colonial, domestic, and spatial discourses bring together the workings of the natural world and comment on British intellectual and mercantile might in an unapologetic and ambitious medieval fantasy. Echoing *The Rape of the Lock*, the poem concerns three young women, Maria, Miranda, and Leonora, who lose their veils, and the three gallant knights who seek the veils' return from Albruno, a giant gnome who rules the world of gnomes and sylphs. Modeled on Erasmus Darwin's *The Botanic Garden* (1789) and *The Temple of Nature* (1803), and written in the Della Cruscan tradition, the poem consists of six "Books," or approximately 4,200 lines in heroic couplets. The Spenserian fairyland tale that drives the poem's dramatic action is part romance, part travelogue, and part scientific treatise, with each of the different registers signaled in different ways. Porden maps the romance on a realist geography of the globe that coexists with an imagined geography below the earth's surface inhabited by gnomes and sylphs. The geographical separation between imagination and reason in the poem is also stylistically expressed in the marriage of its Spenserian elements and its tight heroic couplets which evoke Alexander Pope.[25]

The tension between spaces of rationality and irrationality is also expressed thematically in the poem in complex allegories of chemical reactions and botanical development. The allegories themselves are dense, imaginative flights that feature battling gnomes and sylphs with names borrowed from scientific discourse, such as Sideros (Iron), Zircon, and Strontia. The literal, typographic separation of these allegories from the footnotes that help explain them is underlined by the radically divergent diction in the footnotes, where Porden cites authoritative sources ranging from Hume to Humphrey Davy and Roget. The loss of Miss Denman's veil on the beach at Norfolk, translated into a fantasy of threatened virtue, engenders a quest that in its attempt to understand and tame nature precipitates rigorous scientific investigation—or would, at least, were its excesses managed more deftly. In any case, as a result, the poem places the daily life of women at the center of an interrogation and mapping of the laws of the physical world.[26]

Perhaps not unexpectedly, then, although the poem's actors are pri-marily male—including the knights Henry, Alfred, and Alonzo, the evil Albruno, the good spirit Ariel, and many of the Gnome "elements"—the three women actively shape the plot and resolution of the poem through their actions. Strangers at the outset, the women are quickly bound together by their shared plight, forming a "community of grief" from which they "derive relief."[27] While they lament their precarious situations—their "ravish'd" (IV, l. 103) veils are the outward signs of their virginity and propriety, symbolic of their vulnerability to sexual advances from the Gnome king and his minions—they quickly identify the freedom that the loss of their veils gives them. No longer bound by the uniform of maidenhood and the requirements of English society, they urge each other to

> Think of the joys to range through realms unknown,
> The robes of regal state—the sparkling crown,
> And powers superior trembling at our frown;
> ... Come, mourn no more—we lift our heads on high,
> Examples great of female constancy,
> Resolved in danger's sternest hour to prove
> Our dauntless courage and unchanging love. (I, ll. 899–907)

The "new found friends" (I, l. 914) transform the passive feminine virtue of constancy to their lovers/knights into an active, intellectual quest. Maria, for example, mounts a "white palfry" and "discarding female fear" sets off to find both her veil and Henry, who has gone in search of it. "All day I journey'd, but as evening fell, / Trembling I wander'd thro' a woody dell" (III, ll. 435–36). Leonora, likewise, seeks the volcano at Stromboli in an effort to get her veil, leaving Alonzo, the knight who is ostensibly responsible for her safety and the return of her veil, to seek news of her from a peasant who recounts:

> Alone, at midnight's silent hour, she came,
> The shelter of my humble roof to claim
> No guardian veil conceal'd her lovely face
> From evening blasts, or man's intrusive gaze.
> At morn she left me; Ubald for her guide;
> Eager she climb'd the mountain's rugged side:
> And when she reach'd yon gulf of liquid fire,
> In haste she bade the wondering youth retire. (V, ll. 401–409)

The peasant's account makes clear the risks of publicity to women who leave domesticity behind: Leonora is unprotected, and thus subject to the male gaze and aspersions of sexual impropriety. Yet Porden uses this opportunity to assert that women can circulate easily and confidently in public, an assertion commensurate with another level of allegory that is dormant in the poem, that of women's possible participation in scientific, geographic, and writing projects, which, like traditional romance quests, are widely conceived of as male domains.

While the bulk of the poem describes battles between elements and natural forces, and to a lesser degree, between those forces and the knights, Maria, Miranda, and Leonora all at some point take active roles in the quests and, in at least two cases, the women save the very men who are trying to help them. Despite the putative impropriety of her lone quest, Leonora enters the volcano's mouth where, joined belatedly and rather passively chaperoned by Alonzo, she discovers the secrets of Pyros, the fire lord, tames him, and regains her veil. Later, Miranda saves her knight Alfred from a watery tomb by convincing the sea gnome Marino to replace his (Marino's) desire for Miranda with a desire for Marguerite the sea nymph. Hers is a triumph of language over physical might, a triumph that makes reason—and by extension rationalist scientific projects—dependent on persuasion, a quality Porden aligns in her poem with the imagination and women. Although Albruno is immortal, the combined physical strength of the knights and the intellects of the women eventually conquer him, forcing him to reveal his secrets and surrender the veils at poem's end. The result is an inverted romance wherein active women save passive men and conquer male foes. Maria, Miranda, and Leonora's demystification of the natural world avers women's ability to encounter and know the physical world using intellect rather than physical force. In this way, Porden displaces the primacy of a heroic masculinity based on tests of physical strength.

For Porden, knowledge of the secrets of the natural world renders that world subject to human enterprise. The triumph of the intellect over the natural world is easily extrapolated into one of Britain's rule over the geopolitical world: scientific knowledge is the basis for political might. Porden uses Miranda's discovery of the paper Nautilus—which, as Porden's footnote explains, citing "Roget and Shaw's Lectures" and the Royal Institution, "is supposed to have given to man the first hint of the art of sailing," an art that enables human exploration and eventual domination of other lands[28]—as an occasion for an encomium to Britain's naval supremacy.

The subject seas Britannia's navies ride,
And every wind, that sweeps the foaming tide,
Wafts a rich tribute to her island throne,
And makes the wealth of distant worlds her own. (IV ll. 76–80)

The women's continued searches for their veils are, therefore, at once quests for scientific knowledge and an expansion of Britain's mercantile network. In Miranda's pursuit of knowledge across and through the seas, Porden transforms woman's constancy from a domestic quality (directed toward lover or family), to a more public national purpose, and her poem's emphasis on mercantile power makes Britain's "island throne" the center of a world back to which knowledge and commodities return.

The poem also articulates its imperialist agenda in its orientalized depiction of Albruno's world. He tempts the women with the promise of "boundless riches" "which might Arabia's fabled hoards excell," "diamond palaces, and emerald vales . . . amber streams o'er sapphire beds that rolled, / And silver seas, and lakes of liquid gold" (I, ll. 132–36). His "destined consort" is promised slaves who "in gorgeous robes should round her wait / In halls where luxury all her pomp displays, / And fragrant gums in golden censers blaze" (ll. 139–41). His palace, as well, is emblematic of Eastern excess:

Tall minarets and cupolas of gold;
Such are the piles the wanderer's eye that feast,
Where fancy revels in her favourite east,
O'er Scythia's plains to roving Tartars shine,
Or Moslems bound to Mecca's holy shrine;
Or such the Indian temples, vast and grand,
By Delhi's monarchs raised on Jumna's strand. (III, ll. 72–78)

By figuring Albruno as a sexually predatory oriental despot who controls an exotic realm, the poem both commodifies the mysteries of the Eastern world and justifies Britain's mastery of those mysteries and by extension what Porden sees as Britain's imperialist destiny to wrest them from the East. The realist geography of the romance reveals itself as a global quest mapped onto Britain's trading routes. Echoing Pope's *Windsor Forest*, Porden's poem implicates women in foreign trade.[29] She lists women's cosmetics and jewelry as by-products of the domination of the natural and geographical world, first in a footnote on the mineral sources of cosmetics—"A variety of metallic preparations have been used by the ladies of different countries for this purpose, particularly the oxyds of bismuth, and antimony" (footnote 15)—and later when describing Albruno as the "Monarch of the Mines, whose "jewels sought by men as rich, and rare, / To deck the vain, the stately, or the fair, / With thousands yet to solar light unknown, / Blazed on his gorgeous vesture and his crown" (II, ll. 55–58). Although Porden frequently references Pope—complete with a reference to Belinda in Book III (l. 117)—her placement of women at the center of the imperial trade is not misogynist. Instead of blaming women for mercantilism, as Pope does, Porden understands that women's appetite for commodities enables and justifies women's active participation in Britain's expanding empire.

In the women's and the knight's travels, Porden weds the two geographies of the poem, the one fantastical and the other geopolitical. The mysteries of the natural world (the realm of Albruno) underlie known geography, but become available to humans in places where geographical knowledge ends and an imaginative world begins: the Arctic. Leonora's journey to the realm of fire at Stromboli in Book V, reveals to her that in the heart of the volcano the worlds of fire and ice meet: "Where frost and fire contend for Thule's reign, / Where her vast geysers' boiling fountains flow, / And Hecla burns amid eternal snow" (V, ll. 285–87). Meanwhile, Alfred enters the fantastical underworld that Pyros shares with Albruno through the "Arctic seas," "those seas alike where truth and fancy reign" (IV, ll. 170–71). As the literal geographical end of the world, the Arctic as Porden conceives of it is England's opposite, a place of extremes where the winter "months in darkness roll, / And fogs eternal shroud the frozen pole" are replaced with a rapid summer where "the realms around / Burst into bloom, and flowers conceal the ground" (IV, ll. 189–90, 173–74). Because it is *not* Britain, the Arctic is useful in defining Britain. It is, according to Porden:

> Not, like our isle, with soft transition blest,
> Where gradual beauties gain a higher zest,
> Where with delight, we watch the opening flowers,
> And the soft influence of the vernal showers;
> The expanding fruits in size and flavour grow,
> Till their bright rinds with ripening lustre glow. (IV, ll. 191–96)

In contrast to the careening, masculine unpredictability and challenge of Arctic weather, Britain possesses a fertile climate that enables reflection and observation and, as the stable center that produces Maria, Miranda, and Leonora and to which they hope to return, is a space in which Britons—even those who stay at home either by choice or by societal stricture—are uniquely capable of understanding the world. In positioning a warm and fertile Britain as the center for knowledge gathered in imperial quest, Porden furthers her perceived centrality of women to imperialism.

In contrast to Britain's "white" or "snowy cliffes," the polar landscape is threatening and unstable, a place not for reflection, but for action. Porden's poem reflects the influence of earlier whaling accounts by making the snowy north a male space, visited by the "busy seamen" who "entrap the seal, or wound the unwieldy whale" (IV, l. 190). Yet while men can visit the Arctic in the poem, they are powerless to subdue it. Alfred narrowly escapes an attack by a sea snake only by the timely intervention of Marguerite, a sea nymph. Later, he encounters "new dangers" in a field of icebergs.

> Oh! should the sun's meridian fervour launch
> From yon dread height the threat'ning avalanch;
> Or should the waves impel some floating rock,
> They sink or perish in the dreadful shock!
> And lo! Impatient of the expected prey,
> O'er the firm ice a bear pursues their way. (IV, ll. 222–27)

The same avalanche that threatens Alfred saves him when the iceberg shears away, leaving the pursuing bear adrift, "lament[ing] in pain." Unlike daring young Nelson or resourceful British seamen of the exploration accounts from which scenes like his encounter with a polar bear are drawn, Alfred is passively borne along in the ship. The real Arctic story, Porden contends, is not one of male agency and mastery, but one of female-orchestrated chance and providential delivery.

While Porden concedes that the Arctic may be a male realm, it may only be navigated safely by the female spirit, Marguerite, who distracts an attacking sea snake and midwifes the ship into the underworld through the vortex of the Maëlstrom at the North Pole.[30] The Maëlstrom is gendered female like Charybdis (to which Porden compares it) and its mechanics are a sort of monstrous birth that, instead of delivering Alfred into the world, draw him into a literally suffocating underwater fantasy.

Ere, with redoubled fury, boil'd the main
And whirl'd, with giddy motion, round and round,
The bark absorb'd descends the abyss profound. (IV, ll. 277–80)

Alfred "vainly struggles" and "cries in vain for aid" as he is drawn inevitably toward its center and down into the ocean where, were he not given a magic ring by Marguerite that enables him to breathe underwater, he would die. Instead of gaining access to Marino's secrets by his Arctic trials, Alfred is imprisoned in an underwater cave until Miranda, with her reason and persuasion, can free him.

Alfred's defeat in the Arctic is turned into victory first by Marguerite and later by Miranda. By giving women the agency Alfred lacks, in the form of quick thinking and verbal skill, Porden legitimates women's acts of imagination. The geographical knowledge and physical acumen that enable Alfred to be a hero on the jousting grounds of Britain carry little weight in a space that goes by different rules. Porden's Arctic is fantastic, but no less probable than the Arctic of hero-making exploration narratives. As allegory, the polar section of *The Veils* attributes to women the restoration of balance to the natural world and the domination of the geographical world, a claim for the powers of female imagination that transcends the romance's final recuperation of the three women into heterosexual union.

When Eleanor Porden was herself contemplating heterosexual union with the polar explorer John Franklin in 1823, Franklin objected to her career as a writer and asked her to cease publishing when she became his wife. Porden, by now a well-known poet and longtime host of the London literary salon the Attic Chest, rejected Franklin's request in a letter that explicitly compares her writing to Franklin's exploration of Arctic wastes:

When I requested my sister to mention to you that I expected the full indulgence of my literary pursuits, both as to writing or publication, I certainly considered that I was asking no favour, claiming no concession. . . . When you first named your profession to me, as a possible reason of objection on my part, I answered that I had to return your indulgence to claim for my literary pursuits and I begged you then to consider well whether their pursuit in any way were likely to be unpleasant to you. . . . From all this I should undoubtedly have concluded, that

> if on your return from a Polar, or any other Expedition, I had
> presented to you . . . works fresh from the Printer and the
> Binder I should have brought you an acceptable offering. Imag-
> ine then, (but I believe you will not imagine,) the pain which
> your answer gave me. That you had an objection almost
> amounting to horror to anything like publication in any one
> connected with you, that it was possible your feelings might
> alter but you could pledge yourself to nothing! I have seldom
> received so severe a shock. (108)[31]

Porden imagines their marriage as a place where two sympathetic travelers might meet; the explorer returning from the Arctic and the author
from the printer's shop. Franklin's inability to imagine the pain his
request gives Porden reveals his lack of sympathy; he's unable—selfishly
unwilling, she accuses—to imagine her constricted life caring for a par-
alyzed mother and aging father or to imagine her devotion to writing.
By doubting his capacity to *imagine*, Porden identifies what she perceives
to be the division between the male world of exploration and the world
of women's writing. For Franklin's is the world of concrete, physical
exploration, documented in exploration journals and supported by an
avid nation, while Porden's travels must take place largely in the imagination, due to increased societal circumscriptions of women's behavior
like those behind her future husband's trepidation about her career.

    When in her correspondence with Franklin, Porden compares her
writing to Franklin's national employment, Porden refuses to subordinate her literary explorations to his geographical ones. By asking "no
favour" of Franklin, she asserts her position as one equal to the naval
lieutenant's, and indeed as a financially independent woman, she did not
need the marriage.[32] Despite the risks to his person and her happiness
that his impending second Arctic expedition holds, she is "the last
person in the world that would endeavour to detain" him. Arguing that
"nothing" that she "might publish could possibly" give him "one tenth
part of the uneasiness which that Expedition must necessarily cost" her,
she continues, "It is indeed my earnest hope that you would never suffer
a consideration for me to influence your mind for a moment on any
such occasion; but why should you wish to deprive me of the only
employment that could really interest me in your absence?" (109).

    Porden is keenly aware that Franklin's objections are based not on
her private actions, but on her public notoriety, which conflicted with
his rather strait-laced, Methodist views of proper wifely behavior.

Franklin's request to Porden illustrates what Mary Poovey has identified as the central struggle of the woman writer in the early nineteenth century. "Not only was marriage virtually the only respectable 'occupation' for women (and both learning and writing were frequently seen as threats to domestic duty), but writing catapulted women directly into the public arena, where attention must be fought for, where explicit competition reigned."[33] Porden again likens her desire for fame to Franklin's own:

> And on what plea should you ask me to renounce [my culti-
> vated tastes], or to descend from the place which I hold in soci-
> ety? . . . You say that all desire of literary fame is vanity, simply
> because your own ambition lies in another channel; but if when
> your Book is fairly before the public you do not take somewhat
> of a parent's interest in its fate I shall not think the better of you
> for your apathy. That fame in the way of your profession is not
> indifferent to you I will venture to pronounce. For instance,
> were you in command of a well appointed fleet, you would cer-
> tainly wish to encounter the enemy, to obtain a signal victory,
> and to place your own name with those of Nelson and Duncan
> and Howe and Rodney, etc. etc. etc. Yet your own duty would
> be as conscientiously performed if the first ball that was fired
> carried your head with it; and your country's interests as much
> promoted if your success achieved the Victory, nay, both objects
> would be as effectively attained. If, while you were gazing idly
> on a spotless sea, some brother officer the commander of a rival
> fleet, should obtain the success I have supposed yours, I know
> you would have the generosity to rejoice in his good fortune,
> but if you did not envy it, you are not worth a pin. (110–11)

In her resistance to Franklin's demand, she makes visible the personal stakes in abstract ideals of national duty and heroism. For, like writing, duty and heroism are individual acts that take on meaning only in their publicity. Comparing writing for publication with naval victory in the Napoleonic Wars, Porden not only hopes to make her argument under-standable to her future husband, but by implication, to claim for women and writing some of the power of more easily recognized national acts. The danger to England's Nelsons and Franklins in their naval battles and geographical explorations—heads blown off by cannonballs or limbs missing from frostbite—is available to her only in a public, critical response to her work. Like those heroes, she runs risks, and, like them, is reluctant to turn from the challenge; if successful, she, too, expects the reward of celebrity.[34] Porden's "well-appointed fleet" is her talent, and she is not satisfied with sitting "idly" and letting others take the day.

In her private premarital negotiation, Eleanor Porden articulates the difficulties of women's authorship and the importance of imagination and representation to those who cannot participate in heroic national acts due to their gender. The polar explorations of Franklin and men like him made them famous, validating them as men and citizens, and as visible participants in the making of national spaces. Porden's claims for her poetry are an asseveration of the importance of women's writing in terms of that male national work of military enterprise and geographical exploration. Her comparison insists that women's writing is an analogue of those national acts and that women's writing is a space in which constructions of nation are performed and contested.

Porden's correspondence with Franklin reprises an argument she makes more broadly in her poem *The Arctic Expeditions*. Although as we have seen, Porden opens the poem by urging the sailors to "plant Britain's trident" in "seas unknown," she makes clear that exploration for exploration's sake is only part of a larger rationale for geographical expansion or, for that matter, imperial claims. In her introduction to the poem, she writes that in addition to seeking a passage to the North Pole, the "doubtful fate of the Colony believed to have been once established on the Eastern Coast of Greenland . . . are subjects on which for some years my mind has dwelt with peculiar interest" (Introduction, 1). The colony to which she refers was not British; the Danes had occupied Greenland for several centuries, but their settlements had been silent since the early fifteenth century. Porden's "peculiar interest" is in a populated Arctic, one that would reveal that the empty space that the expeditions hope to map—and on which they depend in order to develop the model of heroic masculinity established by the Phipps expedition in the eighteenth century and even earlier by Henry Hudson and Hakluyt—is not empty at all. Porden's Arctic may in fact be populated by white Europeans. The implications of this belief help Porden to reinsert women into the homosocial project of Arctic exploration and into the center of empire. If there are indeed lost colonies in Greenland, the Arctic is already part of a larger colonial network, and therefore its exploration by Britons is not a new sort of endeavor at all, but rather the extension of an active colonizing impulse already at work in the other parts of the world. At the same time, the rational scientific project of mapping empty space is now transformed into a project of uniting the human family, motivated by a feminine domestic sympathy expressed as "grief for man long sever'd from his kind" (ll. 19–20, p. vi). Thus, Porden's contextualization of her poem anticipates the work's larger argument for women's participation in voyages of Arctic exploration, even if they are at a literal physical remove from them.

In the poem itself, Porden literalizes women's involvement in Arctic exploration by writing of the superintendence of the mission by "Muses" that include the polestar and an "unseen Directress," magnetism. In the tradition of the epic, both muses are gendered female, but it is magnetism, that "lov'st, like Virtue, still to shrink from view / And bless a world, yet shun the glory due," (ll. 15–16) that most actively operates like the female domestic ideal: invisibly, yet forcefully. In "The Esquimaux Girl's Lament," a later anonymous, unpublished Valentine's Day poem written to Franklin in 1823, Porden links the North Star or polestar more overtly to constancy: "Spread thy canvas once more, keep the Pole Star before thee / 'Tis Constancy's type and thy Beacon of Glory" (97–98). The sailors in *The Arctic Expeditions*, guided by these unseen forces—forces that echo the influences attributed to women's virtue and constancy in later texts such as those of Sarah Stickney Ellis—cross a "trackless main," toward both scientific knowledge and a possible lost colony.

Porden imagines the restitution of "civilization" to the colony as effected by the restitution of communication to them, a mix of language and sympathy, and thus an extension of values that Porden identifies as female in *The Veils*. "It will be curious to observe," she muses in a rather anthropological footnote to *The Arctic Expeditions*, "should any of these secluded beings yet live, what changes their situation has produced in their language, manners, and religion. Whether they have deteriorated into barbarism as their climate became more rigorous, or have been roused to new activity by the necessity of contending with the elements" (12–13). By connecting women, language, civilization, and scientific knowledge in both this poem and in *The Veils*, Porden attributes the logic and the means by which nature and geography are mastered to British domesticity, rather than to the martial form of masculinity with which her poem commences.

Yet in *The Arctic Expeditions*, acknowledging the bar to women's physical participation in voyages of discovery, the female remains the "unseen force" behind what must be a male experience of physical hardship and bodily endangerment:

Go forth, brave Seamen, reach the fated shore,
Go! doomed to honours never reaped before,
Nor fear strange tales that brooding ignorance teems,
Wild fictions, borrowed from Arabian dreams;
Fear not, while months of dreary darkness roll,
To stand self-centred on the attractive Pole;
Or find some gulf, deep, turbulent, and dark,
Earth's mighty mouth! suck in the struggling bark;
Fear not, the victims of magnetic force,
To hang, arrested in your midmost course;
Your prows drawn downward and your sterns in air,
To waste with cold, and grief, and famine, there:
Strange fancies these—but real ills are near,
Not clothed in all the picturesque of fear,
Which makes its wild distortions wildly dear. (ll. 70–92)

Here, Porden dismisses the "strange tales" of earlier speculations, including her own in *The Veils*. Paradoxically, however, her dismissal reinforces
the Arctic's status as a storied place, that is, as a space defined through a
history of representations.[35] By repeating the content of "strange fancies" and "wild fictions, borrowed from Arabian dreams," the poet reinforces the links between Arctic landscape and the limits both of
knowledge and the human body. Access to the "real" Arctic is, of course,
only available to the men who explore it, but since its landscape resists
thorough exploration, paradoxically the Arctic exists primarily in fantastical speculation—which is, of course, what Porden's poem is, even as
she attempts to differentiate it from earlier forms of speculation. The
power of these representations—the "picturesque of fear" and "wild distortions wildly dear"—are exactly what makes Arctic exploration so
compelling, and what makes assumptions about the Arctic so difficult to
dismiss. But speculation and fantasy alone bring about neither the reuni-
fication of Britons nor an understanding of the world. The Arctic myths
all end in stasis, with sailors "self-centred," "arrested," or "frozen" in mid-
plunge into the vortex at the "attractive Pole."[36]

The "real ills" Porden lists in the next stanza are indeed "near" to the
imagined ones, for they, too, are images of static bodies trapped in a hostile environment. In a lengthy passage in which Porden graphically
imagines the expedition's failure, the "Frozen air /Seems almost solid"
in the "painful glare" of "endless snow" (ll. 96–97). "Awful it is to gaze
on shoreless seas, / But more to view those restless billows freeze / One

solid plain" (ll. 102–104). The difficulty of Arctic exploration thus lies not in strange and horrifying mythological encounters or imagined terrors, but in the explorers' inability to deal with Arctic reality due to the limits of the male British body. Lacking familiar cues because of the instability of the compass near the pole, the unchanging sun of summer, and the endless dark of winter, the primary discovery of the explorer is his isolation. Cut off from the metropole, his animated body is the only mediating thing between life and death that is all but inevitable, as expressed in Porden's anaphora:

> When fatal slumber comes with dreadful weight;
> When every limb is pain, or deadlier yet,
> When those chill'd limbs the sense of pain forget. (ll. 99–101)

If the explorer is able to resist his "fatal slumber," he is "doomed to roam / Unknowing where, and hopeless of a home" (ll 112–13). Domesticity can only extend so far. Here Porden anticipates the frozen corpses, the desolate wastes, and disorientation of male Arctic exploration accounts—no less fantastic and no less deadly than the imagined phenomena of Arctic fictions. Instead of asserting the nation's claims in the name of Britannia, the iced-in polar explorers are "[them]selves the nucleus of a mighty isle" (l. 125)—not of Britain, but of desolate ice. Gone is the community promised by the lost colony; the mission fails in a solipsistic exile of homosociality.

Porden saves her explorers from these Arctic dangers and "impatient" polar bears by invoking once again the powerful force of community in the form of nation:

> Yet Britons! Conquerors on the subject deep,
> Where'er its islands rise, its waters sweep,
> Fired by our fathers' deathless deeds, defy
> The frozen ocean, and the flaming sky. (ll. 130–34)

Individual acts of hardiness and heroism done in the name of nation are not enough; strength comes not from individual men, but from the idea of nation that includes a history of "fathers' deathless deeds" and the good wishes and support of its female citizenry at home. Guided by the providential appearance of God, who "can guard his creatures and can stay their course" (l. 137) and who "unite[s]" the sailors "on that vast profound" (l. 143), the two expedition ships, one from the west coast of

Canada and the other from Greenland, meet at last in the poem as co-
discoverers of the Northwest Passage. There, the solitude of the freezing,
trapped explorer is transformed into the triumphant singularity of discovery: "Yourselves sole sovreigns of that awful zone, / Sole friends, sole
rivals, on those seas unknown" (ll. 144–45). The success of the mission
affirms the collective, communal values that enable it; the seamen take
"mutual pride" (l. 148) in their "comrades' daring" (l.149).

Importantly, for Porden, the most valuable result of Arctic exploration is the tales it produces. She imagines the two crews of the ships
trading accounts of their encounters, accounts that strangely affirm what
she expects them to find there, those monstrous fantasies she dismisses
earlier in the poem. The crew of the ship that enters the Northwest Passage from the west confirms the cannibal existence "of savage nations
fell with thirst of blood" (l. 154), and the men from "the Arctic main, /
Of all its monsters speak in loftier strain: Strange forms and huge" (ll.
159–60). These are the age-old fantastical accounts of Arctic encounter,
and their confirmation reasserts the place of imagination in Britain's
imperial projects, all the while erasing the vivid image of the frozen,
dead sailor that represents Arctic reality. "So many 'travellers' wonders'
have lately been confirmed, that one might feel tempted to exclaim,
with Antonio in the Tempest, 'Travellers ne'er did lie, Though fools at
home condemn them,'" Porden observes in a footnote (20). Here,
Porden equates the work of Arctic explorers with authorship; stories as
well as acts are part of the foundations and perpetuation of Nation.
Exploration confirms the importance of the imagination even as it discovers material geographical and scientific truths.

The sailors' imagined victory at the Pole literalizes the centrality of
the British male to Arctic exploration:

> . . . centered on the Pole
> Round them the Earth, the Sea, appeared to roll,
> Nay, the bright Sun, and all those first that burn
> With native lustre, seem'd round them to turn. (ll. 171–73)

Yet the triumphant mapping of the North Pole that would afford primacy in national and imperial endeavors to males is neither the literal
nor the most significant end of the expedition. For Porden, the most
valuable and laudable part of Arctic exploration comes when the explorers return to

The heart-felt welcome to your native land,
The dear embrace, the gratulating hand,
When joyful thousands throng the white-cliff'd shore
To greet as brothers men unseen before:
On each strong limb, each storm-worn feature dwell,
Yourselves more wondrous than the tales you tell. (ll. 178–81)

The "well-earned fame" of the sailors expressed in the "dear embrace" of the community that welcomes them "as brothers," confirms that their suffering and achievements both were done in the service of the national community. Yet the triumphant homecoming is Porden's speculation, since the sailors she imagines returning in triumph have not, at the poem's writing, actually left on their Arctic journey. When she turns in the next stanza from this imagined triumphant return to address the departing "undaunted heroes," Porden champions narrative as the real production of Arctic exploration.

Then on! Undaunted heroes, bravely roam,
Your toils, your perils, shall endear your home,
And furnish tales for many a winter night,
While wondering Britons list with strange delight. (ll. 184–87)

"Toils" and "perils" result in a new appreciation for civilization by the sailors and "tales for many a winter night" for their delighted audience. Their stories become the nation's stories, but the returned explorers become a story themselves due to their celebrity. The nation will tell of the men who "dared explore the Pole,/On icy seas the lion flag unfurl'd,/And found new pathways to the Western World" (ll. 189–91). By assigning primacy to stories and their authors, Porden manages once again to assert a role for women's authorship and to transform the consumption of narrative—understood to be a passive act, gendered feminine—into the driving force behind Britain's national endeavors and imperial expansion.

The Arctic Expeditions, with its imagined triumphs in the name of Britain and Britannia and its tales brought back from the edges of known geography, does the same sort of "national work" the sailors themselves do: it provides a "tale" that defines British character and resourcefulness that also gives its teller notoriety. Not only is female authorship nation-building, but its recompense—celebrity or publicity, deemed so suspect by the likes of Franklin and those who demanded "propriety" of women—continues the work of nation by identifying the public woman author with the values of nation. When, at the end of Porden's poem, "Britannia's trident" conquers the "Genius of the North," one hears not only a claim for Britain, but a resonance for the female poet:

> Queen of the Seas! she hails her conquering train,
> Pleased with the prowess that confirms her reign.

That Porden confirms British identity, women's authorship, and the link between them in the same Arctic geography in which Shelley situates her very different critique of the linked masculinist projects of science, empire, nation, and aesthetics underscores the availability of the Arctic to competing narratives. While for both authors the gendering of Arctic experience as male renders it an attractive or important target of critique, Porden's argument for extending women's influence into a superintendence of British imperialism reveals her vision of Arctic exploration and empire to be more reformist than radical. The poet's neatly ordered lines braid together a conservative politics of nation and of gender as she endeavors to "write women back into" a national imperial narrative with poetry that consciously echoes and attempts to rival male predecessors such as Pope while placing women at the magnetic center of the national imperial project. Her reliance on a triumphal aesthetic driven by heroic couplets brings into focus what is at stake in the Gothic "disorder" of Shelley's narration of Romantic and imperialist masculinity. The contrast clarifies not only the fine details of Shelley's feminist critique of Romanticism but her deeper understanding of the manner in which such a vision of masculinity underwrites British imperial expansion. In stark contrast to Porden's "clean" masculine lines, then, Shelley presents an eminently "messy" work, one in which the power of the sublime is set loose within the very structure of the narrative to underscore her unease with both the sublime and the "quest" as forms of male self-realization. In *Frankenstein*'s gothic excesses and its ultimately destabilizing Arctic frame, Shelley rejects any reinsciption of female presence in British imperial endeavor and by extension calls into question women's accepted role in the nation.

The yawning gap between these two critiques of an exclusionary British masculinity united only by their contemporaneous publication underscores the degree to which Arctic space constitutes a surprisingly important substrate for British imaginings of gender and empire in the early nineteenth century. The divergent solutions offered by Porden and Shelley—if rejection can be called a solution—only underscore the salience and unresolved nature of the questions, raised by imperial practices in traditional colonial spaces, of what is necessary for imperial gender formations, and the relation of the domestic and local to national and imperial identities. These questions underpin much of the literature of the later century, and both the strategies Porden and Shelley employ to answer them and their assertions about women's authorship and authority inform the next generation of women writers.

CHAPTER FOUR

A PALE BLANK OF
MIST AND CLOUD

Arctic Spaces in *Jane Eyre*

Much recent criticism of *Jane Eyre* focuses on Charlotte Brontë's use of space in the novel, for as Karen Chase has observed, "Few novels are as spatially articulate."[1] Brontë succinctly establishes the spatial particularities of *Jane Eyre* in its opening lines:

> There was no possibility of taking a walk that day. We had been wandering, indeed, in the leafless shrubbery an hour in the morning; but since dinner . . . the cold winter wind had brought with it clouds so sombre, and a rain so penetrating, that further outdoor exercise was out of the question. . . . I was glad of it; I never liked long walks, especially on chilly afternoons: dreadful to me was the coming home in the raw twilight, with nipped fingers and toes, and a heart saddened by the chidings of Bessie, the nurse.[2]

The bitter outdoors is matched by an equally cold and unfriendly domestic space—"coming home" is even worse than the bitter walk. Feminist critics have tended to focus on the confining domestic interiors that echo Jane's oppression whereas postcolonial critiques look at the

novel's racialized representations of the colonial spaces of Jamaica and
India.[3] But one aspect of the novel that has not received much attention
beyond reductive symbolism is Brontë's use of Arctic space. "The leafless
shrubbery" (68) and "the cold winter wind" (68) are more often read as
physical phenomena that are expressive of social and moral relationships:
the loveless Gateshead is reflected in its grey landscape and Aunt Reed's
"eye of ice" (68); by contrast, Jane's temper burns with a fiery passion.[4]
Yet focusing on the novel's use of heat and cold solely as a symbolic
system tells only part of the story.

   Analysis of Arctic space in *Jane Eyre* reveals a nation-building agenda
at the core of the novel, one which complicates readings that see the
text exclusively in terms of women's spaces and/or colonial space. Tracing a shift in the novel's use of Arctic space from imagined place of identification to physical place of bodily hardship reflects not only Jane's
movement from childhood to maturity, but Brontë's investment in
women's active role in nation-building. By rewriting nation-building,
masculinist rhetorics of Arctic exploration as the domestic experience of
a young woman, Brontë is able to claim political space for women that is
more central to the good of the nation than simple helpmeet or useful
dependent. She asserts for women those qualities developed by male
Arctic explorers: courage, resolution, patience, endurance. As Francis
Spufford points out, these qualities of Arctic explorers are similar to
those demanded of women by domestic ideology.[5] Reading *Jane Eyre* as
a rewriting of the masculine genre of exploration narrative, however,
also enables us to see ways in which Brontë borrows for Jane the authority of Arctic explorers—their place in the national imagination, their
odd combination of singular, lonely, private achievement, super-
freighted with the reactions of an avid reading public who enlisted that
achievement to nationalist ends. By remapping Arctic space onto Great
Britain, Brontë makes a participatory form of symbolic citizenship
accessible to women who previously were denied it. Famously, Robert
Southey—who had given Horatio Nelson's national heroic masculinity
an Arctic origin—had replied rather quellingly to a letter from the
young Brontë that literature "cannot be the business of a woman's life,
and it ought not to be. The more she is engaged in her proper duties, the
less leisure will she have for it, even as an accomplishment and a recreation."[6] Brontë's engagement with Arctic issues in *Jane Eyre* links her to
a tradition of female writing, seen in work by Mary Shelley and Eleanor
Anne Porden, in which Arctic space, incapable of being physically

explored by women writers, is used as an imaginary space in which to enact gendered tales of knowledge.

Composed in 1846 and published in 1847, *Jane Eyre* coincides with a moment of heightened awareness of British Arctic enterprise with the great fanfare and wide documentation in popular periodicals such as the *Illustrated London News* accompanying the launch of Franklin's expedition in 1845. Charlotte Brontë was familiar with the Arctic, and not only because of the surroundings of her family home of Haworth Parsonage, which Elizabeth Gaskell describes as having "sinuous hills [that] seemed to girdle the world like the great Norse serpent," adding intriguingly, "for my part I don't know if they don't stretch to the North Pole."[7] Numerous popular expedition journals and travel accounts published by the century's early Arctic heroes, including Sir John Franklin, William Parry, and John Ross, had made readers familiar with hardship and survival in the polar regions. *Blackwood's Magazine*, to which the Brontës' father subscribed and which the children read avidly, contained two articles in 1821 documenting Parry's 1819 expedition. The younger Brontës' degree of engagement with the expeditions is readily apparent in their juvenilia. In Glasstown, the imaginary world in which they set their juvenile writings, Anne and Emily chose Ross and Parry as names for their characters, while Branwell and Charlotte chose Bonaparte and the Duke of Wellington.[8] The equivalence between these figures is appropriate because Arctic accounts such as Parry's manufactured national heroes whose bravery, courage, and bodily risk put them in the same category as figures from the Napoleonic Wars.

Such interests continue to animate Charlotte Brontë's mature writing, though in a very different form. Thus, as *Jane Eyre* opens, we see Jane sitting in the window seat, curtained off from the library,

> clear panes of glass protecting, but not separating [her] from the drear November day. At intervals, while turning over the leaves in my book, I studied the aspect of that winter afternoon. Afar, it offered a pale blank of mist and cloud; near, a sense of storm-beat shrub, with ceaseless rain sweeping away wildly before a long and lamentable blast. (39–40)

The "pale blank" is a horizon of sorts, and one that *should* circumscribe Jane's existence. But read in terms of the blankness of Arctic space, as a "pale blank" that invites inscription, what is at first understood as a limit opens up as a possibility, a peculiarly fecund space that makes women's action possible through acts of imagination. Contrasted with the snug, orientalized perch in the windowseat from which she "studies" the horizon and to which she retires when excluded from the Reeds' happy domesticity, the blankness of the outside world is both the page on which Jane will write her story and the space in which she will experience it.

After contemplating the "blank" horizon, Jane "returns" to reading *Bewick's History of Birds*. More precisely, she returns to the pictures in the text, for aside from a brief perusal of the narrative, she has no use for Bewick's writing. Significantly, the section that she does read is made up of "certain introductory pages that, child as I was, I could not pass quite as a blank" (40). Jane relates to texts in general as "blanks" unless, as in the case of Bewick, they have special interest to her and to her situation. Not surprisingly, the pages that interest Jane are those that address the enormous blank of Arctic space.

> They were those which treat of the haunts of sea-fowl; of "the solitary rocks and promontories" by them only inhabited; of the coast of Norway, studded with isles from its southern extremity, the Lindeness, or Naze, to the North Cape,
>
> > Where the Northern Ocean, in vast whirls,
> > Boils round the naked, melancholy isles
> > Of farthest Thule; and the Atlantic surge
> > Pours in among the stormy Hebrides.
>
> Nor could I pass unnoticed the suggestion of the bleak shores of Lapland, Siberia, Spitzbergen, Nova Zembla, Iceland, Greenland, with "the vast sweep of the Arctic Zone, and those forlorn regions of dreary space—that reservoir of frost and snow, where firm fields of ice, the accumulation of centuries of winters, glazed in Alpine heights above heights, surround the pole, and concentre the multiplied rigours of extreme cold." Of these death-white realms I formed an idea of my own: shadowy, like all the half-comprehended notions that float dim through children's brains, but strangely impressive. The words in these introductory pages connected themselves with the succeeding vignettes, and gave significance to the rock standing up alone in

a sea of billow and spray; to the broken boat stranded on a desolate coast; to the cold and ghastly moon glancing through bars
of cloud at a wreck just sinking. (40)

Bewick's text contains a geographical list of white lands distant from the
intense redness of Gateshead's interior, enabling Jane to imagine a narrative for the pictures that follow. The images she "reads" are not of
birds—few illustrations in Bewick are, curiously—but of lonely ship-
wrecks and isolated rocks. While these images reflect Jane's own isolation
and her emotional state, Brontë's insistent incorporation of the Victorian
Arctic shorthand in Bewick's text ("bleak," "vast," "desolate") foregrounds Jane's emerging sense of her position, which is linked not to her
social relations (the way it is in the altercation with her cousin John that
follows this scene), but is instead enabled by the Arctic "suggestion" of
the text.

Perhaps most importantly, an *idea of her own* emerges from "that
reservoir of frost and snow." The description of Arctic spaces enables her
imagination to generate its own text; Jane fills in the blanks with imagined narratives. Significantly, it is Jane's propensity to express ideas of her
own that both gets her into trouble and helps her survive, and in this
way, her narrative ability is a mark of her maturation. Since the pictures'
stories Jane supplies are "as interesting as the tales Bessie [the nurse]
sometimes narrated on winter evenings" (40), stories borrowed from
Richardson's *Pamela* and other literary sources, Jane's stories, spawned by
the Arctic, also mark her birth as an author.

The poetry quoted in Bewick links Jane's emerging understanding
of her position as female and as writer to the political and nationalistic
overtones of the Arctic in nineteenth-century discourse. The lines come
from the "Autumn" section of James Thomson's *The Seasons*, a poem
that in its descriptions of landscape, accounts of religious debates, and
political discussions, is deeply concerned with the making and maintaining of the nation. The passage quoted by Bewick connects Britain to the
Arctic by tracing the northern ocean from farthest "Thule" to the
Hebrides. Clearly, this section is used by Bewick precisely because it is
concerned with bird migration, as the lines of the poem that follow the
ones cited in the text attest:

> Who can recount what Transmigrations there
> Are annual made? What Nations come and go?

> And how the living Clouds on Clouds arise?
> Infinite Wings! till all the Plume-dark Air,
> And rude resounding Shore are one wild Cry.[9]

The addition of the birds to the bleak expanse gives the inanimate environment shape and life as we see with the metaphor of "living Clouds." Similarly, Brontë shows that the way to animate the inanimate list of Arctic territories Jane is given by Bewick is to insert herself into these geographical spaces via the imagination. Just as the birds become "Nations" in Thomson, Jane's insertion of woman into the pictures and text of Bewick make it possible for woman to participate in nation. The birds' commotion and "wild Cry" are exactly what is denied Jane in the oppressive domesticity of Gateshead. Similarly, their "transmigration" is a movement that Jane, the dependent orphan, cannot assume. These are the things to which she aspires and which are made possible for her in Arctic fantasy. They are not physically or literally available to her at the moment, but through her Arctic imaginings she is able to envision the potential for action and movement.

The link to a broader series of concerns attaching to Britain's global position and the place of women in its imperial projections becomes more apparent if we consider more fully the context of Brontë's allusion to Thomson and *The Seasons* through Bewick. In "Winter," the final and best-known poem of *The Seasons*, the "Nations" of birds are explicitly replaced in the Arctic with the British nation when Thomson presents the Arctic landscape as a space of Britain's imperial expansion. The poem begins by describing winter arriving in England, then follows the season through Scotland and other parts of Britain, until finally tracing its permanence in the literal Arctic. The ordering of the poem extends Britain's borders outward from England to its farthest reaches by the mechanics of snow and ice, which, like British rule, cover the various geographies. For Thomson, the Arctic belongs to Britain through efforts—albeit failed ones—of imperial expansion. In a famous passage from "Winter" describing the fate of Sir Hugh Willoughby, the "Briton" sent by Queen Elizabeth to explore Meta Incognita, as she called the Arctic, Willoughby and his men encounter

> . . . a bleak Expanse,
> Shagg'd o'er with wavy Rocks, chearless, and void
> Of every Life, that from the dreary Months
> Flies conscious southward. Miserable they!

Who, here entangled in the gathering Ice,
Take their last Look of the descending Sun;
While, full of Death, and fierce with tenfold Frost,
The long long Night, incumbent o'er their Heads,
Falls horrible. Such was the BRITON's Fate,
As with first Prow, (What have not BRITONS dar'd!)
He for the Passage sought, attempted since
So much in vain, and seeming to be shut
By jealous Nature with eternal Bars.
. . . he with his hapless Crew,
Each full-exerted at his several Task,
Froze into Statues; to the Cordage glued
The Sailor, and the Pilot to the Helm.[10]

Arctic space, then, as early as the mid-eighteenth century was linked to nation building and to a particular form of bodily risk. Thus, when Jane then inserts herself into the world of Bewick's birds, she is joining not only the solitary images of Bewick's woodcuts—things that invite her imaginative projection—but also Thomson's much earlier and famous rhetoric of imperial expansion. The Arctic with which Jane identifies is an escape from the social conditions that make her a dependent, but just as the solitariness of the literal Arctic explorer is narrated to the public as nation-building in poems such as Thomson's and in the Arctic narratives of returned explorers, the "Arctic autobiography" Jane Eyre narrates to the public is one of nation building performed by woman within domestic borders of Britain. The national work that Arctic space performs in male exploration narratives thus becomes the national work that British space performs in female exploration narratives. Jane's self-definition using Arctic space is also a declaration of her citizenship in Britain, something Brontë's text further underlines when a servant believes Jane to be "some infantine Guy Fawkes" (58) and when Jane describes her confrontation with John Reed in terms of a slave revolt.

As Jane increasingly comes to inhabit her role as female "explorer," her removal from Gateshead is precipitated by her perceived intractability, vocalized in her confrontations with authority. After driving her aunt from the room, Jane is "left there alone—winner of the field," (69) her solitariness transformed from victimhood to triumph. Instead of enjoying her victory, however, she is overcome with remorse, which she seeks to placate by reading:

I would fain exercise some better faculty than that of fierce speaking—fain find nourishment for some less fiendish feeling than that of sombre indignation. I took a book—some Arabian tales; I sat down and endeavoured to read. I could make no sense of the subject; my own thoughts swam always between me and the page I had usually found fascinating. I opened the glass-door in the breakfast-room: the shrubbery was quite still: the black frost reigned, unbroken by sun or breeze. Through the grounds. I covered my head and arms with the skirt of my frock, and went out to walk in a part of the plantation which was quite sequestered; but I found no pleasure in the silent trees, the falling fir-cones, the congealed relics of autumn, russet leaves swept by past winds in heaps, and now stiffened together. I leaned against a gate, and looked into an empty field where no sheep were feeding, where the short grass was nipped and blanched. It was a very gray day; a most opaque sky, 'onding on snaw," canopied all; thence flakes fell at intervals, which settled on the hard path and on the hoary lea without melting. I stood, a wretched child enough, whispering to myself over and over again, "What shall I do? What shall I do?" (70)

Jane's "strug[gle] out into unhoped-for liberty" (69), her self-assertion, results in the failure of imagined tales to soothe or transport her. In place of the imaginative journeying of reading, she walks out, underdressed, into an Arctic scene of "black frost" and an "opaque sky." Identified by Bessie as "a little roving, solitary thing" (70), Jane's shift from reading to walking, from imagining to "doing" (70), is what marks her removal to school at Lowood, where her internal, imagined journey turns into a polar journey, with Jane cast as active protagonist instead of imaginary or imagined participant transported there by her imagination.

The removal to Lowood is perceived from the start as an exploration narrative in which Jane is taken "away to unknown, and, as I then deemed, remote and mysterious regions" (51).[11] A girl's school, Lowood is an inversion of the male homosocial space of Arctic exploration. It is a place of hardship, and Jane's experience there is related with all the standard details of Arctic narratives: bad food and little of it, bodily hardship, and relentless suffering, mitigated only — and not at first—by the presence of others who experience the same thing. The winter wind penetrates the girls' inadequate shelter and freezes the water with which they are to wash. They shiver in their beds; Jane is "ready to perish with cold"

(63). The burned porridge of her first morning evokes the meals of rancid hides and soles of shoes that Franklin chronicled in *Narrative of a Journey to the Shores of the Polar Sea*, and in days after, although the porridge is not burned, there is too little of it.

Strikingly, Brontë's description of the landscape around Lowood also closely follows descriptions of Arctic spaces by explorers. Take for example, her description of Lowood's grounds in winter:

> laid out beneath the iron sky of winter, stiffened in frost, shrouded with snow!—when mists as chill as death wandered to the impulse of east winds along those purple peaks, and rolled down' ing' and holm till they blended with the frozen fog of the beck! The beck itself was then a torrent, turbid and curbless; it tore asunder the wood, and sent a raving sound through the air, often thickened with wild rain or whirling sleet; and for the forest on its banks, *that* showed only the ranks of skeletons. (92)

The lack of differentiation between earth and sky, between fog and river, echoes the concerns of Sir John Ross, who, on his 1819 voyage, saw uncertainty and the threat of erasure in the indistinctness of the polar landscape: "Those unacquainted with frozen climates . . . must recollect that when all is ice, and all one dazzling mass of white, when the surface of the sea itself is tossed up and fixed onto rocks, while the land is on the contrary often very level, the two cannot be distinguished with accuracy" (69). The "ranks of skeletons" of trees on the river's bank evoke at once the frozen, typhus-stricken bodies of the Lowood students and those of dead explorers in undifferentiated Arctic wastes. Brontë even describes the freezing nights and mornings as having a "Canadian temperature [which] froze the very blood in our veins" (88).

In Lowood's harsh conditions, the girls' bodies are pushed to points of resistance that are the standard fare of Arctic narratives, and in rewriting those conditions Brontë transcribes the traditional masculine narrative of Arctic character building onto a population of schoolgirls. The girls "march forward . . . like stalwart soldiers" into a cold wind that "almost flayed the skin from [their] faces" (72):

> Our clothing was insufficient to protect us from the severe cold; we had no boots, the snow got into our shoes, and melted there; our ungloved hands became numbed and covered with chillblains, as were our feet. I remember well the distracting irritation

I endured from this cause every evening, when my feet inflamed, and the torture of thrusting the swelled, raw, and stiff toes into my shoes in the morning. Then the scanty supply of food was distressing: with the keen appetites of growing children, we had scarcely sufficient to keep alive a delicate invalid. (72)

Importantly, Brontë's use of Arctic hardship and imagery is, necessarily, not merely a transcription of male exploration narratives. Unlike the simple conflation of Arctic hardship and positive character formation found in Robert Southey's *Life of Nelson* and in John Franklin's account, Brontë recognizes that while hardship may form character, it does so at a cost. For the pupils at Lowood, "deficiency of nourishment resulted in abuse which pressed hardly on the younger pupils," when big girls steal the food from the little ones, and close them out from the fire (71). Brocklehurst's mission "not to accustom them to habits of luxury and indulgence, but to render them hardy, patient, self-denying [. . . with the aim of . . .] improving . . . the spiritual edification of the pupils, by encouraging them to evince fortitude under the temporary privation" (75) depends on a one-to-one correlation of moral development and physical hardship. Like the metropolitan readers of Arctic exploration narratives, who granted returned explorers symbolic knowledge that exceeded their bodily distress, Brocklehurst misunderstands the link between suffering and character. The suffering Jane, echoing Franklin's officer Hepburn, who wondered if he should ever recover his "understanding" even should he survive the winter, understands that "whatever [Brocklehurst] might do with the outside of the cup and platter, the inside was farther beyond his interference than he imagined" (76). Brontë rewrites male Arctic adventure from the standpoint of one who understands its subtexts of fragility—that which does not kill the explorer may not make him stronger, but may, in fact, alter him to the point of unrecognizability.

In fact, Jane's privations at Lowood do build her character, but not in Brocklehurst's terms. We can see a useful parallel with the Arctic section of Robert Southey's *Life of Nelson*, where a young Horatio Nelson learns that national character demands both risk taking and appropriate submission to authority. While Jane admires Helen Burns's fortitude in suffering, she "could not comprehend this doctrine of endurance; and still else could [she] understand or sympathize with the forbearance [Helen] expressed for her chastiser" (68). She can respect Helen, but she cannot emulate her. Helen's forbearance is linked to her ability to live elsewhere mentally while she is suffering; that is, it is identified with her belief in the pleasant home she misses and her belief in a heavenly home with God after death. Jane has not such certainties of home and hearth to ground her—she is a wanderer through cold wastes.[12] The demands that national and domestic ideology make upon women, Brontë seems to say, depend on there being a space for women in the nation and the domestic in the first place. Importantly, Jane's active resistance to Brocklehurst's authority takes place in her identification with the very elements meant to subdue and discipline her. In a passage reminiscent of the window seat passage that opens the book, Jane once again looks out at an unwelcoming landscape:

> I . . . lifted a blind and looked out; it snowed fast, a drift was already forming against the lower panes; putting my ear close to the window, I could distinguish from the gleeful tumult within, the disconsolate moan of the wind outside.
>
> Probably, if I had lately left a good home and kind parents; this would have been the hour when I should most keenly have regretted the separation: that wind would then have saddened my heart: this obscure chaos would have disturbed my peace: as it was, I derived from both a strange excitement, and, reckless and feverish, I wished the wind to howl more wildly, the gloom to deepen to darkness, and the confusion to rise to clamour. (65)

At the window, the solitary Jane connects the tumult of the school to nature's ferocity and wishes for its escalation, in order to reflect more accurately the passions she feels. Her projection of herself onto the exterior world is a symbolic expression of her unsettled interior, but the exterior's reflection of her interior back to herself also enables Jane's assumption of masculine Arctic exploration narratives as her own, as woman's. Moreover, we can see in passages such as this how Brontë borrows from and reworks the forms of autobiography and bildungsroman. As an orphan cut off from any sense of domestic origins, or household, Jane essentially constitutes her own origin and composes her autobiography out of and on the elements of the wintery landscape. In this sense, she achieves the goal that Victor Frankenstein had so desperately sought, and, ironically, seen come to naught in the Arctic and the spaces of Britain's northern reaches. Indeed, for Brontë it is perhaps the successful coalescence of an imperial masculinity in the Arctic, however suspect it may be, that enables a female self's creation out of nothingness. Brontë's reworking of autobiography underscores *Jane Eyre*'s generic difference from the romance deployed by Shelley to illustrate the impotent desperation of the masculine attempt to found a self outside of the bounds of domesticity. Jane succeeds in finding such a self precisely because under the terms of the gender politics of the era it is seen as unnecessary and perverse for a woman or girl to do so.

Indeed, after Lowood is reformed, Brontë does not abandon the evocation of exploration narratives. Jane's subsequent dissatisfaction with her teaching position hinges on her yearning for physical experience. "I remembered that the real world was wide," Jane recounts, "and that a varied field of hopes and fears, of sensations and excitements, awaited those who had courage to go forth into its expanse, to seek real knowledge of life amidst its perils" (116). Looking out a window at Lowood, Jane yearns to journey beyond the horizon's limit: "My eye passed all other objects to rest on those most remote, the blue peaks. It was those I longed to surmount; all within their boundary of rock and heath seemed prison-ground, exile limits. I traced the white road winding round the base of one mountain, and vanishing in a gorge between. How I longed to follow it farther!" (99). The "world" of course is not wide for an unconnected young woman without any means, and Jane recognizes that she must exchange freedom for servitude and enclosure. But when she at last surmounts "the hilly horizon," she takes up residence at Thornfield where, "after a day of bodily fatigue and mental anxiety," she understands herself to be "at last in safe haven" (113). Yet the "safe haven" of Thornfield, while it offers the first approximation of equality and family to Jane in the form of Mrs. Fairfax and Adele, is itself remote and cold.

While the mature Jane acts and does, as befits an explorer, she also maintains the space of musing imagination identified in her childhood with the Arctic in her contemplation of *Bewick's Birds*. Jane's mature artwork echoes the scenes that return again and again to desolation and cold, shipwreck, and death. Of the three pictures Rochester looks at, two in particular comment on Jane's identification with Arctic narrative. In one, the Evening Star is a woman, with "dark and wild" eyes, who rises in the sky above the horizon. The other yet is more explicitly "Arctic" in content,

> The third showed the pinnacle of an iceberg piercing a polar winter sky: a muster of northern lights reared their dim lances, close serried, along the horizon. Throwing these into distance,

rose, in the foreground, a head—a colossal head, inclined towards the iceberg, and resting against it. Two thin hands, joined under the forehead, and supporting it, drew up before the lower features a sable veil; a brow quite bloodless, white as bone, and an eye hollow and fixed, blank of meaning, but for the glassiness of despair, alone were visible. Above the temples, amidst wreathed turban folds of black drapery, vague in its character and consistency as cloud, gleamed a ring of white flame, gemmed with sparkles of a more lurid tinge. This pale crescent was "the likeliness of a kingly crown"; what it diademed was "the shape which shape had none." (143)

These are self-portraits, not of Jane's physical appearance, but of a projected interior, with their source in her "spiritual eye" (156), evidence that Jane's affinity with desolate polar expanses is more than symbolic, but is, rather, her primary mode of representing and understanding herself in the world. The cold sublimnity of the icebergs and northern lights are for Jane the natural environment of the soul. "Were you happy when you painted these pictures?" (143), asks Rochester. Jane answers, "I was absorbed, sir: yes, and I was happy. To paint them, in short, was to enjoy one of the keenest pleasures I have ever known" (143). Painting the images is one way in which Jane visits the physically distant Arctic by literally painting her soul as/into the landscape, but it is also a way in which she masters the Arctic. For later, Jane paints to discipline an imagination that she feels has run away into a romance with Rochester. She masters her emotions and her imagination by painting Blanche Ingram's portrait to remind herself of the difference between the physical ideal of woman and herself, and of the ridiculousness of her feelings and hopes for Rochester. The "wholesome discipline to which [she] . . . force[s her] feelings to submit" (184) allows Jane to "fix" both her impressions of outer and interior worlds, by making them match.

Tellingly, Jane's first encounter with the man who will be her "likeness," her "equal" (284), takes place in a scene of desolate, Arctic expanse, in the fields near Thornfield, "whose best winter delight lay in its utter solitude and leafless repose. If a breath of air stirred, it made no sound here; for there was not a holly, not an evergreen to rustle, and the stripped hawthorn and hazel bushes were as still as the white worn stones which causewayed the middle of the path" (127). "I like this day; I like that sky of steel; I like the sternness and stillness of the world under this frost" (173), Rochester later says, further identifying himself with the landscape and nature that defines Jane. In turn, Jane perceives her growing friendship with Rochester as filling in the "blanks" of her existence, blanks previously identified with the Arctic and with Jane's own imagination, but now identified increasingly with Rochester. As the narrative of romance joins her narrative of domestic Arctic exploration, Jane feels her "thin-crescent-destiny seeming to enlarge," and her "bodily health [improve] [as she] gather[s] flesh and strength" (166). Significantly, these are the feelings of the polar voyager who has returned home, as Jane later does from visiting her dying aunt at Gateshead to a Thornfield with hedges full of roses and a waiting Rochester.

Despite her growing physical strength and her confidence that her wandering days of trial are over, Jane persists in employing oceanic images of voyaging as she allows herself to slip into love with Rochester. Romance is a new adventure, perilous because it is a departure from the solitariness that defines Jane, and, crucially, from the solitariness of Arctic exploration that has, until now, served as Jane's appropriated template. After Rochester's near expression of love to her, she envisions herself "on a buoyant but unquiet sea, where billows of trouble rolled under surges of joy."

> I thought sometimes I saw beyond its wild waters a shore, sweet as the hills of Beulah; and now and then a freshening gale, wakened by hope, bore my spirit triumphantly outwards the bourne: but I could not reach it, even in fancy—a counteracting breeze blew off the land, and continually drove me back. Sense would resist delirium: judgement would warn passion. (171)

Heterosexual romance is positioned here as a new adventure, at first seeming to offer itself up as a geographic space to be conquered like any other that the male Arctic explorer might encounter. In the traditional masculine narrative of exploration, "sense" and "judgement" would persevere and result in successfully reaching "outwards the bourne" to the opposite "shore." Because the structures of domestic heterosexual romance are precisely what have bounded Jane and propelled her to assume the role of female "Arctic" explorer, however, a necessary logical reversal comes about: "sense" and "judgement" here do not triumph in a conquering of geographical space, as in traditional masculine narratives, but instead triumph precisely in resisting the "delirium" and "passion" that the thrill of conquering would seem to offer. "Sense" and "judgement" win out for the female explorer in a refusal to vanquish geo-

graphical space, in a refusal to give in to the "delirium" of domestic, heterosexual "passion."

Brontë goes out of her way to describe Rochester as falling short of
the romantic ideal; he is "ugly," "preciously grim," at times possessing a
"frigid and rigid temper" (150). Yet, he is in some ways an ideal of active,
masculine strength. Jane observes he has a "good figure in the athletic
sense of the term—broad-chested and thin-flanked" (140). A flattering
Blanche praises Rochester indirectly when dismissing "the young men of
the present day" as "poor, puny things, not fit to stir a step beyond papa's
park gates: nor to go even so far without mamma's permission and
guardianship! . . . [A]s to the *gentlemen*, let them be solicitous to possess
only strength and valour: let their motto be—hunt, shoot, and fight: the
rest is not worth a fillip" (195). Yet Rochester's physique belies his weak-
nesses, which are attributed in the novel to his connection to colonial
enterprise. Susan Meyer has detailed the way colonialism infiltrates the
novel, not only overtly, as seen in the racialized representation of Bertha,
but in the "dark and imperious" Blanche Ingram and in the thick-lipped
dilettante John Reed. She argues that Rochester himself bears the "taint"
of colonial spaces: "When Rochester decides to leave Jamaica, where he
has taken a wife as a 'slave,' participated in slavery, and become 'black-
ened,' the novel poses the opposition between oppressive Jamaica and
pure England."[13] Rochester thus stands both as the promise of idealized
British masculinity and as the harsh warning of the threat of its dissolution by colonial contamination. An ex-butler describes Rochester to Jane
as "spirited," "bold and keen . . . not a man given to wine, or cards, or
racing, as some are . . . but he had a courage and a will of his own. I knew
him as a boy, you see" (475). But the grown Rochester's marriage and his
subsequent wealth from the colonies, his retreat from the mad Bertha
into the fleshpots of Europe veers far from the English ideal[14]—and he is
transformed from English gentleman to "oriental despot."[15]

As her marriage to Rochester nears, Jane becomes uneasy with the
dependence of her happiness on her subjection, a subjection evidenced
by Rochester's request that she change her dress, which is expressed in
terms of her orientalized subjection to a sultan. As is well documented
by critics such as Gayatri Spivak, Susan Meyer, and Elsie Michie, the
colonial presence erupts decisively into the narrative with the disruption
of Jane's marriage. After the disclosure of Bertha and Rochester's marriage, Jane falls into decline, expelled by the domesticity her love for
Rochester has brought her: "I felt weak and tired. . . . And now I
thought: till now I had only heard, seen, moved—followed up and down

where I was led and dragged—watched even rushed on event, disclosure open beyond disclosure: but *now, I thought*" (330). *Thinking,* Jane immediately casts herself back into her Arctic narrative:

> Jane Eyre, who had been an ardent expectant woman—almost a bride—was a cold, solitary girl again: her life was pale; her prospects were desolate. A Christmas frost had come at midsummer; a white December storm had whirled over June; ice glazed the ripe apples, drifts crushed the blowing roses; on hayfield and cornfield lay a frozen shroud: lanes which last night blushed full of flowers, to-day were pathless with untrodden snow; and the woods, which twelve hours since waved leafy and fragrant as groves between the tropics, now spread, waste, wild, and white as pine-forests in wintry Norway. . . . I looked on my cherished wishes, yesterday so blooming and glowing; they lay stark, chill, livid corpses that could never revive. I looked at my love: that feeling which was my master's—which he had created; it shivered in my heart, like a suffering child in a cold cradle: sickness and anguish had seized it; it could not seek Mr. Rochester's arms—it could not derive warmth from his breast. (330–31)

Here, however, rather than being restorative or invigorating, the cold that accompanies Jane's heartbreak is death-like. Yet if ever there was a woman equipped to navigate death-like regions of cold, it is Jane Eyre. Rochester acknowledges her rationality in her language: "You will say, 'That man had nearly made me his mistress: I must be ice and rock to him'; and ice and rock you will accordingly become," (338) predicting her actions. Yet, even here, ice and rock are not simply symbols of Jane's resolve, but possess, in fact, a nationalist valence. Jane tells herself, "No; you shall tear yourself away, none shall help you. You shall yourself pluck out your right eye; yourself cut off your right hand: your heart shall be the victim, and you the priest to transfix it" (335). In her translation/transformation of Horatio Nelson's heroic war wounds onto herself, Jane turns again to the role of male Arctic voyager and male national figure. Just as male Arctic heroism is based both on exploration and on the suffering resulting from the failure of that exploration, so is female Arctic heroism here based on the exploration of heterosexual romance and the failure of that romance. Thus, "love and the feeling which [Rochester] had created" in Jane are precisely those things that cause her suffering and the "shivering" in her heart. The familiar role of the Arctic voyager enables her to take charge of an emotional, untamed Rochester: "The present—the passing second of time—was all I had in which to control and restrain him: a movement of repulsion, not in the least. I felt an inward power; a sense of influence, which supported me" (340). The sense of influence, however, is neither religious nor does it spring from the language of "women's influence" in domestic ideology, but springs instead from this new formulation of female explorer, as Brontë makes clear with Jane's following analogy: "The crisis was perilous; but not without its charm: such as the Indian, perhaps, feels when he slips over the rapid in his canoe" (341).[16]

This geographic orientation repeats when Jane remarks as she is leaving Thornfield, "I yearned only [for] what suited me—for the antipodes of the Creole" (349) Bertha. Karen Chase reads the difficulties that Jane encounters after her departure from Thornfield as revealing that "escape from confinement offers no solution, only a new problem. The absence of barriers leads to a contrary, but no less pressing, crisis: the self stripped of any protective carapace, defenceless before nature and human society. The self exposed thus becomes as vulnerable as the self confined."[17] The Arctic narratives that structure so much of the imagery in *Jane Eyre*, however, identify those moments of the exposed self as being moments of vulnerability uniquely indicative of Jane's alienation from both the economic and political workings of the nation. In this case, Jane's embodiment of Arctic enterprise enacts her desire for a location within a British society untroubled by the complexities of empire, since throughout the novel, she defines herself against the "antipodal," racialized figures of Bertha Mason, Blanche Ingram, and the Reed family. Read as an Arctic voyage, Jane's flight across the moors and her experience of bodily hardship can be seen as an effort to retrieve and save Britain from the perceived taint of colonial spaces.

Instead of seeing Jane's journey across the heath as a version of the "female plot" described by Sandra Gilbert and Susan Gubar as a flight "from culture (her father's palace) to nature (the great wood), trying to transform herself into a creature of nature, rather than acquiesce in the extreme demands culture is making upon her,"[18] it is possible to read this voyage as a rewritten masculine narrative, the start of a long journey back *toward* Rochester. The journey will enable Jane to assert her agency as a woman and as an equal in his house, but it is no less important ideologically for its retrieval or revitalization of the landowning precolonial Rochester.[19] It is no surprise that the revalorization of British masculinity is coupled with the exorcism of colonial presence and threat.

In Jane's flight, Brontë literally rewrites the Arctic on to Britain's interior. The domestic British landscape, itself already alienated by the British colonial experience, becomes, in that lonely corner of the moor, an Arctic space retrievable and tamable only by virtue of the peril it poses to a woman's physical being—not, as is so common in later sensation novels, by the threat of harm to a woman by a colonial other, but by the woman's experience of space that is perceived (as Arctic space was indeed perceived) as being empty of the social. The moor, like Jane's earlier experience at Lowood, is sketched with an Arctic pencil: the whitewashed stone pillar that marks the lonely crossroads where Jane is deposited by the coach invokes the cairns Arctic explorers put up to indicate their presence in the landscape, constructed traces of human presence which only reemphasized the desolation of the surrounding wilderness.

In the face of this excess of wilderness, Jane is reduced to wandering: "I was weeping wildly as I walked long my solitary way; fast, fast I went like one delirious. A weakness, beginning inwardly, extending to the limbs, seized me, and I fell; I lay on the ground some minutes, pressing my face to the wet turf. I had some fear—or hope—that here I should die; but I was soon up, crawling forward on my hands and knees, and then again raised to my feet" (360). Outcast from society, Jane travels through a landscape that, though physically British, is not only foreign to her, but also unreadable in its lack of civilization: cultivation disappears, fields are "wild and unproductive as the heath from which they were scarcely reclaimed" (362). Jane is confronted by undifferentiated landscape when she seeks shelter: "All the surface of the waste looked level. It showed no variation but of tint: green, where rush and moss overgrew the marshes; black, where the dry soil bore only death. Dark as it was getting, I could still see these changes, though but as mere alternations of light and shade, for colour had faded with the daylight" (370). Here in a familiar echo of the descriptions of Canadian and Arctic landscape discussed in the introduction and in chapter 2, a specific landscape becomes an undifferentiated, limitless space that threatens to extend to and engulf the exploring body.

But "to die of want and cold is a fate to which nature cannot submit passively" (371), and Jane presses on through the wilderness and toward a civilization that cannot understand her. Paradoxically, the people she encounters believe that they understand her all too well. While Jane frets that she will not receive help because people don't know her "character," the more likely reason she doesn't receive help is because people read her character as a version of what she is, a fallen governess, a dependent now without means, perhaps pregnant, who must have done something immoral to get into the situation in which she finds herself. What Jane is denied in the space of the social, she seeks in the alternately "pure," "warm," and "kindly" "Nature": "Nature seemed to me benign and good; I thought she loved me, outcast as I was; and I, who from man could anticipate only mistrust, rejection, insult, clung to her with filial fondness. . . . I was her child" (363). Yet Nature is no mother, the text reveals. Nightfall brings freezing weather that tempts Jane to give in to stasis:

> I sank down where I stood, and hid my face against the ground. I lay still a while: the night-wind swept over the hill and over me, and died moaning in the distance; the rain fell fast, wetting me afresh to the skin. Could I but have stiffened to the still frost—the friendly numbness of death—it might have pelted on; I should not have felt it; but my yet living flesh shuddered at its chilling influence. I rose ere long. (371)

Though Jane imagines death as a "friendly" joining with frost, the threat of too much wandering in wilderness, both to Jane and her Arctic explorer predecessors, is stasis and death, a death that Jane nonetheless resists. In this regard, Jane reiterates the accounts of Arctic explorers who at their lowest moments envision death as a welcome relief. But, like the explorers, she does not ultimately succumb. Unlike the explorers, however, she finds the means of rescuing herself arise from connection to nature and its incapacity for passive submission. In contrast to the adversarial relationship with nature that we see deployed in the explorers' accounts as a means of realizing their defiant masculinity, Brontë shows Jane's resolve and strength as emerging *from* nature rather than through conflict with nature.

Even if Jane staves off her literal death, however, like other Arctic explorers, her physical peril eventually threatens to unseat her reason; the madness that was once the province of the colonial Bertha reaches toward a now uncivilized Jane. Jane's mental instability takes its form from the "dim and misty" landscape, through which she "gropes" (371). With, to borrow the Arctic explorer George Back's language, "nothing to catch or detain the lingering eye,"[20] there is nothing to separate Jane from the physical landscape; she is in danger of being overrun and consumed by it—of joining it as a corpse. What saves her is her recognition of the importance of and her place in the social. Tempted to linger on the moor and die, she nonetheless recognizes that she is "a human being, and has a human being's wants: I must not linger where there was nothing to supply them." Overcoming her pride, on the verge of death, Jane makes toward a light where, confused once again with someone with no or low character, she nearly dies on the step before she is received into the Rivers family cottage.

The apparent end to Jane's Arctic wandering is the Rivers's acceptance of the "thin," "bloodless," "mere spectre" into their family home (377). Jane's entrance into the family is formalized when it is discovered she is their cousin, and finally the solitary Jane has a sense of belonging to a community: "I liked to read what they liked to read: what they enjoyed, delighted me; what they approved I reverenced" (391). Love and community transform the Arctic space that she has ventured through. Seen through new eyes, rural England is no longer a vast tundra, but a projection of "home":

> I saw the fascination of the locality. I felt the consecration of its loneliness: my eye feasted on the outline of swell and sweep— on the wild colouring communicated to ridge and dell by moss, by heathbell. . . . The strong blast and the soft breeze, the rough and the halcyon day, the hours of sunrise and sunset, the moonlight and the clouded night, developed for me, in these regions, the same attraction as for them—wound round my faculties the same spell that entranced [the Rivers sisters]. (391)

Yet the light that leads her there is first perceived as an "ignus fatuus," the same words Jane uses to describe her first inclination of Rochester's love for her as a caution against letting it lure her into a wilderness (370). From the Rivers's cottage, Jane sees her choice as having been between "the luxuries of a pleasure villa . . . to be a slave in a fool's paradise at Marseilles . . . or . . . free and honest, in a breezy mountain nook in the healthy heart of England" (387). The ignus fatuus warns of the danger, however, in reading Jane's recovery of family and her inheritance as a pious recuperation of female bodily excess into women's submission both to God and to domestic ideology.

Brontë's continued caution against such a reading takes the form of St. John Rivers, Jane's cousin who burns with missionary zeal, but not with human passion. Described by his sister as "inexorable as death" (383), St. John Rivers identifies "in [her] nature . . . an alloy as detrimental to repose as that in [his], though of a different kind" (381). Her cousin misreads Jane's heroism when he lists her qualities and invites her to join him in India: "You are docile, diligent, disinterested, faithful, constant, and courageous; very gentle, and very heroic . . . I can trust you unreservedly. As a conductress of Indian schools, and a helper amongst Indian women, your assistance will be to me invaluable" (449). He reads her courage and heroism as, paradoxically, indicating a docile fortitude along the lines of Helen Burns. Jane's reply to his request is foreshadowed by her description of the landscape where he makes his proposal to her, a landscape that speaks to her specific form of dynamic heroism, "where . . . the mountain shook off turf and flower, had only heath for raiment and crag for gem—where it exaggerated the wild to the savage, and exchanged the fresh for the frowning—where it guarded the forlorn hope of solitude, and a last refuge for silence" (446). By invoking the unfriendly, empty, tundra-like heath in order to define herself against the teeming masses of colonial India, Jane's rewriting of British space as Arctic space is complete.

Following the lead of Rochester's old butler, it is easy to read the post-Thornfield-fire Rochester as diminished in wealth, importance, capacity, and sexual potency, diminishments that enable Jane to join him as a financial as well as a spiritual equal. Yet Rochester's disabilities, his knocked-out eye and amputated hand, are a way Brontë inscribes Jane's saving of Rochester into a narrative of national import and empire building, one already linked to Arctic exploration. For like Jane's own imagined wounds of lost hand and eye, Rochester's wounds are a form of national(ist) stigmata that mirror those of that symbol of heroic national masculinity, Horatio Nelson, whose early experience in the polar seas is central to all narratives of character formation through Arctic hardship that follow it—including *Jane Eyre*. At Ferndean, Rochester exists as a shadow Nelson, diminished and distinctly unheroic in the wake of colonial contamination, awaiting Jane's "rehumanizing" influence.[21]

"Worn to nothing," by her Arctic traveling, "a mere spectre," Jane is reborn. It is not a spiritual rebirth, however, but rather one that allows refound social purpose. Though she almost submits to St. John, she resists his proposal to her, knowing that she will reach the limit of her physical strength in India and that her role is in England, to channel her mental and physical resources toward "curing" the nation of the emasculating results of slaveholding and colonialism. In her experience of privation at Lowood and on the moors, Jane conquers the space previously reserved for the male explorer. Her bodily risk through "Arctic " exploration in

Britain thus symbolically defines a new kind of national citizenship for women by recuperating domestic space made foreign by Bertha Mason and corrupted by the spoiled indolence of the upper class in the form of the degenerate Reeds and the morally bankrupt Ingrams.

As Jenny Sharpe argues in a somewhat different way, *Jane Eyre* makes possible a new, domestic female subjectivity, but it does so via its investment in the moral and racial superiority of the colonial.[22] Sharpe's observation succinctly articulates the colonial and racial politics that frame and, indeed, crucially limit the novel's final expression of female agency. Locating *Jane Eyre's* place within the broader discourse of Arctic exploration, however, reveals important nuances in the novel's fundamental relationship to the imperial project, particularly as it pertains to gender and the links between women, nation, and empire. To take full account of Spivak's claim that imperialism is a discursive field in which Jane's struggle for self-determination takes place,[23] we must attend not only to Bertha Mason and to Rochester's and St. John's deep connections to British colonial endeavors in the Caribbean and South Asia. The "feminization" of colonial space as one that invites either the "education" and proseletizing of a St. John Rivers or the commercial and sexual exploitation of a Rochester is obviously grounded in a much longer imperial discourse that genders space. One crucially important but often overlooked aspect of that process during the nineteenth century, as I have been arguing, is the British apprehension of the Arctic as a space for realizing an expansionist British masculinity that is "pure," heroic, and uncompromised by the taints of either feminine domesticity or colonial exploitation.

By remapping this terrain onto a British landscape, Brontë not only reverses the terms of heterosexual romance and women's autobiography but also undermines an important narrative of imperial masculinity. Brontë insists on reversing the imperialist trajectory by reinscribing it onto the domestic landscape of Britain, and in doing so, she calls into question the very notions of definable origins and separate domestic and extranational spaces upon which imperialist logic is based. Confounding "domestic" space in the novel, in other words, carries implications for colonial space as well. Thus, while I do not wish to reject Sharpe's analysis and her implicit admonition about glossing over the novel's troubling racial politics, I would like to suggest that when viewed through the wider lens of nineteenth-century exploration accounts, the *gender* politics of the text lends these issues a significantly different inflection. After all, it is Rochester and St. John who are the colonial "adventurers." To the extent that Jane functions as a "civilizer" as part of her significantly retooled "woman's mission," it is to "civilize" Rochester and British imperialism away from their enfeebling extranational rapacity.

When at Ferndean Jane proclaims, "I hold myself supremely blest— blest beyond what language can express; because I am my husband's life as fully as he is mine" (500), theirs is the union of equals: Rochester, a Nelson restored to health and his place within the domestic, and Jane, home from her long journey in Arctic wastes.

CHAPTER FIVE

ARCTIC HIGHLANDERS AND ENGLISHMEN

Dickens, Cannibalism, and Sensation

When the wind is blowing and the sleet or rain is driving against the dark windows, I love to sit by the fire, thinking of what I have read in books of voyage and travel. Such books have had a strong fascination for my mind from my earliest childhood; and I wonder it should have come to pass that I never have been round the world never have been ship-wrecked, ice-environed, tomahawked, or eaten.
— Charles Dickens, "The Long Voyage,"
in *Household Words*, 1854

We had an act at the North Pole, where the slightest and greatest thing the eye beheld were equally taken from the books of the Polar voyagers. Out of thirty people, there were certainly not two who might not have gone straight to the North Pole itself, completely furnished for the winter!
— Charles Dickens about *The Frozen Deep*,
in a letter to W. F. De Cerjat, Jan. 17, 1857

There is no accounting for tastes, blubber for the Esqimaux, half-hatched eggs for the Chinese, and Sensational novels for the English.
—anonymous reviewer of Wilkie Collins's *Armadale*
in *Westminster Review*, 1866

B oth the exploration accounts of the early century and those gen- erated by the search for the lost Franklin expedition found a nar- rative-hungry audience at home. Tales of resistant British bodies making their way across forbidding frozen landscapes filled lending libraries already packed with volumes of "Voyages and Travels," leading one Buckinghamshire clergyman to lament, "We require duplicates over again of such works as Bunyan's *Pilgrim's Progress*, Defoe's *Robinson Crusoe*, Cook's Voyages, and works of that description."[1] There were so many travel writers published in the first half of the century that one anonymous 1855 reviewer of travel literature wrote "we are fairly wea- ried out with constant additions to our information."[2] Still, the same reviewer reserved a special place for Arctic narratives and their tales of the limits of human experience and knowledge.

> No; there are no more sunny continents—no more islands of the blest—hidden under the far horizon, tempting the dreamer over the undiscovered sea; nothing but those weird and tragic shores, those cliffs of everlasting ice and mainlands of frozen snow, which have never produced anything to us but a late and sad discovery of depths of human heroism, patience, and bravery, such as imagination could scarcely dream of. (589)

The "late and sad discovery"—conjectures about the fate of the 1845 Franklin expedition of the *Erebus* and *Terror* which, as we will see, held unexpected resonances in discussions of the nature and boundaries of national identity in the mid- to late nineteenth century—transformed a blank Arctic into a place of "weird and tragic shores." The conjunction of weirdness and tragedy made the increasingly complex narratives of Arctic exploration one unlikely (and strangely perfect) source of the sensation novel, the mid-Victorian genre that so often examined the strange and the estranged in its mapping of Victorian middle-class values.

While early-nineteenth-century representations of empty and unconquerable Arctic space defined exploration as a project of nation building, the narratives penned by those explorers who searched for Franklin peopled the Arctic with England's dead and transformed the Arctic into a static, panoramic memorial to the British imperial endeavor, even as that empire continued to expand. Not surprisingly, readers increasingly employed representations of Arctic spaces in ideo- logical contests at home. Charles Dickens notably engaged Arctic travel narratives by redeploying tropes they used to construct British identity in potent narratives of racialized national identities in his journalism and, later, the sensation drama he collaborated on with Wilkie Collins, *The Frozen Deep*.

Dickens, the reader, understood the power of travel literature to transport a reader from a chair to the ends of empire and back, without ever leaving the comfort of home. His "wonder" in 1854, expressed in the epigraph to this chapter, at how "it should have come to pass that [he had] never have been round the world never [had] been shipwrecked, ice-environed, tomahawked, or eaten" after reading tales of travel is at once a tongue-in-cheek observation and a precise description of the paradoxical work of travel narratives. For travel narratives asked readers to participate imaginatively in the naturalization of British presence around the globe, demanding, by their nature as representations, that the reader be safe at home (by the fire, in Dickens's case) while simultaneously transported to the edges of empire. Dickens's "wonder" is tied as tightly to the warm fire and the rain beating against the windows outside as it is to the remembered transport of the text: the safety and comfort of home allow him to participate in the appeal and exoticism of travel while it ensures that he will not, actually, ever experience travel's discomforts firsthand. While some readers, like Walton in Mary Shelley's *Frankenstein*, were summoned to actual adventures by reading about exploration and hardship, many more were like Dickens, whose experience of discomfort, of isolation, of assault, of cannibalism *secondhand* as a reader, induces "wonder," a wonder that results at once in a new appreciation for home and for the connection between representation and participation in national projects of citizenship and empire.

Nowhere is Charles Dickens's investment in and recognition of the imbricated nature of reading and citizenship more obvious than in his response to conjectures about the fate of the Franklin expedition. When the Scottish explorer John Rae returned from the Arctic with news of the expedition's reported descent into cannibalism, Dickens responded by staging a debate with Rae about the fate of Franklin in his journal, *Household Words*, in the winter of 1854–55. Dickens's and Rae's journalistic exchange about what may or may not have occurred in the distant Arctic wastes reveals much about the perceived stability of national identities in mid-century as well as about Dickens's investment in readers' vicarious but important participation in the exploration of spaces of empire and nation. While Dickens argued for a stable identity—the English reader by the fireside is no different from the English explorer on the tundra—Rae emphasized unknown exigencies that made explorers different from their armchair-bound contemporaries and situations that might require behavior not readily understood by those at home. Dickens based his conclusion of the immutability of English character on his experience of reading: avid readers of Arctic narratives knew that cannibalism by British military men was impossible, that Englishmen might eat nearly anything, but never each other. If reading Arctic adventure enabled recognition of Englishmen as not-cannibal, more fundamentally it enabled readers to imagine themselves as "British," that is, as participating in a "deep, horizontal comradeship," the "imagined community" that Benedict Anderson famously identifies as being central to the conception of nation.[3] Those readers of *Household Words* who followed the Dickens/Rae debate, therefore, participated in the institutionalizing of shared values of national identity from the privacy of their own armchairs at their own firesides, while reading periodicals and novels that situated them in a community of other Britons who, they could be confident, were doing the same thing.

Anderson ties the rise of "nation" to print culture through the forms of serial and novel. Dickens, however, despite his investment in publication as both a publisher and an author, reveals his understanding of the power of spectacle and performance in the national imaginary in his transformation of the *Household Words* cannibalism debate in his production of the 1857 sensation drama, *The Frozen Deep*. Although Wilkie Collins drafted the play, its subject was suggested by Dickens who, as Robert Brannan compellingly argues, continued to shape the play by actively editing and contributing to it and finally by producing and performing in the play at Tavistock House, and later in public theatres.[4] Dickens sublimates the cannibalism that is the overt subject of his writings on the Franklin mystery in the transformation of his journalism to stage spectacle, shifting his representational strategy from an economy of logic to one of melodrama. As one of many recent critics addressing Dickens's interest in performance and theatricality in his novels, Deborah Vlock convincingly concludes that for Dickens, "novels and theatre . . . have equal access to the real, the genuine."[5] Yet the connection between Dickens's journalism concerning the fate of Franklin and his contributions to and performance in *The Frozen Deep* reveal in this case Dickens's anxiety concerning the power and stability of the written word. In *The Frozen Deep*, cannibalism remains the powerful, if not fully articulated organizing force around which Dickens constructs a stable, white national identity, and by which he concedes that the affective powers of the stage were best to describe to and provoke in his audience that same stable, white national identity in which he was so invested.

The "sensation" provoked by Charles Dickens's performance and felt by all who participated in it on stage and in the audience, relied on the fixed categories of racialized behavior and evidence first established in the Dickens/Rae debate, which were then reestablished by Dickens in every performance of the melodrama. Thus, the constitution of nation, atomized in individual, simultaneous private reading practices in Anderson's model, was instead performed publicly and collectively around the question of an English Arctic explorer's potential cannibalism in each repetition of *The Frozen Deep.* The "symbiosis" between theatre and novel that Deborah Vlock identifies in Dickens is nowhere more identifiable than in the workings of sensation novels, in which stable categories of English/Other and agreed-upon, visible "evidence," so important to the sensation drama, reappear in the novels in complicated plots of mistaken identity, threatened social stability, and problematized knowledge. Transposed to the pages of the Victorian sensation novel, the "felt" and performed resolution of the sensation drama continues to consolidate stable national identities that, paradoxically, are central to the consumption of sensation fiction. For sensation, transgressive as it seems, relies on ideologically conservative, stable categories of reader/citizen in order to generate the shock and repulsion on which its plot depends. Tracing one influence on the sensation novel back to Dickens's *Household Words* articles on cannibalism and stable national identities through his transformation and extension of the same concerns in his contributions to and performance of *The Frozen Deep* enables us to fully recognize the cultural politics of melodrama at work in the evolution of the sensation novel,[6] and to disentangle assumptions about identity and nation which inform the cultural semantics of sensation.

MISSING BODIES OF EVIDENCE

After 1850, when searchers found the first winter encampment of Franklin's third and final Arctic expedition on Beechey Island, few physical traces of the expedition surfaced. In 1854, however, Dr. John Rae, a Scottish employee of the Hudson's Bay Company, returned from a search and mapping mission to report an encounter with Inuit who had seen, several years earlier, a large group of Europeans heading south on

King William Island. In Rae's words, reported on the front page of *The Times* on October 23, 1854:

> None of the [European] party could speak the Esquimaux language so well as to be understood, but by signs the Natives were led to believe that the Ship or Ships had been crushed by ice, and that they were then going to where they expected to find deer to shoot. From the appearance of the Men (all of whom with the exception of one Officer, were hauling on the drag ropes of the sledge and were looking thin)—they were then supposed to be getting short of provisions, and they purchased a small Seal or piece of Seal from the natives. The Officer was described as being a tall, stout, middle aged man.

From these natives, Rae obtained artifacts or "relics" that substantiated their claims of encounter with the British, including pieces of silver plate engraved "Sir John Franklin."

The next day, *The Times* quoted the most inflammatory portion of Rae's report to the Admiralty:

> Subsequently, further particulars were received . . . which places the fate of a portion, if not all, of the then survivors of Sir John Franklin's long-lost party beyond a doubt—a fate as terrible as the imagination can conceive. . . . From the mutilated state of many of the corpses and the contents of the kettles, it is evident that our wretched Countrymen had been driven to the last resource—cannibalism—as a means of prolonging existence."[7]

Predictably, the English public reacted to Rae's revelations with shock and horror. Rae was pilloried in the press by indignant relatives of expedition members who refused to believe that the relics of silverware, uniform buttons, and pocket watches Rae brought back could in any way support his conclusion of cannibalism.[8] Physical evidence supported Inuit claims that they had encountered the Franklin expedition, but the "particulars" Rae relied on for his conclusions of cannibalism were the words of the Inuit as told by interpreters. Rae wrote in *The Times* of November 11, 1854, that the "information" he received from the Inuit sources "by a mode of questioning which they understood" was "perfectly conclusive." Countering those who questioned the relatively few members of the expedition found by the Inuit, Rae wrote, "Nothing is more natural or more easily accounted for by a person of experience in the Arctic Seas, and whose mind is properly constructed." In other words, Rae asserted that he was in a better position to understand both physical evidence and Inuit testimony because of his "experience" as an explorer. In his November 7 *Times* article, he imagines the decision to make an encampment was made by men too taxed to continue until the weather improved. "To show that this opinion is not a mere fancy or fiction on my part, I may mention that my first feeling on hearing the mournful tidings was one of regret that I had not been with the suffering party—a feeling difficult to analyze, but which must have arisen instantaneously and without reflection, from an idea that my greater experience of Arctic travelling and hunting might have been useful to those in extremity and danger."[9] Rae's belief in the Inuit claims emerges from his own "experience" both of Inuit peoples and of extremity. He dismisses a notion of disciplined British seamen and instead envisions— and empathizes with—men struggling to adapt to, and eventually undone by, circumstance.

The most sustained public attack on Rae's conclusion came from Charles Dickens in his magazine *Household Words*, where, in two articles appearing a week apart in December 1854, Dickens argued against the "probabilities" of cannibalism by the Franklin expedition. "It has occurred to me that I am rather strong on Voyages and Cannibalism, and might do an interesting little paper for next No. on that part of Dr. Rae's Report; taking the argument against its probabilities," Dickens wrote to his assistant editor W. H. Wills in November.[10] Dickens knew his strengths; the published pieces showcase his encyclopaedic knowledge of "Voyages and Travels," his detailed knowledge of cannibalism trivia, and a legal reporter's facility with logic and rhetoric (7). By questioning the interrelated categories of evidence and experience invoked in Rae's revelations, Dickens attacks the "probabilities" of Rae's conclusions about the fate of the Franklin expedition. In their place, Dickens asserts a stable identity that privileges narratives originating in the metropole even while defining that identity *against* the cannibal Other found at civilization's peripheries. "Close analogy and mass of experience," Dickens claims in the first of his articles,[11] are all that are necessary to reveal the falsity of Rae's claims, both of a cannibal Franklin expedition and of the instability of national character implied in Rae's claims.

That Charles Dickens should enter into a debate on cannibalism in a family magazine such as *Household Words* should not surprise anyone in the age of tabloid television. As owner, publisher, and editor of the journal, as well as a frequent contributor, Dickens was concerned with circulation numbers. But Dickens's goals for his magazine were also unapologetically ideological. "We aspire to live in the Household affections," he wrote in his introduction to the first issue in March 1850, "and be numbered among the Household thoughts of our readers."[12] Anne Lohrli, who has indexed the magazine, identifies the goal of *Household Words* as bringing "together distinct kinds of family readers: the established middle-class audience of the publishing house journals . . . on the one hand and on the other an expanding lower-middle-class audience."[13] According to Jenny Bourne Taylor, by addressing his readers as part of a "household" or family, Dickens aimed "to consolidate a shared cultural identity by combining fiction, social reportage, and popular accounts of science," in order to generate "a common stock of allusions and references."[14] Dickens saw that work primarily, but not completely, in terms of the mitigation of class differences, declaring as his "main" journalistic object in *Household Words*, "to bring the greater and lesser in degree together . . . and to mutually dispose them to a better acquaintance and a kinder understanding."[15] The miscellaneous nature of *Household Words* articles therefore had a goal of the amelioration of class relations by appealing to a larger category of similarity and shared identity: nation.

In Dickens's responses to Rae's assertions, appearing as "The Lost Arctic Voyagers" in *Household Words* in December 1854, he invokes to the figure of the cannibal to form the "close analogy and mass of experience" essential to his arguments, and in so doing reveals the reliance on racial and cultural difference in the national symbolic economy.[16] From the time of European first encounters with other cultures, cannibalism acted as "a means of creating cultural difference," as Maggie Kilgour points out, with foreigners "frequently defined in terms of how and especially what, they eat, and denounced on the grounds that they either have bad table manners or eat disgusting things."[17] When Dickens counters Rae's specific claims and physical evidence with "analogy," he appeals to shared, "like" values of readers that coalesce in response to the "unlike" values of the cannibal Other. The "one or two facts . . . worth a hundred theories on any subject," that Rae appeals to are countered by Dickens with "theories" turned "fact" (national identity, "duty," "honour")—not by any physical evidence of the fate of Franklin and his men, but by Dickens's alternate appeals to a mythologized figure of the cannibal and a stable national character drawn over the years in Arctic exploration accounts.[18]

Dickens did not dispute the probable demise of Franklin and his men, only their cannibalism. He started by contesting the meaning of Rae's physical evidence, what Dickens describes as "the mute but solemn testimony of the relics he . . . brought home" (361). Immediately leaving aside the material evidence of buttons, timepieces, and silverware Rae had retrieved, Dickens focused on the implications of the kettles, items, by the way, that Rae could not produce. "Was there any fuel in that desolate place for cooking 'the contents of the kettles?'" he asked. "If none, would the little flame of the spirit lamp the travellers may have had with them, have sufficed for such a purpose? If not, would the kettles have been defiled for that purpose at all?" (361). Rae had returned only with word of the kettles, not with the kettles themselves, and Dickens, who had been a legal reporter and understood well that physical evidence relied on its source, seized on the missing kettles as a weakness in Rae's argument.

The kettles and their contents were, of course, the only physical evidence that had a chance of proving beyond doubt the charge of cannibalism. By disputing the kettles as evidence, Dickens made material the connection between "reason" and civilization, deftly opposing the irrationality of the "savage" to the reason of the English reader. For, like cannibalism itself, cooking has long functioned as a distinction between "civilized" and "savage," as Levi-Strauss reminds us in *The Raw and The Cooked*.[19] The very name given the Inuit, "Esquimaux," came from a native word meaning "people who eat raw flesh." How, Dickens implied, could people who didn't cook read evidence in the kettles of people who did? Only a British audience that ate cooked food and understood cooking—the same people who read and understood travel narratives—could understand the character of Franklin and his men. Safe in their kitchens and by their firesides, the readers of *Household Words*—familiar with the role of "duty" and "national character" in earlier Arctic narratives and accounts such as "Unspotted Snow" in *Household Words*—knew what "the nature of men" (as Dickens put it), certainly the nature of Englishmen, was, and could be counted on to agree with Dickens that it "out-weigh[ed] by the weight of the whole universe the chatter of a gross handful of uncivilised people, with the domesticity of blood and blubber" (392–93). It is worth noting, too, that for Dickens national character tended to be subsumed under English rather than British identity. His reliance on "English" as a shorthand for the nation in many ways reiterates the logic of a stable middle-class domestic center set against an unstable and uncivilized periphery. The

Celtic fringes of Britain (and it is not insignificant that Rae is a Scot) may be seen to pose some of the same challenges to the sober solidity of the "English" nation as more exotic locales of empire and exploration do. It was the ethnic or cultural unevenness paralleling that of class that further legitimized the mission Dickens assigned to *Household Words*.

Inuit "domesticity of blood and blubber" certainly contrasted with the domesticity of Dickens's middle-class readers, but blood and blubber were important to Dickens's argument in other capacities. Inuit blubber could refer not only to disgusting (uncooked) fat, but to what Dickens termed the "incoherencies" of native accounts. Blubbering was another way to describe the "improbabilities and incoherencies of the Esquimaux evidence: which is itself given, at the very best, at second-hand" (361). The "word" of the Inuit was problematic, presumably, because, as well-read Victorians knew from earlier accounts of Arctic travel, including John Franklin's *Narrative of a Journey to the Shores of the Polar Sea*, Inuit language lacked the structural capacity to communicate complex notions of history and time. By linking "reason" or under-standing to race and language, Dickens effectively declared all of the Inuit testimony untrustworthy. He further declared that "ninety-nine interpreters out of a hundred, whether savage, half-savage, or wholly civilised, interpreting to a person of superior station or attainments, will be under a strong temptation to exaggerate" (361). So even if the Inuit had possessed the linguistic capacity to be clear about what they saw, it wasn't necessary to believe them. When Dickens pointed out that Rae's evidence was "collected at 'various times' as it wandered from 'various sources,'" he evoked comparison of what was believed to be nomadic, unstructured, and uncivilized culture to a structured, stable British soci-ety (361). To accept the variousness of Inuit explanation, Dickens implied, would be to call into question not only racial categories, but all things precious to Victorian middle-class readers. The ideological high stakes explain at least in part the hyperbolic nature of Dickens's xeno-phobic and racist response to Rae's conjectures.

Not satisfied with discounting Inuit versions of the fate of the Franklin expedition, Dickens actively sought to implicate the Inuit in that fate. In one of his *Times* articles, Rae related that the Inuit had communicated the "very dreadful alternative" of cannibalism by "signs."[20] Dickens in the first of his articles described the "gesture" as "the informant setting his mouth to his own arm" (362), and in so doing reverses the charge of cannibalism—thus far only implied—back onto the "savage" where, for English Victorians, it belonged.[21] The violence of the arm-eating gesture could easily be extended to violence against, and possible consumption of, British bodies. Far from simply misinterpreting the fate of Franklin, Dickens accused the Inuit of actively participating in Franklin's end: "We believe every savage to be in his heart covetous, treacherous, and cruel; and we have yet to learn what knowledge the white man—lost, houseless, shipless, apparently forgotten by his race, plainly famine-stricken, weak, frozen, helpless, and dying—has of the gentleness of Esquimaux nature" (362). In this graphic reversal of the editorial policy responsible for the benevolent representations of nose-rubbing, cheerful fat natives in earlier pieces on Arctic exploration in *Household Words*,[22] Dickens's adjectives divide Inuit and English into different categories of weakness, with the Inuit as morally weak and the English as physically weak, and by implication, their strengths are opposite ones: the Inuit is physically strong and the Englishmen morally strong.

Dickens appears careful to separate his assessment of Rae's conclusions from Rae's character, which he described as "manly, conscientious and modest" (361). However, his invocation of racialized stereotypes of cannibalistic behavior foregrounded Rae's own foreignness. As a Scot who worked for a commercial monopoly, he was not, in fact, English, nor was he pledged to the patriotic, empire-building aims of the military. Historians remind us that "Britain" as a unified nation was new and continually coalescing in the eighteenth and early nineteenth century.[23] Dickens's attempts at crossing class lines in readership were certainly part of that nationalist project but, when push came to shove, the Welsh, the Irish, and the Scots were *not* English. It was no accident that the Arctic explorer John Ross called the Inuit "Arctic Highlanders" when he encountered them early in the century. Like their Scottish and Irish counterparts, Arctic Highlanders lived in squalor and ate disgusting food.[24] Thomas Macauley called the "Wild Scotch " "northern savages," and in his *History of England*, claimed that an English traveler in the Highlands, would "have had to endure hardships as great as if he had sojourned among the Esquimaux or the Samoyeds."[25]

Thus when in two subsequent issues of *Household Words*, Rae responded to each of Dickens's hyperbolically patriotic claims by pointing to *his* experience in the Arctic, the shadow of the savage—perhaps even the cannibal—lay across his words. Rae tried valiantly to combat Dickens's racialized rhetoric with plain-spoken assertions of how his experience as a British explorer in the Arctic gave him a better understanding of the evidence than an arm-chair-bound citizen of Empire such as Charles Dickens. For his part, though, Dickens had been careful not to impugn Rae's character overtly because to do so would bring into question the claim at the base of his reasoning, that Arctic trial produced men of sterling qualities, a claim that he even extends to Rae, writing of him, "He has all the rights to defend his opinion which his high reputation as a skilful and intrepid traveller of great experience in the Arctic Regions—combined with his manly, conscientious and modest personal character—can possibly invest him with" (361). Yet Rae's "skilful" (*sic*) adaptation of Inuit techniques of survival made him suspect in Dickens's eyes. While in the Arctic, Rae, like most Hudson's Bay employees and unlike the Royal Navy, assumed native dress, lived in igloos, and traveled by snowshoe and dogsled. By "going native," Rae was susceptible to the same character defects Victorians saw in the Inuit. Still, Rae persisted in positing his personal experience against Dickens's "close analogy and mass of experience."[26]

Rae wished to narrow the distance between "English" and "Other," taking great pains to portray the Inuit as a people marked by exceeding domestic warmth and filial piety. Therefore, if cannibalism was anathema to the middle-class readers of *Household Words*, so too must it be to the Inuit, whom they resembled in everything but looks and diet:

> In their domestic relationship they show a bright example to the most civilised people. They are dutiful sons and daughters, kind brothers and sisters, and most affectionate parents. So well is the first of these qualities understood among them, that a large family is considered wealth by a father and mother—for the latter well know that they will be carefully tended by their offspring, well clothed and fed, whilst a scrap of skin or a morsel of food is to be obtained, as long as a spark of life remains; and, after death, that their bodies will be properly placed either on or under the ground, according to the usage of the tribe.[27]

In doing so, Rae overlooked—or at least underestimated—the powerful way the binaries of "us" and "them," "home" and "away" functioned in the construction of mid-Victorian bourgeois ideology; he also underestimated the powerful presence of cannibalism in the binary of "civilized" and "savage." Responding to Dickens's depiction of the Inuit as unreliable translators, Rae teased Dickens's readers by describing his interpreter as speaking "English fluently; and, perhaps, more correctly than one half of the lower classes in England or Scotland," some of whom were the very readers of *Household Words* to whom Dickens appealed. As for the Inuit lying, Rae observes, "When the Esquimaux have an object to gain, they will not hesitate to tell a falsehood, but they cannot lie with a good grace; 'they cannot lie like truth,' as civilised men do" (458). It is difficult to read Rae's assertion about lying Englishmen without thinking of it as directed at Dickens's own elaborate argument, which Rae knew was entirely specious. Rae's take on "civilized men" differed decidedly from Dickens's. He responded to Dickens's near deification of Franklin's crew in his rebuttal: "Their conduct at the very last British port they entered was not such as to make those who knew it, consider them very deserving of the high eulogium passed upon them in *Household Words*" (456). The Inuit, on the other hand, Rae argued, despite their rugged nomadic existence, shared the same categories of domestic behavior, familial duty, and "home" as the English reading public did.

Rae's decision to defend the Inuit on the same domestic turf Dickens had used to condemn them, however, played to the rhetorical strengths of Dickens's articles. Proof to *Household Words* readers that Rae was well on the way to savagery would have been his own slipping use of "home" when he answered Dickens's accusations of vagueness with the following concrete details of Arctic life. "Having completed my observations, and filled in rough tracings of the coast line, which I generally did from day to day, we started for home at eight thirty, p.m" (460). "We," for Rae, includes his native guides and translator, and "home" is their camp. Such a lack of differentiation, of course, only enforced Dickens's insinuations that the "experience" that Rae claimed to support his "evidence" was not the experience of an "Englishman," but of a potential cannibal, a savage-loving Scot who embraced the "domesticity of blood and blubber" that Dickens so fiercely dismissed. Rae's assertion that the Inuit were "like" their English counterparts, moreover, could be read by an English audience as not only an offense, but as an unacceptable and offensive accusation that the English, too, were capable of cannibalism.

The second article of Dickens's defense of Franklin addressed the impossibility not only of Franklin's cannibalism, but of all British cannibalism, in an extensive, xenophobic catalogue of maritime disasters. Dickens elaborates on the by now well-established division between civilized and savage by recounting hyperbolic tales of cannibalism at sea, generally performed by Americans, West Indians, and (of course) the French. Although the article is again titled "The Lost Arctic Voyagers," its only reference to the Arctic for the first several pages is the perfunctory and oblique opening line, "We resume our subject of last week" (246). The link between cannibalism and the Arctic went farther back than Rae's recent disclosures. The seeming disjuncture between the two halves of Charles Dickens's argument is a silence that speaks; the juxtaposition enlists John Franklin on Dickens's side of the debate, for it was Franklin's widely read *Narrative of a Journey to the Shores of the Polar Sea* (discussed in the second chapter) that originally conjoined cannibalism to the Arctic experience. The story of the "savage" cannibal Michel, who, after tricking his British companions into eating their dead companions, was killed by Richardson, remained in national memory, and was refreshed by Dickens's invocation of Richardson in the closing lines of his first article.[28]

What is the meaning of the second article's peculiar catalogue of the cannibal horror, of "raving mutineers," and bloodthirsty Frenchmen? Why, when he has already effectively refuted Rae's evidence and assertions, does Dickens turn away from the specifics of the Franklin expedition to seemingly unrelated cases of maritime suffering and survival? H. L. Malchow reads Dickens's "conflation of the European savage with his nonwhite counterpart, of class with race" in the second article as "anticipating . . . cannibalism as the realm of the 'nonwhite.'" In understanding Dickens as contesting images of the cannibal working class in circulation in the 1800s by racializing the cannibal so that "any instances of white cannibalism that might be proved [would lie] in the category of madness and criminality,"[29] Malchow overlooks, however, the performative aspect of Dickens's reliance on horror in his accounts.

Dickens may relate the tales as evidence of the relative rarity of cannibalism, but the sheer number of cases he chronicles would seem instead to indicate a thriving cannibal culture. No fewer than twenty separate incidences are spread across nine pages, each full of descriptions of practicing cannibals who are "delirious," "ferociously wild" "raving mutineers" (385, 387). Certainly the racialized nature of the description indicates the impossibility of English cannibalism: if white, the cannibals are French, Spanish, or American; more often, they are "negro" or "Asiatic" ("of a colossal stature, with short curled hair, an extremely large nose, an enormous mouth, a sallow complexion, and a hideous air") (387). But cannibal discourse was by definition already racialized in the nineteenth century and Dickens himself had already conflated cannibal and Inuit in his earlier article. One might explain his hyperbolic repetition as a hysterical underlining of the racial otherness of the cannibal, but this seems reductive. Emphasizing instead the *repetition* of the tales themselves brings to light Dickens's investment in the affective mechanics of cannibal tales, as well as in their ideological content.

The vividly visceral quality of the tales (the hacking off of legs and siphoning blood from near-dead bodies), each one more horrible than the next, seems designed for the delectation of Dickens's readers. The chronicle of terror works by provoking affect, what Caleb Crane describes as a "double-bind of attraction and repulsion" which produces "delicious shudders" both in the writer and the reading audience.[30] That "shudders" of disgust are also part of the voyeuristic pleasure of reading cannibal accounts does not take away from the conservative nature of Dickens's article. Paul Lyons identifies the social regulation at work in hyperbolic cannibalism accounts as follows:

> The cannibal is what Slavoj Žižek calls a *subject presumed to enjoy*: the viewer feels that the object is enjoying a guilt-free forbidden behavior and that such enjoyment should be stopped. Reading such accounts, then, reinforces social practices of self-mastery (continued regulation of the subject's own boundaries and practices) and cultural mastery (a redrawing and reassertion of the superiority of the viewing culture's values).[31]

Horror, then, reassures readers by reaffirming their place in opposition to the cannibal; thus, Dickens's descriptions do not only "intellectual" work, but performative work as well.

The danger of reading cannibal accounts, however, lies in the privacy of the act of reading. D. A. Miller argues convincingly for a model of interpellation and self-policing at work in mid-Victorian fiction that introduces subversive elements only to have them recontained by "dispersing" discipline from the state onto the private reader.[32] A version of that subversion and recontainment occurs in "The Lost Arctic Voyagers"'s reliance on chaotic transgression to determine and control English identity in contrast to what it is not, but Dickens himself worries that mechanisms of self-policing might not be strong enough. He returns again to the seductive nature of cannibal stories in "The Wreck of the 'Golden Mary'," which he co-wrote with Wilkie Collins and which appeared in the Extra Christmas Number of *Household Words* in 1856, two years after Dickens's Arctic articles.[33] The shipwrecked Captain Ravender is obsessed by cannibalism and worries that other survivors of the wreck may have ideas about it, too:

> Although I had, years before that, fully satisfied myself that the instances in which human beings in the last distress have fed upon each other are exceedingly few, and have very seldom indeed (if ever) occurred when the people in distress, however dreadful their extremity, have been accustomed to moderate forbearance and restraint—I say, though I had, long before, quite satisfied my mind on this topic, I felt doubtful whether there might not have been in former cases some harm and danger from keeping it out of sight and pretending not to think of it. I felt doubtful whether some minds, growing weak with fasting and exposure, and having such a terrific idea to dwell upon in secret, might not magnify it until it got to have an awful attraction about it. This was not a new thought of mine, for it had grown out of my reading. However, it came over me stronger than it had ever done before—as it had reason for doing—in the boat, and on the fourth day I decided that I would bring out into the light that uniformed [*sic*] fear which must have been more or less darkly in every brain among us. (6)

Ravender—whose name, Harry Stone reminds us, teeters between ravenous and provender—must "satisfy" himself not with a cannibal act that will allay his hunger, but by talking about cannibalism to others in the lifeboat. The anxious repetition of his assurances—"Although I had . . . I say, though I had"—disavows his certainty of the impossibility of cannibalism even as he claims it. The workings of the "awful attraction" of cannibalism are private, developed by "dwell[ing] upon [it] in secret," and first suggested by reading. Ravender fears that the secret of cannibalism, repressed, will cause literal acts of cannibalism. He is thus compelled, by the same mechanism that causes him to obsessively ponder the possibilities of cannibalism, to make public his fear, with the belief that publicity will avert the attraction of the cannibalistic impulse. He does so by relating the famed shipwreck of Bligh (in pre-*Bounty* days):

> They listened throughout with great interest, and I concluded by telling them that, in my opinion, the happiest circumstances in the whole narrative was that Bligh, who was no delicate man either, had solemnly placed it on record therein that he was sure and certain that under no conceivable circumstances whatever would that emaciated party, who had gone through all the pains of famine, have preyed on one another. I

cannot describe the visible relief which this spread through the boat, and how the tears stood in every eye. From that time I was as well convinced as Bligh himself that there was no danger and that this phantom, at any rate, did not haunt us. (6)

"Bringing to light" the cannibal potential "more or less darkly in every brain," along with reasserting the racial implications of light/dark, civilized/savage, are motives that are certainly present in Dickens's language, as this diffuses the cannibal threat. Important to understanding how stories of cannibalism work in Dickens is the revelation in this passage of how public performance, here in the form of story-telling and "tears," safely dissipates the potential for disruption posed by privately brooding individuals. Ravender consolidates and controls the lifeboat "community" in a shared moment of sentiment, brought on by a narrative of example.

Dickens's list of cannibal tales in his second "Arctic Voyagers" article is of course a narrative of counterexample, but its mechanics are the same as those of "The Wreck of 'The Golden Mary'." The tears (of recognition? relief?) Ravender's tale elicits in his audience do the same work as the "shudders" prompted by "The Lost Arctic Explorers." By contrast, John Rae's careful point-by-point refutation of what he perceived as Dickens's naive nationalist diatribe returns again and again to the impossibility of truly understanding the position of another without having experienced the conditions of that position: "analogy" for Rae does not answer; experience does. Dickens counters with a different kind of "experience," the experience of repulsion that allows readers to explore the boundaries of national character imaginatively, but no less (for Dickens) concretely. His last installment of his Arctic articles concludes, "Therefore, teach no one to shudder without reason, at the history of [the English sailors'] end. Therefore, confide with their own firmness, in their fortitude, their lofty sense of duty, their courage, and their religion" (392–93). The invitation to "confide" with the "firmness" of Franklin's sailors—the slip from the singular reader to the plural "their" of the sailors—recognizes both the performative nature of Dickens's rhetoric and his investment in the stability of national character. "Being there" made no difference to Dickens. An English reader in an armchair was, for all intents and purposes, an English explorer. For English identity in the mid-nineteenth century, for the readers of *Household Words* at least, was defined by its stability and civility in the midst of the most savage of extreme conditions, be it in the wilds of Africa, the Arctic, or at home.

THE FROZEN DEEP: ARCTIC MELODRAMA
AND THE PERFORMANCE OF NATION

The shudder-provoking power of cannibalism resurfaces in *The Frozen Deep*, written by Wilkie Collins at Dickens's suggestion over the summer of 1856 and first performed by a cast including Collins and Dickens in January 1857 at Dickens's residence, Tavistock House. It was a great hit, and Dickens appeared in it before packed houses in Manchester and London in July and August, even performing it for Queen Victoria on July 4, 1857. Until recently, critics have been generally reluctant to read *The Frozen Deep* as a play about cannibalism per se, since there are no overt references to cannibalism in the text, yet due to Dickens's debate with Rae, Arctic exploration and cannibalism remained linked in the public mind.[34] Cannibalism, however, was a stock trope of melodrama by mid-century: *Sweeney Todd* was first staged in 1847. Dickens himself reestablishes the connection by invoking the "Voyages and Travels" genre, of which the cannibal encounter was a staple, with the shadowy presence of Crusoe and Friday in the play's prologue, which he wrote for Collins:

> One savage footprint on the lonely shore,
> Where one man listen'd to the surge's roar;
> Not all the winds that stir the mighty sea
> Can ever ruffle in the memory.
> If such its interest and thrall, O then
> Pause on the footprints of heroic men,
> Making a garden of the desert wide
> Where PARRY conquer'd and FRANKLIN died.[35]

The links between cannibalism and Arctic hardship seem to have held Dickens in "thrall," to the point where he acted the role of Richard Wardour, the play's potential cannibal. Yet writing—at least significantly rewriting Collins's drafts—and acting in *The Frozen Deep* also provided Charles Dickens with a way to answer once again Rae's assertions about "experience" and the instability of identity, as we see in Dickens's return to the subject and his repeated and anxious inhabitation of Wardour's character on stage.

In theatre, Dickens found a way to make the private shudder of recognition and horror, on which he had depended to recruit and consolidate his English readership in "The Lost Arctic Voyagers" articles, public and shared. *The Frozen Deep* enabled Dickens and his co-author Collins to demonstrate how the "sensation" produced by melodrama—that horror, the surprise, the *frisson* of seeing—worked to shape, regulate, and stabilize social identities.[36] Dickens's prologue makes explicit the link between polar exploration and "inner" qualities: "The secrets of the vast Profound / Within us, an exploring hand may sound, / Testing the region of the ice-bound soul, / Seeking the passage at its northern pole" (97). As we have seen in previous chapters, Arctic exploration was about mapping not only geographical space, but personal and, by extension, national character. Like all "secrets of the vast Profound," when made visible, character could somehow be fully understood. As if Rae's appeal to "experience" still rankled, Dickens makes concrete the lack of distance he sees between explorer and reader/viewer by transporting his audience to the Arctic.

> We had an act at the North Pole, where the slightest and greatest thing the eye beheld were equally taken from the books of the Polar voyagers. Out of thirty people [in the audience], there were certainly not two who might not have gone straight to the North Pole itself, completely furnished for the winter![37]

Just as the set relies on Arctic exploration accounts for its realism, the audience's familiarity with those texts enables them to imagine themselves as ready for an Arctic winter. The transport of drama, "furnished" to the audience by their knowledge of Arctic travel narratives, the set's realistic detail, and Dickens's melodramatic script, becomes the "experience" Dickens knew was lacking in his earlier arguments about cannibalism and national identity. As Joseph Roach observes, "Vicariousness suggests the derivative nature of experience from some prior authenticity."[38]

While recent critical work celebrates the "Dramatic Dickens" by erasing the high/low culture distinction between genres of drama and the novel, most critics still seek to explore the influence of theatrical effects in Dickens's novels.[39] *The Frozen Deep*, however, reveals Dickens's theatricality as being important in and of itself, in its demonstration of Dickens's deeply held belief in the role of publicly performed affect in moral and social transformation and even, perhaps, revealing his distrust of the effectiveness of narration on private readers: he could write novels, but would they act on their readers as he hoped they would? As Joseph Roach puts it in his explanation of the nature of performance,

The social processes of memory and forgetting, familiarly known as culture, may be carried out by a variety of perform-ance events, from stage plays to sacred rites, from carnivals to the invisible rituals of everyday life. To perform in this sense means to bring forth, to make manifest, and to transmit. To perform also means, through often more secretly, to reinvent.[40]

The "enacted" nature of the theatre demands embodied, "felt" response by both audience and player. *The Frozen Deep* thus allowed Dickens to enact and embody claims of shared national values, appealing to affect in moments of sentiment or melodrama, in order to prove and reinforce the perhaps-unconvincing "rational" claims he had made in his *House-hold Words* articles.

Dickens embraced the theatre as a powerful vehicle for social change, describing in detail the "unquestionably humanising influence in all the social arrangements of the place."[41] In the persona of Mr. Whelks in "The Amusements of the People," Dickens articulates the need for drama that could work for the social good. People would always frequent the theatre, he reasoned, so"[w]e had far better apply ourselves to improving the character of their amusement. It would not be exacting much, or exacting anything very difficult, to require that the pieces in these Theatres should have, at least, a good, plain, healthy pur-pose in them" (quoted in Schlicke, 202). Dickens's/Whelk's interest in regulated, rational recreation was typical of the period, when moral reformers turned their attention to public entertainment out of "sympa-thy with the plight of the urban masses" and "practical considerations of social stability."[42] It is no surprise then, that *The Frozen Deep* is deeply concerned with the struggle between good and evil.

In the persona of Mr. Whelks, Dickens may have dismissed melo-drama as "an incongruous heap of nonsense,"[43] but over its three acts, *The Frozen Deep* covers nearly all of melodrama's traditional terrain:

strong emotion, both pathetic and potentially tragic, low comedy, romantic colouring, remarkable events in an exciting and suspenseful plot, physical sensations, sharply delineated stock characters, domestic sentiment, domestic settings, and domestic life, love, joy, suffering, morality, the reward of virtue and the punishment of vice.[44]

The play establishes its domestic concerns at the beginning, starting "before we cross the troubled Seas, [at] an English hearth and Devon's waving trees" (97). Four women in Devonshire wait for news of men on an Arctic exploration mission who haven't been heard of for more than a year. One of these men, Richard Wardour, perceives himself as having been "jilted" by his childhood love, Clara, and has declared publicly that he will kill her new sweetheart. The sweetheart happens to be Frank Aldersley, also on the mission, who has no idea of Wardour's existence. The tension arises from the men being "together—away [in] the eternal ice and snow" on "the same Expedition—to share the same perils, to be united in one ship, if an accident happens to the other." The resulting drama, as Clara perceives from her safety at home, will occur if her "name is ever mentioned between them" (114). By grounding both play and audience in Britain, Dickens links the Arctic action that will follow to the welfare of both home and state. The fate of those in one arena are linked to the fate of the others, as Clara develops a nervous illness clearly linked to Aldersley's being missing and the women disagree in hushed, fragmentary debate about the best way to handle both Clara's ill health and the probable loss of their loved ones. When the first act ends with Clara's Scottish nurse declaring that, using "second sight," she sees Frank "i' the grasp" (116) of Wardour, the link between the domestic and the Arctic is made complete.

The Scottish Nurse's second sight acts as dramatic segue to the Arctic scene opening Act II. Instead of Frank being in Wardour's "grasp," however, the men practice an orderly naval discipline—junior officers keep watch, complete assigned tasks, and reply respectfully to their seniors—to maintain their good spirits after the loss of their ships to the ice pack. This is no doubt Dickens's vision of a possible stage in the fate of the Franklin mission, a *tableau vivant* of his position against Rae. Included in this retrospective commentary on Rae's credibility is the falsity of the Scottish nurse's hysterical vision: the connections between Scot and Inuit established in the debate are certainly at work here, and the nurse's irrationality and her desire for the men's destruction—the scene read by Lillian Nayder as the racial displacement of a class-based cannibal desire—were both positions ascribed to Rae during the debate. That Dickens, not Collins, was the author responsible for moving the action from Britain to the Arctic, and from the troubles of women to the trials of men, seems significant, as does his repetition of descriptors from his articles.[45] "Valour," "honour," and the "spirits" Dickens employs and appeals to throughout the play possess nationalized valences, accrued during the lengthy public debate he had held with Rae.

If, as Michael Booth suggests, "familiarity" is "an essential aspect of melodramatic appeal,"[46] we see "familiarity" in *The Frozen Deep* cohere in its self-conscious reference to Arctic narratives. In addition to borrowing the stage set from "the books of the Polar voyagers," the second act borrows the activities of the ice-bound men from the pages of Arctic accounts. By dramatizing official Admiralty accounts, the play not only continues Dickens's earlier arguments about the fate of the Franklin expedition, but participates in what Homi Bhabha labels the "pedagogic" temporality of nationalism. The performance on stage serves not as a singular present moment but as a "rhetorical figure of the national past."[47] Therefore, the dramatic finale of the end of Act II, when Wardour and Aldersley set out into the bleak unknown in search of aid for their companions, is at once the moment of crisis for two of the play's main characters *and* an imagined, narrated reenactment of such moments in Arctic survival literature. Wardour loads his gun, rams the ammunition home and cries, "Come then! Come over the snow and the Ice! Come over the land that no human footsteps have ever trodden and where no human trace is ever left!" (140).

Will Wardour, played by Dickens, resort to the "last resource"? Will he kill and eat Frank Aldersley? The unanswered question introduced by the end of the second act reveals how the reassurance of the familiar and the dread of anticipation work together in the logic of melodrama. The fixed form of melodrama, Michael Booth argues, "presents . . . not social documents but images of crime, enactments of personal and social transgression in which the enactor is defeated and his crimes nullified."[48] In the schematic nature of melodrama, there can be only one conclusion: the reassertion of social norms. The potential for transgression in performance makes theatre a potent political site, but in the melodrama, transgression is recuperated by its conservative mechanics to unify audiences into the reaffirmation of shared values. In performance halls throughout Britain and beyond, audiences of *The Frozen Deep* experienced the familiar anew, and embraced it more strongly than ever.

Rearticulations of the "familiar" in melodrama have such constitutive power, Peter Brooks argues, because the form literalizes the centrality of the body as site of meaning in its truth-affirming performance of moral statements. Drawing on Foucault's model of the modern body as the primary location of control and discipline, Brooks identifies the role

of the body—of both audience and actor—in melodrama as "pre-emi-
nently invested with meaning, a body becomes the place for the inscription of highly emotional messages that cannot be written elsewhere, and
cannot be articulated verbally."[49] In other words, as a melodrama, *The
Frozen Deep* substitutes its own embodied experience for the "experience" of polar exploration and bodily suffering that Rae had privileged
in his assertions about Franklin's cannibalism. It is as if Dickens, wary of
a possible lack of containment of transgression in the cannibalism
accounts in "The Lost Arctic Voyagers" and bothered at the weakness of
"analogy and the mass of experience" in his earlier argument, needs to
perform his message once again to ensure its appropriate, affirming message of stable national identity. The function of melodrama, as Christina
Crosby describes, is to "[create] this collective 'we,' an audience that
bears witness by its tears to the truth of the representation before it"
(73). *The Frozen Deep* is Dickens's attempt to have the last word.

There is of course, only one real answer to the unspoken question of
Wardour's cannibalism at the end of Act II. Conventions of melodrama
and conventions of Arctic narrative come together to disallow any devi-
ation from the anticipated ending. This not only reaffirms a solid English
civility, but in a way akin to Captain Ravender's discussion of cannibalism acknowledges and confronts the unease arising from British penetration into remote parts of the globe. Explaining this expiatory
function of melodrama, Nadine Holdsworth observes that "[a]s a cultural response . . . melodrama attempts to impose logical solutions and
moral order on a disorderly universe, to provide a vision of certainty in
an uncertain world. In its adherence to rigid moral structures and
monolithic character definition, melodrama consoles its audience by
intimating that the world can be understood."[50] So whether or not Wardour is a cannibal is not so interesting as *how* the impossibility of his
cannibalism is revealed. How does Dickens supply an answer everyone
already knows, and still manage the "theatrical excess" (of both spectacle
and emotion)—or as Booth puts it, the "apprehension, suspense, and
fear"—so central to melodrama's constituting of a "collective 'we'"?

One way in which Dickens manages both to create and manage the
necessary "excess" is by cultivating standard essentialized traits of the
cannibal Other throughout the play. In contrast to the other sailors who
step directly out of a tradition of nautical melodrama, Wardour the
potential cannibal makes his name and his fortune in Africa in order to
come home to claim his childhood playmate, Clara, as his wife. His
violence thus is linked to his colonial experience, rather than to his

disappointment at Clara's dismissal of his suit. Like racial difference, Wardour's capacity for violence can be read in "his face" by Clara, and "his awful, awful look of fury and despair" betrays his lack of mastery over his emotion (110). At work are the two categories of cannibal seen in Dickens's earlier catalogue of cannibalism in *Household Words*—race and madness. (Clara by contrast is set up as pure—her presence with friends in England is due to her mother marrying a foreigner and Clara not wanting to leave England.[51]) Although Captain Crayford recognizes that "under all [Wardour's] outward defects there beats a great and generous heart," and describes him as "one of the best officers and one of the hardiest men in the Queen's Navy," Wardour is identified with the cannibal Other long before a cannibal act becomes a real possibility in the play (125). Like his non-English counterparts, he is a monstrous bogeyman who "comes across [Clara] in [her] dreams and makes [her] as frightened in the darkness as a child" (113). When later an emaciated Wardour "hunger[s] for the life" (158) of his rival Frank Aldresley, the "hunger" is read by the audience as cannibal desire.

The synonymous mastery of appetite and morals in *The Frozen Deep* furthers the cultivation of the cannibal subtext. Wardour goes to the Arctic to forget Clara, but there his desire is surpassed by the true and pressing hunger of Arctic survival situations, starvation. Dickens takes the opportunity to insist on the impossibility of cannibalism by English sailors at every turn, including the cook, John Want's, description of a seasickness cure on his first voyage. While making bone soup for the remaining men—perhaps Dickens's explanation for what was truly in Franklin's kettles—Want lists the foods he was forced to eat on his first voyage until he could neither eat more nor vomit. His seasickness cure was pronounced complete when the Captain declared, "Never give in to your stomach and your stomach will end in giving in to *you*" (123). Want is able to make his career on the ocean and in service of his country only when he learns to discipline his appetite. Want's name, of course, underscores this point in its evocation of a desperate hunger that could nevertheless be mastered.

John Want reminds the audience of the men's predicament both by his position as a cook with no provisions and by his comedic, rueful observations on the crew's probable eventual death by starvation. Additionally, through the cook, Dickens is able to once again explore the power of narrative as an instigation to travel, describing Want as lured into his career by "reading Robinson Crusoe, and books warning [him] not to go to sea" (122). The books warn him, but also draw him to it, reminiscent of the dynamic between the safety of home and the promise of adventure in Dickens's 1854 observation of his own relation to travel literature. Want is the reader to whom adventure does "come to pass," and as cook, he is responsible for what, or whom, gets eaten, or doesn't get eaten in the course of the play. Dickens plays once more with Rae's cannibal kettle when the men use John Want's saucepan to determine who will go for help: lacking a hat in which to place lots, they put slips of paper, each representing a man, in the pot.

Despite this reference to the lurking possibility of cannibalism, Dickens makes his audience wait for the resolution to the unspoken—not because it is unspeakable, but because it is understood—question of cannibalism. The third act opens with the women and the survivors of the Arctic camp together in Greenland, with all accounted for except Wardour and Aldersley. Wardour's first utterance on his reappearance, "Let me eat," reminds the audience of his appetite, while his appearance—the stage directions read, "He is clothed in rags; his hair is tangled and gray; his looks and gestures are those of a man whose reason is shaken, and whose bodily powers are sinking from fatigue" (156)—powerfully evokes the loss of reason on which Dickens both blamed "white" cannibalism and identified as a side effect of cannibalism in his second article. When Wardour slowly answers his fellow shipmate's query about Frank Aldersley, saying, "I think I know your meaning. I think I dimly understand," the shipmate responds, "Confess, unhappy ruin of a man! Tell us how it was done!" (156). Wardour's response is to flee, proof to those assembled of his guilt of Aldersley's murder and of his cannibalism, since to survive, he would have to eat something (or someone).

Wardour's innocence is proven in his production of a living, though enfeebled Aldersley. After leaving time for speculation and accusation, Wardour returns, staggering under the weight of an insensate but still-breathing Aldersley, whom he restores to Clara in front of an assembled crowd saying, "Saved, saved for *you*" (158). The manuscript stage directions, in Dickens's hand, read "Great sensation." As a stage direction, this is no doubt directed at actors—a message for them to show reaction or a stir—but "sensation" also anticipates the audience's reaction. Significantly, the sensation arises *not* at Wardour's possible cannibalism, so effectively has Wardour been portrayed by turn as un-English and mad, but at the evidence that he has not cannibalized Aldersley. Wardour's reappearance as an "upstanding naval man" produces the sensation, which arises from the audience's release from the threat of fractured identity (a cannibal Wardour) and reaffirmation of the social code (in the return of

Aldersley). Here the affective mechanics of melodrama evoke comparison to Susan Stewart's analysis of nostalgia.[52] For Stewart, nostalgia, in its appeal to the "lived" and the affective, allows a suturing of subject into discourse via a mythic past that somehow joins experience to linguistic description. Similarly, for Dickens the moment of sensation allows audience and actor to experience "truth" in the melodramatic *present* with the same effect of erasing linguistic instability.

Whereas Rae's consistent calls to "experience" indicted Dickens's powers of description to truly capture "what it was like" and thus brought into question Dickens's conclusions about a stable national identity no matter how compellingly argued, *The Frozen Deep* effectively responds to this by producing a present experience that trumps that of Rae's experience, mediated as it is by memory and geographical distance, as well as by linguistic and cultural translation. In the play, the melodramatic present is also a moment evocative of the national mythic past—Bhabha's national "pedagogic temporality"—since Wardour's resistance to cannibalism connects to sources as pervasive as popular travel literature, as explicit as the Dickens/Rae debate, and as deeply held as English national identity itself.

In his dying moments, Wardour examines his struggle against his desire to harm Aldersley. The moment of "sensation" may be past, but Wardour's lengthy speech is still melodramatic in that it privileges sensation over cognition,[53] as evidenced by one reviewer's judgment that Dickens's acting in the scene "moved his audiences more intensely than the dialogue or situation could account for."[54] Wardour's speech restates the conflation of unregulated desire with cannibalism: "There was a time when the fiend within me hungered for [Aldersley's] life" (158). This observation leads Aldersley to recognize how Wardour has turned the cannibal charge inside out by sacrificing his physical and mental well-being for Aldersley's. Aldersley cries out as Wardour dies, "I should never have been here but for him! He has given all his strength to my weakness; and now, see how strong I am and how weak *he* is" (160). Wardour's final speech makes clear the character-affirming nature of Arctic hardship:

> I took him away alone—away with me over the vast expanse of snow—he on one side, and the tempter on the other, and I between them, marching, marching, marching til the night fell and the camp-fire was all aflame. If you can't kill him—leave him while he sleeps—the tempter whispered to me—leave him

while he sleeps! I set him his place to sleep apart; but he crept between the Devil and me and nestled his head on *my* breast, and slept *here*. . . . I heard the night-wind come up in silence from the Great Deep. It bore past me the groaning of the icebergs at sea, floating, floating past!—and the wicked voice floated away with it—away, away, away forever! (158–59)

The image of Aldersley as a suckling child at Wardour's breast is itself strangely cannibal, especially since Wardour dies of malnutrition and weakness. But Wardour's aid to Aldersley is cast as self-sacrifice, and thus his affections for his mate are maternal, the values of the domestic sphere summoned out of and reasserted in privations suffered outside of civilization. In championing domestic values at such a moment, Dickens once again puts forth the stable identity he embraced in his *Household Words* debate with Rae.

Wardour's revelation also privileges sensation over cognition, employing pathetic fallacy to identify his moment of revelation and change as inextricably related to Arctic hardship. Isolated in the Arctic wastes, he chooses to embrace Aldersley, and discovers to his surprise the "great depths" of moral character. Dickens described the power of Wardour's return to a friend in January, writing in a letter, "I certainly have never seen people so strongly affected by theatrical means."[55] The moment of potential transgression is swept "away" simultaneously by the Arctic winds, by affirmation of the social bond, and (for the audience) by a wave of "felt" recognition. "It's a great sensation to have an audience in one's hand," Dickens wrote to Miss Coutts, claiming for himself as writer and actor some of the sensation that so moved his audience.[56]

Just as the play provided English audiences with the "experience" of polar exploration in its transporting stage sets and the equally transporting and affecting writing, Charles Dickens found in playing Wardour the "experience" that Rae had held over him. Reviewers and friends all noted Dickens inhabited the role to powerful effect. Wilkie Collins wrote of the touring company that in the role of Wardour, Dickens " terrified [the actor playing] Aldersley to that degree, by lunging at him to carry him into the cave, that he said Aldersley always shook like a mould of jelly, and muttered, 'This is an awful thing!'"[57] He also described his co-author's acting to a friend, "The trite phrase is the true phrase to describe that magnificent piece of acting. He literally electrified the audience" (834). Unanimously, reviewers of *The Frozen Deep* judged the performances to be superior to anything on the professional

stage; some thought the acting "so unusual that its example might revo-
lutionize the professional theatre."[58] Transported from his fireside and
from the streets of London into the Arctic wastes for an evening, Dickens finally had an answer to his earlier idle "wonder" at not being tomahawked or eaten and, for that matter, to his own cannibal potential.

In placing himself in the role of a possible cannibal nightly while on
public tour with the play in the summer of 1857, Dickens was able to
affirm the stability of his character—and by extension, national identity—again and again. The very power of melodramatic performance is
in its transitory, always escaping nature—paradoxically the very feature
that fixes the body as the space described by Brooks as "a place for the
inscription of highly emotional messages that cannot be written elsewhere, and cannot be articulated verbally" (131). Repetition remains the
only way to recapture the moment of sensation that reveals, in Dickens's
words "actual truth without its pain." In describing the experience of
creating the play, Dickens writes,

> As to the play itself; when it is made as good as my care can
> make it, I derive a strange feeling out of it, like writing a book
> in company; a satisfaction of a most singular kind, which has no
> exact parallel in my life; a something that I suppose to belong to
> a labourer in art alone, and which has to me a conviction of its
> being actual truth without its pain that I never could adequately
> state if I were to try never so hard.[59]

In his production of *The Frozen Deep*, Dickens seems both to recognize
the limits of print to transport and transform—limits so vigorously
denied by him in his debate with John Rae—and to exorcize that
recognition in order to stabilize the categories he so rigorously deter-
mines and defends in his journalistic work and fiction. In wistful recognition of the transitory transformative power of melodrama and his
desire to recapture it, Dickens wrote to Collins in August 1858, "I miss
Richard Wardour's dress, and always want to put it on."[60]

III

Charles Dickens's 1860 serialization of Wilkie Collins's *The Woman in
White* in *All The Year Round*, regarded by many as the inaugural, defini-
tive sensation novel, was one way in which he continued to perform

Richard Wardour. The Franklin expedition of 1845 had been a high-profile endeavor of the historically specific moment in reaction to which Margaret Oliphant situated the sensation genre in an influential 1862 review:

> Ten years ago the world in general had come to a singular crisis in its existence. The age was lost in self-admiration. We had done so many things that nobody could have expected a century before—we were on the way to do so many more, if common report was to be trusted. . . . [W]e had invented everything that was most unlikely, and had nothing before us but to go on perfecting our inventions.[61]

Not surprisingly, controversies and speculations surrounding Franklin's disappearance, articulated in debates such as Dickens's and Rae's cannibalism exchange, seemed equally concerned with the issues of national identity, uncertain social conditions, and vexed causalities that Oliphant identifies with sensation. "Saturated with the climate of the stage," as Martin Meisel describes them, sensation novels borrowed their affective mechanics from sensation dramas such as *The Frozen Deep*.[62] Possibly even more than Dickens, Collins actively viewed his fiction as an extension of the pleasures (and power) of the stage, writing in his prologue to his early novel *Basil*—a novel in which one sees explorations and anticipation of techniques perfected in sensation fiction—in 1852, that he believed

> that the Novel and the Play are twin-sisters in the family of Fiction; that the one is a drama narrated, as the other is a drama acted; and that all the strong emotions which the Play-writer is privileged to excite, the Novel-writer is privileged to excite also.[63]

Identified by Oliphant as the "simple physical effect" of the sensation plot, the excitement of strong emotions was vilified by disapproving critics as an addictive stimulant. Negative critical reaction stemmed from the power of sensation to reach and move its readers not through rational appeal to the intellect or moral faculties, but by eliciting the physical responses we associate with theatre. By publishing the sensation novels of Collins and others (including Charles Reade's *Hard Cash*) and by writing novels such as *Great Expectations* that were identified with the genre, Dickens was able to reproduce the identity-stabilizing effects of shock and repulsion in print, rather than rely on nightly repetitions of theatrical performance as Richard Wardour. Thus, the profoundly domestic sensation genre has an unlikely genealogy that includes a tradition of using the distant Arctic as a proving ground for male national identity—a peculiar footnote in its genesis that deepens one's understanding of the ideological work of sensation, particularly when the Arctic reappears in the late work of Wilkie Collins.

Plays such as *The Frozen Deep* worked in performance but not on the page due to their overdetermined dialogue and schematic plots, but sensation novels could afford more nuanced investigations of character and motivations over several hundred tightly plotted pages. If *The Frozen Deep* defined national identity by staging its stability outside England, sensation fiction pointed out threats to national identities in largely domestic plots concerning urban social issues such as bigamy, contested wills, and illegitimacy. Indeed, in their interrogations of gender concerns linked to the "woman question," class difference, and larger issues of national identity, sensation plots pushed at accepted norms, leading critics to fear that indulgence in reading sensation fiction contributed to social destabilization and moral degeneracy. Early sensation plots involved a threat to the status quo, often in the form of a foreign evil penetrating the middle-class home. These threats—what Cannon Schmitt identifies in *Alien Nation* as the "violation[s] of the English ideal of domesticity"—did not succeed, as their critics feared, in subverting the "domestic, middle-class version of Englishness." Instead, the inevitable, repeated defeat of threats to domestic order entailed the (re)institution of "an expanded Englishness—one that recuperated for professional middle-class manhood the signs of a chivalric, rural, and aristocratic national identity."[64] In their tidy resolutions, sensation novels perpetuated and reinscribed the domestic values displayed by men in faraway places like those represented in *The Frozen Deep*.

Schmitt bases his discussion of how "Otherness" functions in national identity formation in sensation fiction on his reading of Collins's *The Woman in White*, in which foreign threats force an interrogation and defense of English values and national identity. Earlier ideas of "Britishness," and more specifically "Englishness," evolved as defined against a foreign Other that was kept outside of the physical nation, as Linda Colley so insightfully traces. In sensation fiction, however, foreign influences (such as the evil Italian Fosco in *The Woman in White*) infected the nation until they were purged by diligent middle-class heroes. Yet as the genre evolved, new plots and a heightened consciousness of the problems and demands of empire required more complex models both of the interaction between the nation and what lay outside it and of the kind of citizen who could make sense of this new world. The certainty of a stable, masculine national character found in Dickens and in Collins's earlier novels, gave way, in Collins's work at least, to a British-ness more difficult to identify and define.

Collins's 1868 novel, *The Moonstone*, for example, appears to follow the course that Schmitt identifies with sensation novels: possession and subsequent theft of an Indian gemstone threatens the happiness and health of the heiress Rachel Verinder until the gem is taken back to India and Rachel is restored to her fiancé. The guilty party of the novel, however, is not the "Other" (a troupe of malevolent Indian acrobats), but Godfrey Ablewhite, the English son of a wealthy banker. And in a further twist, the English detective Sergeant Cuff can only solve the mystery with the help of Ezra Jennings, a mixed-race opium addict who alone possesses the ability to decode the clue that explains the disappearance of the gem. Granted, the novel ends with the eradication of the threat to what Oliphant, in her *Blackwood's* review, had identified as "the safe life we lead at home":[65] the removal of the jewel to India and the restoration of solidly English values with the marriage of Verinder and her fiancé Franklin Blake. But the resolution depends on the "piebald," miscegenated colonial product Jennings, someone who is not identifiably "English" at all and yet in whom resides the "unsought self-possession which is a sure sign of good-breeding" of a "gentleman."[66] In *The Moonstone* at least, Collins cautions against easy, racialized generalizations about what is and is not Britishness, and what can and cannot be enlisted and encompassed in a stable, shared sense of nation.

The Moonstone's plot is removed in every way from the Arctic, but its preoccupation with mutable, indeterminate identities and their relation to domestic stability recurs in one of Collins's last sensation works, one in which he once again invokes the Arctic to explore complicated national subjectivities. John Ruskin immortalized *Poor Miss Finch* (published in *Cassell's Magazine* in August 1871) as typical of the worst of "the loathsome [*sic*] mass" of contemporary literature, dismissing it in *Fiction, Fair and Foul* as an "anatomical preparation" in which "the heroine is blind, the hero epileptic, and the obnoxious brother is found dead with his hands dropped off, in the Arctic regions."[67] No matter that at the end of *Poor Miss Finch*, Nugent Dubourg's hands are still attached to his frozen body; for Ruskin, death by freezing was just another outrageous plotting folderol. Other critics agreed, including M. W. Townsend who described the novel (anonymously) in his obituary review of Collins's work as a "repertory [*sic*] of wasted cleverness."[68] More recent critics have been engaged by the novel's representations of race and disability. Yet Collins's involvement with *The Frozen Deep* invites a closer look at the seemingly random Arctic finale of *Poor Miss Finch* and, in turn, at the rest of the novel. Although *Poor Miss Finch* was written and serially published in 1871, the action of the novel takes place "back as far as the years 'fifty-eight and 'fifty-nine,"[69] precisely when Collins and Dickens were working through issues of national character and domestic stability in *The Frozen Deep*.

In the Dickens/Collins collaboration, *The Frozen Deep*, the Arctic served as a stage on which to realize the stability and legibility of national character. *Poor Miss Finch* takes up issues of character and nation explored in *The Frozen Deep* in a plot that vexes the simplistic correspondence between racial and moral categories that were at once so comforting to Dickens and so much a part of the mechanics of both sensation and nation. More than a decade after *The Frozen Deep*, *Poor Miss Finch* redeploys the Arctic and the figure of the cannibal. Both works end with a character's death in the Arctic, but while the triumphal end of Richard Wardour revealed the impossibility of English cannibalism and the victory of domestic morality, the lonely death of Nugent Dubourg reflects Collins's suspicion of the indeterminacy of national character, and reminds us that the threat to nation comes from cannibals who walk among us, unrecognized. Appropriately in this late sensation novel, the threat to England and the domestic is not foreign, not easily identifiable as different in race or class, but is instead a moral rot found within the nation's borders. Sensation, Collins suggests, arises from failing to recognize the phantasmic nature of the supposed "fact" of British character—which in Dickens's view, is stable in all circumstances—instead of acknowledging its cultivation in moral education and experience.

Poor Miss Finch is a strange novel, with overlapping plots of a love story and an interrogation of identity. The novel is narrated by Madame Pratolungo, the French widow of a South American revolutionary who is the paid companion of "Poor Miss Finch." Lucilla Finch is blind, in her early twenties, and falls in love with a visiting artist, Oscar Dubourg. Oscar and Lucilla are engaged to be married, but their bliss is ruined when Oscar is knocked on the head by an intruder and as a result acquires epilepsy, a condition he treats with silver nitrate. While it cures him of fits, the medication turns him dark blue. Oscar's identical twin brother Nugent shows up, bringing with him a German surgeon whom he hopes can cure Lucilla's blindness. Oscar, knowing that Lucilla fears and loathes "dark" people, switches identities with Nugent, at least until she gets used to her vision. But Nugent falls in love with Lucilla and decides to elope with her, leaving a brokenhearted, still-blue-skinned Oscar to travel the continent in despair. Oscar and Lucilla are eventually restored to one another, but Lucilla loses her sight permanently. The Arctic appears overtly only in the final few pages of the novel, when Nugent is found frozen to death on a lost Arctic exploration vessel, hunched over a letter he is writing to his brother and his bride.

The plot offers enough moral lessons for one critic to have dismissed it as "a sensation novel for Sunday reading."[70] Ruskin's categorization of the novel as an amended "hospital report," however, recognized the centrality of sensational diseased bodies to the work and their uneasy juxtaposition with the novel's morally uplifting aims.[71] How, the author of *Modern Painters* wonders, can a catalogue of grotesquerie purport to perpetuate British values? Collins described his purpose in his introduction as an attempt to show that "the conditions of human happiness are independent of bodily affliction . . . it is even possible for bodily affliction itself to take its place among the ingredients of human happiness" (xi–xii). Echoing tropes of earlier Arctic exploration literature, Dickens's cannibalism articles and *The Frozen Deep* had linked steadfastness of character to resistant, healthy English bodies, a connection perpetuated by Victorian theories of physiognomy and phrenology. Collins's novel, in contrast, rebuts these claims, revealing an uneasy and undependable coupling of character and physicality. By doing so, Collins brings into question not only the legibility and immutability of moral and national character so forcefully articulated by Dickens, but also categories of gender and race upon which both sensation and the nation had come to rely.

In a world of traded, mistaken, and stolen identities in the English countryside, the sensational body in *Poor Miss Finch* is not Lucilla's, around whose vulnerability the plot revolves. Rather, the sensational body takes the form of the Blue Man, a grotesque body shared between identical twins Oscar and Nugent. When Oscar contracts epilepsy, his intellect is subordinated to his physicality. Silver nitrate restores Oscar's command over his body, and indeed reveals a strength of character that was not visible before, but it replaces his flawless white exterior with a dark blue one, "so like death," Oscar remarks, "that I sometimes startle myself when I look in the glass" (93). In describing the work of the medicine as "saturation" (93), Collins expresses the connection between surface and interior, a connection extrapolated by Lucilla into a link between appearance and character. But where Lucilla in her horror of dark-skinned people sees the connection as one of exact correspondence, the mechanism of "saturation" reveals instead an uneasy and unpredictable relation between the body's interior and exterior.

Oscar's blue skin not only is a physical declaration of his disease, but also brands him as racially Other, and as such, repulsive to Lucilla, who though blind, expresses a "terror" of "dark" people. Lucilla herself is so perfectly white that she doesn't blush or flush, and her relation to dark things (and dark people) is exemplified by her encounter with a "Hindoo" whom she imagines as "a kind of monster in human form" (94). She ascribes her prejudice to her blindness, which gives her "a false view of persons and things" (94). Lucilla's fear, however, is not simply of the external unknown, but of her own self-division. Her outer whiteness contains an inner darkness; "my darkness" constitutes a sexualized unknown that she cannot "resist" "peopl[ing]" with brown demons" (52). Her reaction to the Indian and her resistance to a "dark" husband reflect her uneasy entry into womanhood and sexual awareness from a circumscribed life of modest propriety. By locating the source of Lucilla's bias in the social as well as the psychological, Collins suggests that distrust of others is caused as much by projected fears as it is by literal physical difference. Further, by presenting the "Hindoo" as a gentleman and in so doing revealing Lucilla's own psychological darkness, Collins complicates the easy equation of reading the "foreign" or racially Other as not representing British values.

The racializing of Oscar's difference indicates that Collins's concern is not one of individual character only, but also one of national character. When Lucilla's preconception and the twins' interchangeable bodies lead her to mistake Nugent for Oscar, her duping reveals the fallacy of "the English proverb, [that] what's bred in the bone" (246) will out in the flesh. For not only are the brothers perfect physical copies of one another despite being dissimilar in character, they are also perfect copies of English gentlemen, a fact that enables their easy absorption into the Dimchurch community. Despite appearances, Oscar and Nugent, like the piebald doctor's assistant Ezra Jennings in *The Moonstone*, are British, but not entirely English. Oscar's "foreign name" comes from his Jersey-born mother, and "Dubourg" (39) is not his last name at all, but a pseudonym taken by the twins in response to Oscar's highly visible trial for murder, which occurs before the novel starts. But if in *Poor Miss Finch* a mutable, indeterminate British body replaces the role the foreign threat to safe domestic bodies plays in other sensation fictions, questions of the indeterminacy of national character are not limited to the visible "Other" that takes the form of the blue body in the novel. The villainous Nugent, after all, is not physically different from others in the novel; Dimchurch itself and its inhabitants reveal the difficulties in identifying all that is English as being all that is good.

The threat to domestic order represented by the "foreign" in other sensation novels is for Collins already resident in the English countryside. Beautiful as it is, however, the countryside is an untracked, uninhabited desolation. The cart "heave[s] and roll[s] like a ship" (5), and Madame Pratolungo claims that "a stranger to this neighbourhood could only have found his way by the compass, exactly as if he had been sailing on the sea" (6). By making the local and familiar uncanny, Collins extends a strategy from his early travel writing, *Rambles Beyond Railways* (1855), in which he described England as being as exotic as any holiday destination on the continent, and therefore worthy of visiting by middle-class readers. By describing rural England as an accessible version of England's past, works such as *Rambles* provided readers with a way to imagine themselves as connected to that national past. Yet in its colorful portraits of rural peasantry and their nearly incomprehensible speech, *Rambles* also represented the interior of the nation as foreign to itself or, more specifically, foreign to its middle-class reading public. The representation of the countryside and its inhabitants in *Poor Miss Finch* participate in this second strategy, where provincialism is dangerous to the idea of nation.

The threat to the blind Lucilla comes from Nugent, whose ability to pass as an irreproachable gentleman due to his appearance and manner once again reveals the dangers of reading male British exteriors as indicative of the moral qualities that lie within. Nugent is "irresistible" because he is the white, masculine version of his twin: "So utterly different in his manner from Oscar—except when he was in repose—and yet so like Oscar in other respects, I can only describe him as his brother completed" (107). In addition to making him racially suspect, Oscar's disease and his consequent blueness mark him as being of indeterminate gender. Epilepsy renders his sensibility subordinate to unconscious phys- ical forces, a state traditionally gendered female, and consequently he is reduced to feminine tears. Furthermore, his profession as an artist in the decorative arts and his "delicate" appearance ("more like a boy than a man") (30) feminize him. His inability to confront Lucilla with the truth is also seen as evidence of feminine weakness by Madame Pratol- ungo, who tells Oscar, "Be a man! Own it boldly. . . . She will see her stupid prejudice in its true light, when she feels it trying to part her from *you*" (98). Pratolungo's emphasis on *you* is consistent with her republi- canism, but it also realizes Oscar's individualism—he is unique, if also flawed (by social standards at least), and his individuality is precisely what enables Lucilla to fall in love with him.

Oscar's inability to "be a man," Lucilla's "stupid prejudice," and Nugent's amorality collude to enable Nugent to steal both Oscar's iden- tity and the girl. Lucilla's confusion between the two brothers when she regains her sight arises from her inability to see past an imagined ideal of British masculinity: the moral man in the beautiful body. The ease with which Nugent perpetrates the switch reveals the problem in believing in a stable national masculinity at the expense of allowing for individual difference. Nugent is both insidious and dangerous in his ability to pass, not simply for Oscar—"exactly alike in their height, in their walk, in their features, and in their voices . . . the same coloured hair and the same beardless faces. Oscar's smile exactly reflected on Nugent's lips" (107)—but as a man of character.

Nugent's deception rewrites the threat of literal cannibalism at the center of *The Frozen Deep* into a metaphorical cannibalism of Oscar's identity, and from empire's edge to the center of England. Cannibalism, so long enlisted to define what was *not* British, is in this case the result and logical end of Britishness. The stable national character so important to Dickens requires not only the expulsion, but the cannibal consump- tion of the un-British, be it in the form of effeminate males or visibly "Other" individuals. Paradoxically, here the perfect Briton is the canni- bal: Nugent's visible "Englishness," readable in his manners and appear- ance, allows him to absorb Oscar's identity. Nugent is the scary result of national character taken to its limit: the imagined, shared values that allow the nation to cohere find their ideal in a facsimile of ideal British masculinity, a copy devoid of those same values. In the end, there is no center to Nugent. "Blame the passion that has got me body and soul: don't blame *me!*" (230) he cries to Pratolungo.

Nugent's exile to the Arctic is a voyage of atonement. His removal imitates the established Arctic romance of the heroic man who leaves a woman behind in England, but while "the absent Nugent dwelt a little sadly in their minds," Oscar and Lucilla marry, and Nugent has no one to whom to return. His geographic exile makes physical and extreme the social exile he brought on himself. Expedition accounts and popular representations such as *The Frozen Deep* presented the Arctic as a place of extremity where English values are realized, and indeed it is only there that Nugent can articulate his guilt, writing to Pratolungo, "Forgive me—if you can. I have not escaped without suffering; remember that" (339). Ironically, Nugent's death further perpetuates the national story of Arctic heroism and romance that he does not qualify for in life. As recounted in a public report "in case it may meet the eyes of his friends," the distinctly unheroic Nugent is rewritten as a tragic Arctic hero who is found "with open eyes . . . still fixed on the lock of hair" (339) presumed to belong to his beloved at home.

Oscar's return to England from his exile on the continent to claim Lucilla unifies the plots of love story and national identity. Lucilla acknowledges the irrationality of her repulsion when she encounters another blue man on the beach at Ramsgate: "There he is . . . with a fine woman for a wife, and with two lovely children . . . and a happier family you couldn't lay your hand on in all England" (270). The "retired Indian officer" and his happy family prove that reincorporation of difference, both of physical difference and the Englishman's experience in the colonies, is not only possible, but necessary. "I will live out of the world," Oscar tells Madame Pratolungo when he learns that his treatment for epilepsy will have the side effect of turning him deep blue (90). Like Walter Hartright in *The Woman in White*, who travels abroad in the middle of the novel and comes back from "the stern school of extremity and danger" with a "will that had learnt to be strong . . . as a man should" (183), Oscar returns from the continent a changed man or, rather, changed into a man. His newfound agency and discovery of "hidden reserves of strength in . . . character," however, are not due to the traditional male pursuits of adventuring or soldiering, but are credited instead to his nursing of injured soldiers in Italy:

> Ancient despair (especially of Oscar's sort) used to turn soldier, or go into a monastery. Modern despair turns nurse; binds up wounds, gives physic, and gets cured or not in that useful but nasty way. . . . [I]t implied, as [Pratolungo] thought, both courage

and resolution to have conquered the obstacles which he must have overcome, and to have held steadily on his course after he had once entered it. (307)

Readers in the 1870s would have associated war nursing with Florence Nightingale's Crimean campaign, but instead of confirming Oscar's suspect gender, the "courage and resolution" he gains by his experience confirm his masculinity. Merging his "super-sensitive" nature with a "stronger . . . nobler side" (209), Oscar is able finally to claim his identity, and in so doing, to save Lucilla. Their marriage and the birth of children confirm the role of a new kind of national masculinity in Victorian Britain, one that is less determined by a physical ideal confirmed by heroic acts abroad than by self-knowledge gained by acknowledging difference and weakness. In place of a static, unchanging male national character realized for Dickens in the alien geography of Arctic extremity, Collins proposes multiple, adaptable, substantive domestic masculinities, wrapped up in Pratolungo's final words, "Long live the Republic!"

Preserving this new order requires the exile of the smooth-talking facsimile of British masculinity. Nugent's death on an Arctic exploration ship literalizes the exchange of the brother's positions via the blue body: Oscar is, in Lucilla's blindness and by his own actions, no longer primarily identified and defined by his blue skin; Nugent is literally blue with cold and frozen to death in the Arctic. In death his frozen, static exterior finally matches his morally frozen interior. Paradoxically, the man-making work of the Arctic, that staple of nineteenth-century exploration accounts, comes too late for Nugent because he comes to it too late—the kind of men the Arctic makes belong to an earlier era. For Collins, Britishness exists first and best in the increasingly miscegenated and complex bloodlines that appear in the gardens of home. Like Walton in *Frankenstein*, Nugent voyages in search of an "open Polar sea," but instead of encountering Frankenstein's monster, he dies while contemplating Lucilla's hair, the evidence of his own monstrous self.

CHAPTER SIX

ENDS OF THE EARTH,
ENDS OF THE EMPIRE

R. M. Ballantyne's Arctic Adventures

In their tales of global adventure, writers of boys' adventure novels including R. M. Ballantyne and George Henty sought to locate and delimit British heroic masculinity. Like the reassuring combination of frisson and familiarity that travel writing offered to Charles Dickens, what Graham Dawson terms the "narrative pleasure" of boys' adventure novels relies on "endless repetition" and the "comfort of a known reading experience."[1] In this genre, boys venture to unmapped parts of the world where, challenged by new geographies and native peoples, they vanquish material and human foes on their way to claiming new lands for empire and becoming men. As Joseph Bristow succinctly describes it in *Empire Boys: Adventures in a Man's World*, the scope of the boys' adventure genre is "fearless endeavour in a world populated by savage races, dangerous pirates, and related manifestations of the 'other' to be encountered on voyages towards dark and unexplored continents."[2] That some novels by R. M. Ballantyne, George MacDonald, and H. Ryder Haggard take place in Arctic space does not contradict Bristow's assertion that these novels are always about "dark" continents. For, if the repetition so central to the adventure genre had the effect of stabilizing and naturalizing British heroic masculinity, it also erased geographical difference. The tropical and polar edges of empire may have had different climates that

151

presented different challenges, but in adventure novels they similarly called up in their youthful explorers the very same, replicable schoolboy pluck, superior British intellect, and triumphant Christian values.

A close look at Arctic boys' adventure fiction written by R. M. Ballantyne, however, reveals that despite the surface coherency in the genre that perpetuated such easy geographical conflation and naturalized attendant conclusions about British imperial masculinity, the Arctic persisted in asserting its difference from other imperial spaces and displayed a capacity to rupture rather than bolster the genre of the boys' adventure story. Taught to read Arctic space by the exploration accounts and journalism discussed previously,[3] adventure readers knew what to expect from the northern regions. Across a decade in which expeditions actively continued to search for traces of John Franklin's final expedition, R. M. Ballantyne published several novels that attempt to tie Arctic space to the global narrative and network of empire. Indeed, such efforts underlay Ballantyne's work from its earliest days. In one of his first published works and the first of his Arctic novels, the 1853 *Ungava*, Ballantyne attempted to bring the Arctic under British domination by means of his documentation of the daily life of a new Hudson's Bay Trading post on the Arctic Sea. Similarly, the mid-career *The World of Ice* (1858) depicted the Arctic as a largely empty space in which to dramatize the triumph of British masculinity in its revision of failed Franklin search missions. Yet despite its confident conclusions about British masculinity, *World of Ice*, with its plot and setting borrowed from expedition accounts and popular journalism, threatens to reveal the limits of Arctic usefulness to domestic and imperial projects outlined in the earlier *Ungava*. For although it employs the standard tropes and details of expedition journals (familiar shipboard scenes of domesticity, the threat of being crushed in an icefield, the effect of cold on the human body), the novel documents the unsuccessful extension of British civilizing forces to wild nature and reveals how Arctic geography threatened the cultural and racial superiority upon which both empire and boys' adventure relied. As a result, despite its happy ending, the novel reveals an Arctic sapped of its cultural puissance in a way that draws attention to the inadequacies and the forced, manufactured nature of the masculinity discovered there. It is this exhausted Arctic we find in Ballantyne's 1887 *Giant of the North or Pokings Around the Pole*, a novel that finally and spectacularly concedes the limits of the masculinity that both fueled and perpetuated boys' adventure—and of the genre itself—in the fantastical plot and equally fantastical geography he employs in his fictional account of the discovery of the North Pole.

By 1887, the many missions that had gone in search of Franklin in the 1850s through 1880s, while never locating the bodies of most of the missing men, had thoroughly mapped navigable Arctic space. The North Pole alone remained unknown. When H. Ryder Haggard asked, "Will the romance writers of future generations find a sage and secret place, unknown to the pestilent accuracy of the geographer, in which to lay their plots?"[4] he articulated the adventure genre's reliance on unknown geographies, both as sources of inspiration and as locales in which to make new the traditional plot and similarly dated masculinity of adventure novels. Like imperialism itself, the adventure genre demanded new geographies on which to unroll the same old tales and in which to discover or reveal predictable, unchanging qualities in adventuring British males. As a meditation on the symbolic stakes of Arctic exploration, *Giant of the North* anticipates the fierce competition for the North Pole and Scramble for Africa of the late nineteenth and early twentieth centuries, imperial competitions fueled by a sense of diminishing unmapped and unclaimed geographies.[5] Thus, paradoxically, even as Arctic geography was better understood, Ballantyne in *Giant of the North* writes the most fantastical tale of his career. While continuing to assert the nobility and greatness of Arctic exploration, British domestic values, and an adventurous, heroic masculinity documented in Ballantyne's earlier Arctic novels, *Giant's* unrealistic geography and its increasingly implausible search for the North Pole further expose stable British imperial masculinity to be a fantasy, and reveal the incipient exhaustion of the boys' adventure genre and nineteenth-century polar narratives alike. In the novel's fanciful resolution, Ballantyne comes very close to subverting not only the genre he had helped to define,[6] but the British imperial project in which that genre played such an important part.

BALLANTYNE, BOYS' ADVENTURE, AND IMPERIAL MASCULINITY

Robert Michael Ballantyne published more than one hundred novels during a writing career that spanned over forty years—years that included the Crimean War, the search for John Franklin, the Indian Mutiny, and the fall of the Sudan, as well as the zenith of boys' adventure fiction. Indeed, Ballantyne's widely popular novel *The Coral Island* (1858) is understood to be the quintessential adventure novel, a genre-defining blueprint of homosocial desert island adventure in which three boys reenact *Robinson Crusoe*, subdue cannibal others, and, having become men in their isolated paradise, board a passing ship to return to civilization. This general narrative arc, retold with different details and participants in various world geographies throughout Ballantyne's career, is present in his earliest work, *Hudson Bay or Everyday Life in the Wilds of North America* (1848). An account of his six-year tenure with the Hudson's Bay Company in Canada, the text reveals little of the day-to-day life of a clerk, concentrating instead on establishing the foundational structure that Ballantyne would augment in later works. "A boy" at the narrative's outset, Ballantyne anticipates a Hudson Bay that he has read about—even citing the early English explorer Samuel Hearne and John Rae—and thus finds himself disappointed not to encounter the Inuit as they near the icy Straits of Hudson.[7] As the plot follows his different postings and adventures, Ballantyne portrays his work as a clerk at the edges of empire as an extended sporting adventure, a more domesticated version of John Franklin's *Narrative of a Journey to the Shores of the Polar Sea*. By-now-familiar challenges of ice fields, sudden storms, and freezing temperatures—at one point, Ballantyne touches his tongue to the frozen flintlock of his gun and tears it away, "leaving a piece of skin the size of a sixpence" (183)—are interleaved with digressions on the behavior of natives, the architecture encountered in settlements, and "welcome" reminders of home.

For the young Ballantyne, the rigors and dangers of Arctic life are relieved by the presence of a settler society that insistently connects the adventuring youth to commerce and domesticity, and by extension to Britain. At the Oxford House outpost on the Trout River, Ballantyne comes across an unused barrel-organ, something he admits to loathing in "Auld Reekie" but, he explains, "four years' residence, however in the bush had rendered me much less fastidious in music, as well as in many other things . . . so that it was with a species of rapture I now ground away at the handle of this organ . . . and played . . . 'God Save the Queen,' 'Rule Britannia,' 'Lord McDonald's Reel,' and 'The Blue Bells of Scotland'" (242). The songs, which he plays "over and over again," sound "like the well-known voices of long, long absent friends" (243). His happy appreciation at empire's margins of "old and threadbare" songs (243) that at home he would have dismissed as either excessively patriotic or maudlin outlines how geographic distance functions in his later works: geographic remove and the physical and moral challenges of life at the edges of empire reinvigorates the Briton, both in his appreciation for home and in his sense of his affiliation to the home country. Listening repeatedly to "God Save the Queen" and "Bluebells of Scotland" in Northern Canada may comfort and reassure Ballantyne, but it also reinvigorates his sense of national affiliation, producing it as he has never experienced it before.

That the tunes that trigger Ballantyne's delight here are equally split between British imperial anthems and Scottish traditional songs reflects Ballantyne's own positioning in terms of imperial and national narratives. His writing career was directly linked to national narrative—and the failure of that narrative in Scotland. Ballantyne's once-wealthy family had been Walter Scott's publishers, ruined when the author went bankrupt.[8] Scott, of course, made his money on historical novels that produced a vision of a modern United Kingdom through their representation of Britain of the past. It was literally an overinvestment in those novels by Ballantyne's family—and by extension their overinvestment in the national myth—that led to Ballantyne's participation in mapping empire as a Hudson's Bay Company employee, an experience that in turn generated Ballantyne's very popular books. The commercial failure of the national-narrative-making Scott (due, it must be said, to his financial mismanagement rather than a lack of popularity of his books) directly engendered Ballantyne's own imperial exile and citizenship and the successful imperial narratives that resulted. The link between a failure of coherent national narrative and the birth of imperial enterprise found in this biographical detail is also found in Ballantyne's adventure novels and his (and their) investment in larger questions of imperial identity. For in place of the bankrupt Scott's fictions of Great Britain's national history, Ballantyne's novels posited a triumphal British imperial future rehearsed in repeated narration of British domination of foreign spaces and peoples.[9]

Time and again in Ballantyne's novels, the British masculinity discovered or revealed in hardy, curious, and brave boys at the geographical margins of empire is reimported to Britain upon the heroes' return at novel's end. If in their fictionalization of expedition accounts and rewriting of *Robinson Crusoe*,[10] adventure novels made overt the embedded ideological and pedagogical goals in those earlier narratives, they extended those goals in their conversion of the unknown into the known or familiar in their tightly scripted plots and their mapping of alien geography into the space of empire. The novels' dependence on the resistant bodies and stable subjectivities of their characters—and by extension, of their readers—strongly links them to imperial practices, as has been well documented.[11] In adventure novels, the production of masculinity is at once rationale for and productive of empire, and imperial margins and other spaces once again reveal themselves to be essential to how Britain understands itself at home. As Martin Green puts it, the "adventure narrative [is] the generic counterpart in literature to empire in politics," with the imperial space important primarily as "a place where adventures took place and men became heroes."[12] The genre thus both justifies and (re)produces empire; it produces Great Britain as necessarily imperial, since it is in imperial expansion that British qualities of pluck, honesty, bravery, and strength are starkly revealed.

In boys' adventure novels, imperial geography plays an important role as the place in which boys become men, or, as Joseph Bristow writes, as a space where the British boy is "placed . . . at the top of the racial ladder and at the helm of all the world."[13] Paradoxically, however, despite the importance of exotic geographies to boys' adventure, the stability and force of the genre is such that differences—geographic, climatic, and cultural—are attenuated, if not outright erased. The reasons for this are twofold. First, the familiar oft-repeated plot of these novels reproduces its model of a stable heroic masculinity that predictably responds to all situations and geographies.[14] It should not surprise us that narrative repetition also produces and perpetuates racial and cultural stereotypes, for the pressures of the genre are such that individuals who are culturally and/or racially different cannot be depicted as fully realized characters without threatening the predictable outcome, in which the challenges and threats encountered by the boy heroes are vanquished or contained by the novel's end. Second, since the product of boys' adventure is the imperial masculinity documented above, the genre insists on every space being encompassed by empire. In other words, geographically different spaces in these novels are all similarly available to Great Britain's domain and, once enfolded into empire, *are* all the same, as part of the larger geography that is the British Empire.

This erasure of geographic difference as part of the imperial project is at once perpetuated by and reflected in the reliance of adventure novels on narrative repetition. In addition to making imperial spaces and the native peoples who inhabit them essentially the same, and thus equally available to imperial domination, the repetition that is the hallmark of boys' adventure novels also results in a curious de-historicizing of empire.[15] Despite surface differences between texts, the shared plot always resolves in the same triumphal way, with the inference that, as imperial expansion and logic is dramatized (again and again, invariably) in the novels, so it has always been. In *The Coral Island*, for example, the shipwrecked threesome of Ralph Rover, Peterkin Gay, and Jack Martin find evidence of a Crusoe-like precursor on their desert isle when they come across his initials carved in a tree, and later, the hut of the marooned sailor who has died. Just as *The Coral Island* rewrites in some fashion the text of *Robinson Crusoe*, the previous British presence on the island indicates that empire has no originary date. As a result, the repetition of the predictable adventure plot remarks on the stability of empire, even as that empire must be extended into new geographies—and more adventure novels must be written—in order to reassert that stability.

BALLANTYNE'S ARCTIC ADVENTURES

Ballantyne's Arctic novels show how this logic of geographic, chronological, and generic stability can be extended to northern geography, while at the same time revealing a limit to such assertions of stability. Near the beginning of his late novel *Giant of the North*, the following curious exchange occurs between Chingatok—the "Giant of the North" after which the novel is named—and his mother, Toolooha. In it, Chingatok tries to comprehend and explain what, exactly, the men of the Arctic expedition ship, *Whitebear*, are doing in the north. Chingatok admits that he worries that the British polar explorers are insane:

> "Why would you think so, my son?" asked the old woman, sneezing.
> "Because he has come here to search for nothing."
> "Nothing, my son?"
> "Yes—at least that is what he tried to explain to me. Perhaps the interpreter could not explain. . ."
> "But it is not possible to search for nothing," urged Toolooha . . . "Has he not come to search for new lands here, as you went to search for them there?" . . .
> "No, I tell you. It is nothing! Yet he gives it a name. He calls it Nort Pole!"
> . . . "Nort Pole!" repeated Toolooha once or twice contemplatively. "Well, he may search for nothing if he will, but that he cannot find."

      "Nay, mother," returned the giant with a soft smile. "If he
will search for nothing he is sure to find it!"[16]

This humorous discussion echoes a tradition in the adventure novel of
having racial others supply humor through their misunderstanding and
misapplication of white British language. Chingatok and Toolooha's
inability to understand an abstract concept consolidates the imperial
identity of the British boy reader who in his laughter recognizes not
only a familiar racial stereotype at work, but his own racial and cultural
superiority. Yet, as we shall see, like so much else in *Giant of the North*,
this exchange exceeds the structural familiarity or stasis of the genre and
brings into question the ends of boys' adventure fiction. Chingatok
breaks stereotype in that he is not a passive and naïve native but, like the
British seamen themselves, an intrepid and brave explorer, having
encountered the *Whitebear* on his own voyage of discovery to the south.
The passage also addresses and mocks the rationale of Arctic exploration—if not for financial or physical territorial gain, then for what,
exactly? Chingatok's conclusion that if one searches for nothing, one is
sure to find it, uncomfortably captures the relationship of boys' adventure fiction to imperial masculinity. For generic claims and overdetermi-
nation aside, what is British masculinity except an abstraction, and by
extension, "nothing"? That is the fear, of course, and if in *Giant of the
North*, Ballantyne diffuses that fear by putting it into the mouths of
native "others" as something at which to laugh, Chingatok's musings on
the use value of the North Pole haunt the novel and indeed the boys'
adventure genre itself.

     By the time he articulated his unease with the ways in which Arctic
geography confounded and called into question the underlying assumptions and values of the adventure genre in *Giant of the North*, Ballantyne
had made repeated attempts to extend the geographic scope of boys'
adventure to the Arctic. On the one hand, the Arctic would seem to be a
perfect backdrop for boys' adventure, with its harsh climate determined
to either make a boy's character, as was the case, we are asked to think,
with the real-life Horatio Nelson, or kill him, as with the real-life John
Franklin. Indeed, Ballantyne seemingly needed only to reproduce the
tropes of Arctic blankness and manly British conquest of alien territory,
as established by Franklin and Parry in the early century and reproduced
in the multiple narratives produced by the mid-century searches for the
Erebus and *Terror*, to capitalize on the symbolic role the Arctic historically played in imperial narratives. On the other hand, as Franklin's *Nar-*

rative documented and John Rae's discoveries about the lost Franklin expedition revealed, British masculinity and bodily integrity were hardly stable, and the complete conquest of Arctic space continued to elude explorers. Certainly, Britons in the Arctic could triumph, if triumph meant surviving to narrate their Arctic journey. But Franklin's final disappearance, the inability of more than twenty separate search missions to locate him and his men, and the fruitless search for a navigable Northwest Passage[17] indicated that the Arctic continued to escape British domination, a domination that underlay the standard boys' adventure plot.

Whereas in the logic of imperial adventure, interpretable physical traces of British presence—the initials on the tree and the abandoned hut on the Coral Island—naturalized the imperial aspirations of boy adventurers by placing them in a legible history, the Arctic, despite offering up occasional cipher-like relics of the Franklin expedition, confounded attempts at British mastery and, as a result, vexed the conflation of imperial geography and the attendant de-historicization of imperial conquest so central to the boys' adventure genre. As the redoubled yet still unsuccessful efforts to find more than scant traces of Franklin in the 1850s through 1880s reveal, the Arctic's capacity for confounding British penetration refused to build on or comply with a palimpsested history of conquest. In temperate imperial margins, initial defeat of British expansion efforts (due to disease or armed native resistance) gave way, almost ineluctably, to successful conquering missions. The slow building of British presence and colonies abroad in other parts of the empire had enabled early failures and deaths in India and the Pacific—including the very recent 1857 Indian Mutiny—to be folded into the larger narrative of British imperial triumph. In contrast, the Arctic engendered no such victorious narrative, and offered in its place no physical product, be it property or commodity. Instead, the Arctic offered up narrative—not just any narrative, but the same predictable account of an encounter with undifferentiated white space that revealed or evoked heroic masculinity.

In the nonfictional Arctic expedition accounts of the early century, it had been possible to read the imperial masculinity produced by discomfort and dislocation at the edges of empire as a successful conclusion to or outcome of otherwise failed imperial explorations or endeavors. During the search for Franklin, the predictable discovery and documentation of what Britons had encountered before in the Arctic—the chilblains, paraheliae, ice blinks, frostbite, endless days of summer and endless nights of winter—again affirmed the discovery of a potent imperial masculinity that, when combined with newly precise maps of Arctic coastlines produced by these voyages, seemed to supply the place of Franklin's missing body. Paradoxically, however, as boys' adventure novels reiterated their foundational plots and tropes in ever more diverse environs, these very repetitions that seemed to assure the solidity of their conclusions about imperial masculinity also demanded resolutions—the domination of geographies and peoples, the easy naturalization of British superiority—that Englishmen in the Arctic could not convincingly deliver. As we shall see, in boys' adventure fiction set in the Arctic, the repetition of the boys' adventure plot of certitude, progress, and the inevitability of empire collided uneasily with the repetition of the more ambivalent narratives engendered by Arctic exploration and the Arctic's teasingly elusive geography. Over almost a century of reiteration in Arctic exploration accounts, the resistant and resilient British body that housed a unique national character, identified with pluck, courage, and intellectual and cultural superiority, had promised to eventually unlock the Arctic's secrets. Yet, even as it became more thoroughly mapped as the century wore on, the Arctic remained an abstract space incomprehensible to all but the most dedicated Arctic aficionado, a list of Anglo-Saxon names applied to a landscape that for metropolitan readers remained undifferentiated white space.

What to Ballantyne must have been the tauntingly perfect merger between genres that were dedicated—Arctic exploration account and adventure novel alike—to producing legible, reproducible imperial masculinity instead called into question the basis and productivity of that masculinity, as an examination of his serial efforts witnesses. His repeated return to northern Canada and the Arctic in novels that span his career indicates the persistent cultural presence of the Arctic in imperial narration. Ironically, although Ballantyne's oeuvre will forever be associated at least as much with the icy climes of the Canadian north and the Arctic as it is with tropical islands and rainforests, his several novels with Arctic settings document his many (largely unsuccessful) narrative attempts to enfold Arctic space into imperial space and consequently into triumphal imperial narrative. Writing *Hudson Bay* enabled Ballantyne to use his own experience as empire's agent to feel his way toward what would later be the standard narrative technique and plot of his later fictional works. In the fictionalization of his own Arctic experience in his first truly Arctic novel,[18] *Ungava*, Ballantyne pushes the edges of empire farther north. Yet his attempt to extend British domestic life by creating a trading post on the Arctic Ocean fails—at novel's end, the nascent colony is no more—as if in acknowledgment that Arctic space, to remain symbolically powerful, must remain the forbidding, homosocial geography found in expedition accounts.

In *Ungava*, Ballantyne merged the familiar tropes of Arctic narrative that had established and consolidated British heroic identity in earlier expedition accounts with an assertion of an exportable British domesticity that made the imperial margin seem an extension of Britain. The resulting novel is an episodic dramatization of the technical and anthropological details that had filled exploration accounts, in which a middle-class family at an Arctic trading post serves as proxy for Ballantyne's readers with the somewhat less than satisfying result that the Arctic, once domesticated, threatens to become like everywhere else. Yet Ballantyne encountered a larger generic difficulty: how to borrow from the tradition, established by Southey's *Life of Nelson* and other texts, that asserted the Arctic as a space of radical alterity in which to realize a stable heroic masculinity, while also confirming the spread of civilizing forces, including an imperial trading system and Christianity, into unknown and wild geographies and cultures. In a way, the problem Ballantyne confronted was a version of a larger problem in the genre: its dependency on repeated plots and tropes threatened the excitement and tension promised by the quest narrative at the heart of the text.

Ballantyne was unable to manage this tension: while sharing the ideological investment of the adventure genre *Ungava* becomes a settler-colony novel. In this transposition of his first-person narrative of *Hudson Bay*, Ballantyne supplies the legible "success" missing in earlier expedition accounts by means of the establishment of a prosperous and happy Hudson's Bay Company trading post on the shores of Ungava Bay. Here, we see the proprietors Mr. and Mrs. Stanley, their young daughter Edith, and a young HBC agent Frank Morton interacting peacefully and productively with various French Canadian, "Indian," and "Esquimaux" laborers. Life at the margins of empire here reproduces British society, in which Britons stand out as superior not only to the Inuit and native populations, but to the French as well. Domestic security tempers and resolves Arctic hardship in the narrative: when the novel's two heroes, the young clerk Frank and a ten-year-old girl, Edith, get lost and disoriented in the snow, Edith's gentle nursing revives Frank and saves his life.

As part of writing Arctic space as colonial space, Ballantyne inserts Mrs. Stanley and Edith into the traditionally all-male narratives of expedition accounts.[19] Yet rather than perpetuate a vision of full female participation in active colonial and imperial enterprises—a kind of geographic literalization of the sorts of claims Eleanor Porden earlier made for British female participation in Arctic exploration—Ballantyne finally restricts the participation of Edith to the domestic, thus delimiting "true" imperial citizenship to males and foreshadowing the homosocial world of his later adventure fiction. In her interactions with the Eskimos, Edith acts as a civilizing agent who urges her playmates to give up eating raw food and "to wash their hands and faces before going out to play."[20] Despite the quick thinking that results in the rescue of Frank, the hardiness of British character associated with males in adventure tales and expedition narratives is extended to Edith only in the feminized value of constancy. When Edith disappears into the snowy landscape, she maintains her propriety and values when rescued by an Eskimo family—expressed in her maintenance of a tidy igloo, her reluctance to eat raw flesh, and her care for an Eskimo baby who is neglected during an enthusiastic seal hunt—until her discovery by a search party. At novel's end, with the colony long abandoned, Frank and Edith, both made strong by their youthful adventures in the barren north, reunite in a Canadian agricultural settlement: the symbolic role of the Arctic as a space in which to perpetuate British qualities is here reified in a heterosexual union that will populate the agricultural center of British Canada.

Although *Ungava* was a popular success, it failed as a narrative of triumphant adventure. As if to recoil from the northern boundary of the adventure genre he tested in *Ungava* back to a safe "middle ground" near the equator, Ballantyne followed its publication immediately with *The Coral Island*. Though *The Coral Island* is widely identified with the inception of the boys' adventure genre, its indebtedness and that of the larger genre to the failures of *Ungava* are typically overlooked. It would appear that *Ungava*'s unwieldy combination of exploration account, colonial report, and domestic life is as untenable in imperial genre fiction as it would be in the real icefields of the Arctic. In his reimagining of the imperial plot in *The Coral Island*, Ballantyne not only jettisons British women, but rewrites the "blank space" of imperial potential that the Arctic had always promised—but had failed to deliver on—onto the already heavily inscribed British imperial space of a tropical paradise. This stripped down, homosocial setting that proved to be a signal element of almost all boys' adventure fiction thus can be understood as a more richly elaborated rewriting of the stripped-down, homosocial setting of Arctic exploration accounts. Ballantyne's early attempts to fictionalize those accounts in the Arctic landscape, however, reveal that what had been pre-

viously read as triumphant accounts of human survival that naturalized
and located a British identity could not be transferred to the imperial
novel. To address this difficulty, Ballantyne turns to the most salient literary example of isolated, homosocial imperial triumph from British fiction, and uses *Robinson Crusoe* in order to invigorate his vision of late
imperial triumph, in so doing discarding Arctic geography.

Ballantyne's decision to follow *Ungava* with the publication of *The
Coral Island* indicates his rejection of that novel's unwieldy marriage of
adventure and domesticity in preference for the clarity of the adventure
genre. The tale of Ralph, Peterkin, and Jack's survival on and dominance
of a desert island is also an allegory of settler colonialism and the spread
of empire, but in Ballantyne's refusal to import the baggage of a literal
settler colony—the families, architecture, and daily life of the Hudson's
Bay Company outpost on Ungava Bay—here instead an empty, foreign
space produces "natural" (and naturally superior) British subjects. Necessarily, it seems, in *The Coral Island*, Ballantyne writes Edith (and other
women) out of the plot, distributing instead the domesticity and civilizing agency attributed to females in *Ungava* among the boys who otherwise would not discover these capacities. On the island, domesticity is
not just the source of a clean face, but is, moreover, the foundation of a
Lockeian rationale by which the unpopulated land becomes the boys'
possession. As Peterkin says when they first drift onto the empty shores,
"We'll build a charming villa, and plant a lovely garden round it, stuck
all full of the most splendiferous tropical flowers, and we'll farm the
land, plant, sow, reap, eat, sleep, and be merry."[21] These boys do not need
their mothers and sisters to remind them to be industrious, or to wake
them from dangerous sleep, as Edith Stanley does Frank Morton on the
icy plains in *Ungava*: the imperial gesture in *The Coral Island* depends not
on the civilizing moral force of womanhood, but rather on the boys'
resourceful responses to hardships endured in homosocial isolation, a
reiteration of the conclusion of Arctic expedition texts. Thus, in *The
Coral Island* Ballantyne returns in his discussion of British character and
imperial masculinity to the resistant male body cultivated *in extremis* that
we see in Southey's *Life of Nelson* and Franklin's *Narrative*.

When Ballantyne returned a few years after *The Coral Island* to the
frozen north with the publication of *World of Ice* more confident in fic-
tionalizing boys' experience in a standard adventure plot, he discovered
that although the heroic masculinity affiliated with Arctic exploration
was in fact transportable to other imagined geographies, Arctic geography continued to interfere with a geographic mastery that was the

driving telos of the adventure genre. So strongly did the Arctic resist enclosure in the imperial atlas and plot that when Ballantyne finally depicts the successful British discovery of the North Pole in *Giant of the North*, his fantastical resolution to the puzzle of Arctic geography brings into question the logic underlying Arctic exploration, the adventure genre, and imperial endeavor. Thus, Arctic narrative and its irreduceable failures both mark the inception and signal the impending unraveling of boys' adventure novels.[22]

Revisiting an Arctic setting in his mid-career novel *World of Ice* (1860), Ballantyne reclaims the Arctic as a male space following the formula perfected in *The Coral Island*. Influenced by and capitalizing on the popularity of the many Franklin search missions and the texts they produced, the novel imagines a successful discovery of a lost Arctic explorer. An adventurous, orphaned Fred Ellice—having lost his mother to pirates as a child—ships out on a whaler to search for his father, the lost Arctic explorer. Fred's experiences in the ice are the standard fodder of Arctic exploration accounts: descriptions of natural phenomena such the ice blink and the effect of cold on the sailors' bodies, encounters with "jolly Eskimos," and an ongoing catalogue of shipboard effects and routine. The unfriendliness of the Arctic climate makes discipline a more conscious part of the Arctic-imperial adventure than it is in tropical tales, with the ship serving as a microcosm of Great Britain (complete with Irish and Scottish sailors). The "written code of laws" gives the English captain "supreme and absolute command" over a British and international crew.[23] Scientific routines and watches are detailed, and the value of moral discipline, as well as bodily, is described with a rule that "Prayers shall be read every morning before breakfast" (113). Shipboard structure, Ballantyne suggests, is perhaps as important as Arctic hardship in shaping Fred's masculinity. In this close documentation of Arctic shipboard life and in the fictitious rescue of Captain Ellice, Ballantyne contributes to Dickens's vociferous defenses of the Franklin expedition against social disorder and an accompanying descent into cannibalism. For not only does Ballantyne supply us with a Franklin substitute in Captain Ellice, but Fred himself is understood to be a future Franklin as he grows from boy to man in his search for his father.

Fred Ellice's mature masculinity is the discovery we witness in *World of Ice*. This complies with the generic demand of boys' adventure fiction—that over the course of the narrative, boys become men. But in temperate tales, the discoveries of land, resources, and savage peoples accompany and solidify that discovery of mature masculinity. In *The*

Coral Island, for example, Ballantyne firmly establishes the link between masculinity and imperial domination. The boys' physical prowess enables them to climb to the topmost peak of the island in order to survey their new land. As Ralph describes it, "We found this to be the highest point of the island, and from it we saw our kingdom lying, as it were, like a map around us," at which he pulls out a handkerchief "with sixteen portraits of Lord Nelson printed on it, and a Union Jack in the middle" (45). The confident conferral of imperial possession afforded the boys on the Coral Island is nowhere to be found in an Arctic geography that persistently confounds attempts to map it. In *World of Ice*, Ballantyne seems to concede that British masculinity is the only discovery available in Arctic exploration, be it in the recovery of lost sailors or the training of new ones. That the blank whiteness of Arctic space provides no correlative to masculinity that can be brought back as the product or proof of that discovery had not been an issue in nonfiction expedition accounts—indeed, heroic masculinity was the acknowledged and accepted product of Arctic exploration—but the persistent conflation in boys' adventure fiction between masculinity and geographical dominance exerts a generic pressure to which *World of Ice* must concede.

The resistance of the Arctic to mapping, for Ballantyne, at once brings into question the rationale the British sailors have in being there and potentially disrupts the ship's discipline, that microcosm of an orderly British society, as we see in the following exchange in *World of Ice*:

> "We're far beyond the most northerly sea that has ever yet been reached," remarked Captain Guy to Fred . . .
>
> "I beg your pardon for differing, Captain Guy, but I think that Captain Parry was farther north than this when he attempted to reach the Pole," remarked Saunders, with the air of a man who was prepared to defend his position to the last.
>
> "Very possibly, Mr. Saunders; but I think we are at least farther north in this direction than any one has yet been; at least I make it out so by the chart."
>
> "I'm not so sure o' that," rejoined the second mate positively; "charts are not always to be depended on, and I've heard that whalers have been up hereabouts before now."
>
> "Perhaps you are right, Mr. Saunders," replied the captain, smiling; "nevertheless, I shall take observations, and name the various headlands, until I find that others have been here before me." (74)

Mapping and naming, of course, are the acts by which the imperial adventuring subject is typically realized. By suggesting here that they may be futile acts, therefore, Ballantyne suggests that in ways distinct from other imperial places, the Arctic interrogates the very subjectivity that it brings into being. The captain's uncertainty about the ship's location extends to the precarious situation of agency and the individual body in the Arctic. While on a hunting expedition, Fred almost freezes to death when he stops to rest, "the frost seiz[ing] hold of his frame" (163). As in other Arctic narratives, the promised legibility and mobility of the British subject in polar regions quickly vanishes when the explorer joins the landscape.

Just as the challenging geography and climate of the Arctic confounds easy exploration, they also erode another form of legibility: racial and cultural difference. As *The Coral Island* establishes clearly, in imperial adventure difference is understood by a "natural" hierarchy that places the British over any native peoples they encounter. As early as the morning of their shipwreck, Peterkin in *The Coral Island* observes, "We've got an island all to ourselves. We'll take possession in the name of the king; we'll go and enter the service of its black inhabitants. Of course we'll rise, naturally, to the top of affairs. White men always do in savage countries. You shall be king, Jack; Ralph, prime minister" (15). The stability of this position, where, as Andrea White describes it, "the civilizers remain strangely untouched" and the adventurer "remains stolidly unaffected by his experiences" is a central feature of the adventure genre.[24] The story of Fred's father would appear to follow Peterkin's imagined trajectory. Having joined the Eskimos, Captain Ellice is soon elevated to chief. When Fred and the crew finally encounter him, the captain throws "back his hood [to] reveal a face whose open, hearty, benignant expression shone through a coat of dark brown which long months of toil and exposure had imprinted on it" (261). Fred immediately recognizes his father, suggesting that the stability and legibility of Britishness is such that exterior markings of it—uniforms and insignia— may be considered extraneous. Yet the captain himself is changed by his stay with the Eskimos: he doesn't recognize his own son, his words are "few" and "unintelligible" (261), and he suggests that his life among the natives has been haunted by hallucinations. Unlike Dickens, Ballantyne concedes that Arctic survival demands "going native," and even suggests that the Eskimos are ideally adapted to the Arctic environment in a way that Britons are not. The sailors survive only because they learn to hunt walrus from the natives, and eventually to "relish raw meat, and to long for it" (164). Imagine the recoiling horror of *Ungava*'s Edith Stanley at the white sailors' consumption of raw meat and at Ballantyne's following conclusion: "We would have [our readers] henceforth refuse to accept that common opinion and vulgar error that Esquimaux eat their food raw *because they are savages.* They do it because nature teaches them that, under the circumstances, it is best" (165). The easy racial superiority that informs *Ungava* and *The Coral Island*—as well as the imperial project itself [25]—here is problematized by a native culture in which Eskimo tools and skills outstrip British technology in Arctic environs.

Ballantyne further dramatizes the unstable nature of cultural and racial affiliation in *World of Ice* through his account of a shipboard theatrical. Famously, Arctic expedition accounts by William Parry and others documented the long, iced-in winters passed by their crews, and readers expected scenes of adolescent hi-jinks on the ice, as well as lecture series, theatre productions, and pantomime nights. In Ballantyne's version, the play concentrates on an Eskimo woman who is pursued by amorous polar bears that, after eating her baby, threaten her with sexual advances until a passing British tar attacks "the two bears at once" and claims her as his native bride. Such enactment of British virtues is hardly reassuring, as it confuses identities almost as much as it asserts them: Fred Ellice, the young British sailor, plays the "Esquimau woman" so well that the audience looks around to make sure Aninga, a native woman whom the crew of the *Dolphin* has taken hostage, is still seated in the audience. After the marriage between a British sailor and Fred-as-native-woman takes place onstage, the curtain drops and the narrator comments, "It was left a matter of uncertainty whether Ben Bolt and his Esquimau bride returned to live happily during the remainder of their lives in England, or took up their permanent abode" (226) in the Arctic. The remark, although tongue-in-cheek, acknowledges the larger ways that the Arctic effaces difference and shows how the very strategies used to assert homely values ultimately unsettle them.

Although the muddiness or confusion of identity and imperial rationale that surfaces in *World of Ice* reveals itself in earlier nonfiction works such as Franklin's *Narrative*, its appearance in a boys' adventure novel indicates that the limited number of standard Arctic tropes and plots available had by this point in the century undermined their very value in clarifying British masculinity. Despite trying to make these tropes new by linking them to the triumphal genre of adventure, Ballantyne's repetition of them in an otherwise confident genre only gestures at their exhaustion and the potential exhaustion of the values they were understood to perpetuate. Ballantyne's later *Giant of the North* (1887) thus signals his dissatisfaction with both an Arctic plot that had revealed itself as static and circular and a genre that in its repetition had become stale. No longer could Ballantyne convincingly write the pseudo-realist imperial fantasy, represented by *The Coral Island*, for which he was known. Instead, *Giant of the North* is overtly fantastical in its depiction of an imagined British expedition that discovers the North Pole.

Presented as the transcription of an actual expedition in an introduction that asserts the veracity of the events that follow, *Giant of the North* is the tale of the spirited boy Benjy and his industrious cousins Alf ("a scientific-Jack-of-all-trades") and Leo ("a doctor, almost"), who accompany Benjy's father, Captain Jacob Vane on his mission to discover the North Pole. The three boys, rewritings of Ralph, Peterkin, and Jack from *The Coral Island*, are introduced to shipboard life and discipline in the manner Ballantyne documents in *World of Ice*. Yet from its outset, the novel defies what for Ballantyne is by now a convention. Instead of opening with the embarkation of the polar exploration vessel, *Whitebear*, from an English port or joining the expedition *in medias res* on its Arctic expedition in the opening pages, the narrative begins with a description and biography of Chingatok, the "Giant of the North." Chingatok is himself an explorer who—having heard rumors of "a race of men" who travel the sea on "floating islands" and whose "faces [are] whiter than Eskimo faces" (6)—decides to discover this new "tribe" himself. This reversal of white exploration into unknown spaces and the acknowledgment of a native perspective destabilizes the imperial perspective of the genre even as it attempts to exploit the conceit for humorous purposes: Chingatok has decided these "Kablunets" (the native term for White Europeans) must be poor and has undertaken his mission as one of humanitarian aid, with the desire to lead them to his home to "show them this land of plenty" (17). His rationale for exploration thus reveals his humanity while also calling into question the rationale for the discovery of the North Pole. Therefore, when, shortly after encountering the British expedition and learning of their plans to map the North Pole, Chingatok and his mother have the exchange about "nothing" in which "nothing" and "the North Pole" are interchangeable, Ballantyne is not only playing humorous linguistic games and exploiting the widely used stereotype of the Eskimo as childlike and incapable of complex thought, but commenting at the same time on the abstract or imagined nature of empire. As a boys' adventure novel, its telos is the naturalization of empire documented in the recruitment and instruction of future imperial subjects, Benjy, Alf, and Leo; yet the text's humor and fantastical elements also point out the absurdity or impossibility of the imperial endeavor. Joseph Bristow has asserted that the confident conclusions of standard boys' adventure novels stabilized a male heroic identity that did not exist in empire, but "could, momentarily, cohere" in texts.[26] In *Giant of the North* we see the miasmic and constructed nature not only of that masculinity, but of imperial rationale itself.

When Ballantyne directly addresses the vexed reasoning behind polar exploration in the exchange between Chingatok and his mother, Toolooha, he questions all British exploration. From that point on, the possible bankruptcy both of Arctic exploration as imperial endeavor and of the larger ideological claims and work of the adventure genre itself uneasily inhabit *The Giant of the North*. It is not surprising, then, that when, thirty pages later, the English sailors themselves question the viability of Arctic exploration upon seeing an "apparently illimitable" ice plain, they invoke Chingatok's language:

> "These will stop us at last." [Alf commented].
> "No they won't," remarked the Captain quietly. "Nothing will stop us!"
> "That's true, anyhow, uncle," returned Alf; "for if it be, as Chingatok thinks, that we are in search of nothing, of course when we find nothing, nothing will stop us." (104)

Once again, Ballantyne's linguistic dexterity, although played for humor, holds in it a darker and revealing truth. The juxtaposition of "nothing" with the "apparently illimitable" ice plain presents the paradox of British imperialism. The potential expanse of the British Empire is limitless, so long as the British male sent to map it maintains a resistant body that houses limitless reserves of character and daring. These interior resources, mapped so well in accounts such as Southey's *Life of Nelson*, contrast with the vast blankness of the Arctic canvas, which to untrained or undisciplined eyes is "nothing." Alf's wry observation that if they "are in search of nothing, of course when [they] find nothing, nothing will stop [them]" draws upon the de-historicized, containing logic that *The Coral Island* expressed: one that communicated the always, already, and thus justifiable and natural, status of empire.

This logic is troublingly expressed once more when the men of the *Whitebear* come to Chingatok's land and take formal "possession" of it, naming it "Home-in-Sight Island" and raising a Union Jack, "while the

Captain made a careful note of the latitude and longitude" (129). The name of the island itself raises questions about empire's ends. The question of whether or not Chingatok has a name for his island never comes up; this is, of course, the way empire works and it is not questioned in this or any other of Ballantyne's novels. Yet even if it is granted that Chingatok's home is indeed in sight, if that is the "home" to which the name refers, then why do the British name it "Home" when they raise the Union Jack? Generously, we could interpret Chingatok's service to the sailors in the form of his generous sharing of his survival skills and local knowledge with them after their ship has been broken apart by the icepack as making him a vested, honorary citizen of empire. Another explanation for this curious name lies in the possibility that Captain Vane imagines their ultimate destination of the North Pole being potentially "in sight." The result is a conflation between the as-yet-unachieved geography of the North Pole and the *idea* of the pole, the apparently inevitable conquering or discovery of which is central to the British imaginary even as it exceeds British grasp. In other words, the North Pole, that abstract and elusive goal, is already understood as "home" to the Briton. For in the pole, the British imperial imagination fully realizes itself and is brought home. Having achieved such mastery, the imperial wanderer can then return to domestic ease. "Home-in-Sight" is thus a means for Ballantyne to indicate the necessary terminus of the British imperial imagination while at the same time showing the desperate folly of ever being able to reach it. The strangeness of the name that emerges from its very homeliness aptly captures the condition of adventure fiction and the imperial imaginary in the late nineteenth century, as the confident assertion of domination and imperial sameness that reconciles the metropole and the imperial periphery has reached almost to the level of absurdity.

It is not so much Ballantyne's recognition of the paradoxical rationale for and the accompanying nature of empire but his literalization of it that is remarkable in *Giant of the North*. If empire is possible because it has always, inevitably, been so, at the end of *Giant*, Ballantyne literalizes this paradox. Unlike Walton in *Frankenstein*, the remaining crew of the *Whitebear* find a temperate pole. At Ultima Thule, the symbol of empire's consolidation as the final blank space to map and deliver to the metropole, the temperature rises to 50 degrees, causing Captain Vane to remark, "Summer, boy; it's like India" (421). To be "like" India is to bring the North Pole into the empire as India was under Victoria. The confidence of the analogy on the one hand suggests the stability of British imperial rule as the final blank space is made legible, while on the other hand it telegraphs imperial collapse. In Ballantyne's depiction of the pole as temperate if not tropical, he succeeds in the geographical conflation we have seen is a mark of the successful imperial narrative. Yet in his realization of his desire for a successful Arctic boys' adventure, he simultaneously registers the untenable nature of all of the assumptions that underlie his work. Like the Arctic explorers in search of "nothing," Ballantyne's resolution of his narrative problems conjoining Arctic space with the boys' adventure novel requires him to plumb the void that lies at the heart of the imperial imagination. For not only does *Giant of the North* devolve into absurdity, but it reveals how the genre itself is unable to realize its goal of geographical and cultural containment, which is the driving force of empire.

Further extending this strange fantasy of imperial endorsement at world's end, Ballantyne populates the North Pole with a native shaman, Makitok, who keeps the sacred Eskimo texts. Paler and taller than the Eskimos, the shaman not only looks suspiciously like "the living embodiment of 'Old Father Christmas'" (377), but his name "Makitok" is revealed to be a bastardization of "Mackintosh." The "Esquimaux" holy man, it turns out, is clearly a Robinson Crusoe figure: a descendent of a Scottish sailor marooned with Henry Hudson two hundred and fifty years earlier. By presenting the embodiment of John Ross's "Arctic Highlander," Ballantyne reverses the model employed in *The Coral Island* and has a very-much-alive (if somewhat comical) colonial survivor presiding over this last outpost of empire. In so doing, Ballantyne brings to a close the form he perfected with *The Coral Island* by inserting the voyage of the *Whitebear* in a clearly discernable history. Unlike the "timeless" imperial chronology of *The Coral Island* where the industrious adventurers build on the efforts of the colonial predecessor who recedes into the mists of time, here we see imperial rhetoric presided over by a "Father Christmas" figure reading from "sacred" texts that are supposed to be the basis of all Eskimo religion but are in fact compiled from documents of Hudson's last, mutinous expedition. This depiction of Makitok is almost a parody of the familiar trope of white rule being enabled by invocations of near-supernatural authority over an excessively credulous and supine native population.

Thus, at the end of *Giant of the North*, the North Pole, so long thought to be outside of British domination and to represent the limit of imperial masculinity, is discovered in fact to be already British. This recognition enables realization that empire is not timeless, but may in fact have an end as it had a beginning, and so is fallible rather than always triumphant. The final erasure of geographic, cultural, and religious difference in *Giant* verges on the absurd, with the effect of unraveling all of the claims that rest on the reassuring repetition of the genre and especially the (re)discovery of British infallibility in adventure novels. Because of their shared narrative elements, the Arctic adventure reveals the impossibility of the fantasies of empire's projects in other adventure novels located in other spaces.

The "happy" collapse of imperial narrative in *Giant of the North* strangely parallels the darker conclusion to Mary Shelley's *Frankenstein*. Whereas Shelley draws upon the gothic to reveal the bankruptcy of a national masculinity based on imperial adventuring and the attendant dangers of ignoring the domestic, the unspeakable horror for Ballantyne is to be found in imperial narrative itself. Ballantyne unearths a discrepancy at the heart of the adventure novel that is akin to the return of the repressed at the heart of the gothic. In the reliance of the genre on a closed narrative circle of a known plot inhabited by stock or stereotypical characters whose discoveries are by definition not "real" discoveries but are instead foreordained and thus foreclosed narrative events, adventure novels show how the nongenerative aspect of imperial homosociality that constitutes the terror at the heart of *Frankenstein* has metastasized into the very structure of imperial narrative.

The narrative dissolution of Ballantyne's fantastical novel strangely foreshadows Conrad's relationship with the genre displayed in novels such as *Lord Jim* and *Heart of Darkness*, where, as documented by Andrea White, he employs and deflates the conventions of adventure in order to reveal the exhaustion and shortcomings of the genre as well as of the imperial ideology and practices it espouses and perpetuates. White perceptively links Conrad's fiction with the discernable decline of imperial fortunes in the late nineteenth and early twentieth centuries. She observes that in his work to dismantle adventure novels, Conrad attempted "to demythologize a genre that had so influenced him . . . due to his public and personal awareness that the dream was over, that the possibilities for great aspirations and noble deeds were closing down."[27] Supplementing Conrad's sense of the historical moment and his own experiences participating in imperial seafaring that White documents so well, however, is Conrad's keen perception of the concomitant decline of imperial narrative that emerges so clearly in adventure novels. The exchange about "nothing" that the Giant has with his mother anticipates the "white places" of Conrad's *Heart of Darkness* in a way that extends beyond the "once-inspirational white space" Marlow invokes as his child-hood stimulus for imperial voyaging. For in the threadbare quality of British imperial narrative that registers so clearly in late Arctic narratives—fictional and nonfictional—we can begin to discern the gloom of the "dark places of the earth" that Conrad identifies with Roman Britain and the descending twilight of British imperialism. By century's end, the promise of "unspotted snow" as an Arctic space in which a triumphant British imperial masculinity could realize itself had been foreclosed.

NOTES

CHAPTER ONE. HEART OF WHITENESS

1. Joseph Conrad, *Heart of Darkness* (Oxford: Oxford Classics, 2002), 104. Text references are to page numbers of this edition.

2. L. P. Kirwan, *A History of Arctic Exploration* (New York: W. W. Norton, 1960), 161.

3. Francis Spufford and Robert G. David explore the cultural ramifications of Arctic exploration. *I May Be Sometime: Ice and the English Imagination* (London: Faber and Faber, 1996); *The Arctic in the British Imagination, 1818–1914* (Manchester: Manchester University Press, 2000). Eric G. Wilson documents the metaphorics and poetics made available to Romantics through new understandings of the science of ice, as well as the imaginative possibilities of the empty poles. *The Spiritual History of Ice: Romanticism, Science, and the Imagination.* (New York: Palgrave Macmillan, 2003). Tim Fulford, Debbie Lee, and Peter Kitson in *Literature, Science, and Exploration in the Romantic Era* (Cambridge: Cambridge University Press, 2004) document more fully the relations between science, geography, and Romantic culture, and specifically address polar geography and science in chapter 7, "Theories of Terrestrial Magnetism and the Search for the Poles," 149–78.

4. Ian Baucom, *Out of Place* (Princeton: Princeton University Press, 1999), 4.

5. For this chronology of empire, see Catherine Hall, "Of Gender and Empire: Reflections on the Nineteenth Century," in *Gender and Empire*, ed. Phillipa Levine (Oxford: Oxford University Press, 2004), 48.

6. *The Times*, quoting John Rae, (24 October 1854).

7. Gary Kelly, *Women, Writing, and Revolution 1790–1827* (Oxford: Clarendon Press, 1993), 177–78.

8. The distinction between British and English is at times difficult to sustain: some nineteenth-century English writers use them interchangeably; modern critics often use "British" to speak of either a Four Nations identity *or* an imperial identity and "English" to speak of dominant, metropolitan identities. Indeed, as Arjun Appadurai points out, "Englishness" defines itself both as Britishness (in the sense of imperial identity) and as different from the larger Empire. See Arjun Appadurai, "Sovereignty without Territoriality: Notes for a Postnational Geography," in *The Geography of Identity*, ed. Patricia Yaeger (Ann Arbor: University of Michigan Press, 1996), 48. For the purposes of my argument, which seeks in part to show how a form of national identity produced elsewhere was important to domestic identity, and to reveal how that identity was in turn used in imperial projects, I employ British. While I agree with others that the identification of the ruling class and dominant culture with "England" made Englishness often elide or trump Britishness, I am interested in how extraterritorial space was useful to enlarging—or limiting in some cases—that identity. Certainly in Charles Dickens's discussion of Franklin's disappearance, he is arguing for "English" identity as a basis for a larger stable "British" identity (see chapter 5).

9. See Alan Bewell, *Romanticism and Colonial Disease* (Baltimore: Johns Hopkins University Press, 1999).

10. Mary Shelley, *Frankenstein*, ed. Johanna M. Smith (New York: Bedford Books of St. Martin's Press, 1992), 26, 29. Text references are to pages in this edition.

11. Mary-Louise Pratt, *Imperial Eyes: Travel Writing and Transculturation* (New York: Routledge, 1992), 5.

12. From *Advice to an Author*. Quoted in Ray W. Frantz, *The English Traveller and the Movement of Ideas, 1660–1732* (New York: Octagon Books, 1968), 8. See also Phillip Edwards, *The Story of the Voyage* (New York: Cambridge University Press, 1994), 7, 139–40.

13. Henry Morley, *Household Words* 8 (1853), 241. "Unspotted Snow" was the leading article in Charles Dickens's *Household Words*, November 12, 1853. 8: 241–46. Text references are to pages in this issue.

14. The native groups who inhabit the polar north were collectively known to nineteenth-century Britons as Eskimaux, or Eskimos. The largest groups call themselves Inupiat or Yupik in the Alaskan Northwest and in the Bering Strait and Inuit in the Canadian North

and Greenland. While they shared wilderness and water skills and some social and cultural traditions, groups had distinct garments, facial tattooing, and social customs. In encounters with British whalers and explorers, however, these differences were overlooked, as evidenced in the collapse of many different groups into "Esquimaux." Perhaps paradoxically, in order to recognize the diversity of different Arctic populations, where I cannot be certain of their affiliations in my argument, I refer to them rather generically as "natives." I employ Esquimaux or Eskimo on occasions where I am discussing metropolitan constructions or perceptions of these cultures.

Native social organization was not easily understood by nineteenth-century explorers. Eric Cheyfitz's analysis of European epistemological reliance on Locke's discussion of property in native encounters may be helpful here. See: Eric Cheyfitz, *The Poetics of Imperialism: Translation and Colonization from the Tempest to Tarzan* (New York: Oxford University Press, 1991), ch. 6. Francis Spufford documents and discusses popular representations of Inuit encounter in Arctic exploration literature in "Imagining Eskimos," ch. 8 of *I May Be Sometime.*

15. Lauren Berlant, *The Anatomy of National Fantasy: Hawthorne, Utopia, and Everyday Life* (Chicago: University of Chicago Press, 1991), 4, 19. Elizabeth Helsinger, *Rural Scenes and National Representation: Britain 1815–1850* (Princeton: Princeton University Press, 1997), 11; Helsinger expands this definition to include "cultural institutions and traditional, habitual practices and rituals, images and representations, narratives, and modes of narration."

16. Benedict Anderson, *Imagined Communities: Reflections on the Origin and Spread of Nationalism* (New York: Verso, 1991), 6. Raphael Samuel goes even farther: "The idea of the nation, though a potent one, belongs to the realm of the imaginary rather than the real. It occupies a symbolic rather than territorial space" (16). *Patriotism: The Making and Unmaking of British National Identity* (London: Routledge, 1989).

17. Antony Easthope's *Englishness and National Culture* (New York: Routledge, 1999), dismisses the persistent attachment to some idea of a "real" nation as being coextensive with an "imagined" one. Ian Baucom in *Out of Place*, attempts to assert the spatial component of national imagining in his readings of locations.

18. David Harvey, *Justice, Nature, and the Geography of Difference* (Cambridge, MA: Blackwell, 1996), 112.

19. This is not to say that Colley's influential history of British identity does not engage with geography. Indeed, one of her main

contributions is to question a narrative of Britain's history as an insular island nation. *Britons: Forging the Nation, 1707–1837* (New Haven: Yale University Press, 1992). Her primary focus, however, is on ways in which differences of language, race, gender were conceived and mobilized in order to coalesce a collective identity that then ameliorated tensions of class and local linguistic and cultural difference.

20. quoted in L. P. Kirwan, *A History of Arctic Exploration*, 158.

21. Simon Gikandi, *Maps of Englishness: Writing Identity in the Culture of Colonialism* (New York: Columbia University Press, 1996), xviii, xii.

22. The confluence of race, gender, class, nation, and empire has produced recent influential critical work that informs my approach and analysis. Representative work on the Romantic era includes *Romanticism and Colonialism, Writing and Empire, 1780–1830* (Cambridge: Cambridge University Press, 1998), edited by Tim Fulford and Peter Kitson, as well as Nigel Leask's *British Romantic Writers and the East: Anxieties of Empire* (Cambridge: Cambridge University Press, 1992). Influential texts concerning the later century are Patrick Brantlinger's *Rule of Darkness: British Literature and Imperialism 1830–1914* (Ithaca: Cornell University Press, 1988), Cannon Schmitt's *Alien Nation* (Philadelphia: University of Pennsylvania Press, 1997), and Jenny Sharpe's *Allegories of Empire* (Minneapolis: University of Minnesota Press, 1993), among many others. In addition to Gikandi, some works that seek to complicate the hegemonic metropole/periphery binary that informs early scholarship include Anne McClintock's *Imperial Leather: Race, Gender, and Sexuality in the Colonial Context* (New York: Routledge, 1995) and Inderpal Grewal's *Home and Harem: Nation, Gender, Empire, and the Cultures of Travel* (Durham: Duke University Press, 1996).

23. In *Making A Social Body: British Cultural Formation, 1830–1864* (Chicago: University of Chicago Press, 1995), Mary Poovey documents the movement toward abstraction in the eighteenth and nineteenth centuries, linking it to capitalism, the market, and production. Her insightful and careful history helps us understand how literary representations that rely on abstraction are also, then, related to the means of production. By revealing how modes of production enable abstraction, which in turn structures social and spatial organizations, Poovey renders yet more complex and important the relationships between the many categories—nation, empire, race, gender—addressed in this project.

24. Lisa Bloom, *Gender on Ice* (Minneapolis: University of Minnesota Press, 1993), 2, 3.

25. Trevor Levere's careful examination of science, exploration, and the Canadian Arctic shows how Arctic exploration (and by extension other forms of exploration used for imperial expansion) both relied on and developed new technologies. *Science and the Canadian Arctic: A Century of Exploration, 1818–1918* (Cambridge: Cambridge University Press, 1993).

26. Felicity Nussbaum's *Torrid Zones* (Baltimore: Johns Hopkins University Press, 1995) argues convincingly for the link between these categories, linking the "invention of the 'other' woman of empire" to "the consolidation of the cult of domesticity in England." She solidifies the connection between the two by arguing that at the same time, colonial expansion demanded reproduction by women at home (1).

27. Parry was second-in-command to Sir John Ross. While John Franklin mapped the seacoast by land, Ross and Parry captained ships seeking both a Northwest Passage and magnetic north. Tim Fulford, Debbie Lee, and Peter Kitson discuss Ross and the quest for magnetic north more fully in *Literature, Science, and Exploration,* ch. 7. Although Ross commanded the sea portion of the 1819 expeditions, Parry's expedition account, *Journal of a voyage for the discovery of a north-west passage from the Atlantic to the Pacific: perfomed in the years, 1819–20* (London: John Murray, 1821), like Franklin's, became a bestseller.

28. Spufford argues that the feminizing demands the Arctic made on explorers enabled women at home to be more invested in their endeavors than they were in other forms of imperial exploration. *I May Be Sometime,* 101–103.

29. Quoted in Spufford, *I May Be Sometime,* 125.

30. Ibid., 126.

31. Clements R. Markham, *Franklin's Footsteps; a sketch of Greenland, along the shores of which his expedition passed, and of the Parry Isles, where the last traces of it were found* (London: Chapman and Hall, 1853), 60. Eric Wilson documents the prismatic optics of ice in *Spiritual History,* 15 and following.

32. In eerie coincidence, the name of the man who finally completes the Northwest Passage echoes that of the Antarctic-seeking protagonist of Edgar Allan Poe's 1838 *The Narrative of Arthur Gordon Pym.*

33. R. Browne, review of *Yachting in the Arctic Seas,* by James Lamont, 1876. *Appleton's Journal of Literature, Science, and Art* 15 (1876): 385.

34. John Tillotson, *Adventures in the Ice* (London: James Hogg and Son, 1869), 276.

35. Joseph Conrad, "Geography and Explorers," in *Last Essays* (New York: J. M. Dent and Sons, 1926), 11. Text references are to this edition.

36. Douglas Hewitt also reads Franklin's presence in the novel as evidence of a cannibal subtext. See "'Heart of Darkness' and Some 'Old Unpleasant Reports,'" *The Review of English Studies* new series 38, no. 151: 374–76. See also Diana Ben-Merre, "Conrad's Marlow and Britain's Franklin: Redoubling the Narrative in *Heart of Darkness*," *Conradiana* 34, no. 3 (Fall 2002): 211–26.

37. Conrad's choice of "militant" is an interesting one, chosen perhaps in order to capture the relationship he saw between explorer and land in which mapping the unknown is a form of conquering. See Conrad, "Geography and Explorers," 6–12. See Felix Driver, "Geography Triumphant? Joseph Conrad and the Imperial Adventure," *The Conradian* 18, no. 2 (1994): 103–11 and *Geography Militant: Cultures of Exploration and Empire* (Oxford: Blackwell Publishers, 2001), passim.

38. I share with Benita Parry and others the conviction that Conrad's text employs conventional imperial imagery, tropes, and assumptions in order to interrogate and critique imperialism. See Parry, *Conrad and Imperialism: Ideological Boundaries and Visionary Frontiers* (London: Macmillan, 1989), introduction. Bill Ashcroft, Gareth Griffiths, and Helen Tiffin outline the links between imperialism and modernism in *The Empire Writes Back: Theory and Practice in Post-Colonial Literatures* (London: Routledge, 1989), 156–60.

39. Conrad, *Heart of Darkness*, 105. Joseph Bristow discusses the importance of this passage to understanding Conrad's narrative technique in *Empire Boys: Adventures in a Man's World* (London: HarperCollinsAcademic, 1991), 154–66. Ian Watt links Marlow's model of narrative to Impressionism. Ian Watt, *Conrad in the Nineteenth Century* (Berkeley: University of California Press, 1979), 170.

40. Conrad, "Geography," 12. *The Voyage of the Fox* was the account of McClintock's unsuccessful expedition in search of Sir John Franklin. Andrea White documents McClintock's relation to Lady Jane Franklin, and reads Marlow's mission to rescue Kurtz as a rewriting of idealized searches for Franklin. *Joseph Conrad and the Adventure Tradition: Constructing and Deconstructing the Imperial Subject*, (Cambridge: Cambridge University Press, 1993), 18–23 and 190–91.

41. Marlow's "lie" to the "Intended" about Kurtz's last words—the substitution of her name for "The horror! the horror!"—reveals that her clean, white, complacent metropolitan remove from Kurtz's world is implicated in if not central to that horror (186).

42. See John Tierney, "Explornography," *New York Times Magazine*, July 26, 1998.

CHAPTER TWO. NATIONAL BODIES

1. For example, as Tim Fulford documents in "Races, places, peoples, 1800–30," an introductory essay to Fulford and Peter J. Kitson's *Romanticism and Colonialism*, Anna Letitia Barbauld's 1791 *Epistle to William Wilberforce, Esq.* conceives of the East "as an infectious and sybaritic luxury which corrupted and feminized civilizations and encouraged despotism" (44). In the same volume, similar arguments are forwarded about Mary Shelley by Joseph W. Lew and the Jamaican journals of M. G. Lewis by D. L. MacDonald. Fulford and Kitson's volume seeks to understand the mutually constitutive and possibly subversive relations between Romantic cultural productions and colonialism. Alan Bewell's *Romanticism and Colonial Disease* discusses how disease structured metropolitan understandings of tropical colonies. In part, this chapter seeks to extend what Fulford labels the "complex geo-political imaginary" of Romanticism (47), and in doing so extend the mapping of what Nigel Leask has labeled "the anxieties of empire" (*British Romantic Writers and the East*, 6–12). Thus, the Arctic origin of Nelson's national masculinity that is a focus of this chapter also reinforces and extends Tim Fulford's compelling argument in "Romanticizing the Empire: The Naval Heroes of Southey, Coleridge, Austen, and Marryat," *Modern Language Quarterly* 60, no. 2 (1999): 161–96, that Southey's *Life of Nelson* and the public's subsequent understanding of the hero are linked to orientalist fears of the effeminizing effects of colonialization on the court aristocracy.

2. John Tosh has argued that a male interiority that matched a male exterior was a newly emergent model of masculinity in the late eighteenth and early nineteenth centuries in "The Old Adam and the New Man: Emerging Themes in the History of English Masculinities, 1750–1850," in *Manliness and Masculinities in Nineteenth-Century Britain*, ed. Michael Roper and John Tosh (New York: Routledge, 2005). I do not wish to claim that the model discussed in this chapter is the only model of masculinity in circulation at the time. For discussions of other forms of Romantic masculinity see Anne K. Mellor's *Romanticism and Gender* (New York: Routledge, 1993) and Marlon Ross's *The Contours of Masculine Desire: Romanticism and the Rise of Women's Poetry* (Oxford:

Oxford University Press, 1989). See also Ellen Brinks, *Gothic Masculinity: Effeminacy and the Supernatural in English and German Romanticism* (Lewisburg, PA: Bucknell University Press, 2003) and Charles Donelan, *Romanticism and Male Fantasy in Byron's Don Juan* (New York: St Martin's Press, 2000).

Although one focus of this argument is to define a specific masculine national subject and to discuss that subject's importance to and deployment in perpetuating a national and imperial ideal and practice, I do not wish to suggest the absence or unimportance of women in these discourses. Rohan McWilliam has argued that "citizenship was defined in male terms during the [nineteenth] century," but just as clearly women participated in national imaginings and politics, as I discuss in the following two chapters. Rohan McWilliam, *Popular Politics in Nineteenth-Century England* (New York: Routledge, 1998), 99.

3. In the introduction to *Imagined Communities*, Anderson defines the nation as "imagined" and "limited," and as " a community . . . always conceived of as a deep, horizontal comradeship." Benedict Anderson, *Imagined Communities*, 7.

4. While Linda Colley argues this in detail in *Britons*, her article "Britishness and Otherness: An Argument," *Journal of British Studies* 31 (1992): 309–29, argues this most concisely. See also Eric Hobsbawm, *Nations and Nationalism since 1780* (New York: Cambridge University Press, 1990), 91.

5. Arctic space in the nineteenth century was persistently read as uninhabited and empty despite ample evidence to the contrary in expedition accounts. This misreading only serves to underline how pervasively and persuasively broader national and imperial practices and ideologies structured the experience and representations of the Arctic. Erica Behrisch addresses the political effect of this persistent misapprehension on representations of native peoples in the mid and late nineteenth century in her dissertation "Voices of Silence, Texts of Truth: Imperial Discourse and Cultural Negotiations in Nineteenth-Century British Arctic Exploration Narrative." PhD diss., Queen's University, 2002.

6. Etienne Balibar and Immanuel Wallerstein, *Race, Nation, Class. Ambiguous Identities* (New York: Verso, 1991), 93.

7. In separating patriotism from nationalism, I am following the lead of Gerald Newman, *The Rise of English Nationalism: A Cultural History, 1740–1830* (New York: St. Martin's Press, 1997), 52; Newman is careful to point out the differences between patriotism and nationalism.

He defines patriotism as a less organized, more generalized affiliation with and affection for a homeland or locality that nationalism recruits and transforms into coherent ideology. In the early 1800s however, "patriotism" often was used to describe what we now define as nationalism, as specific national identities and subjects emerged. As David Eastwood's work on Southey, as well as his article "The Age of Uncertainty: Britain in the Early-Nineteenth Century," makes clear, these categories were unstable, and as a result these categories and terms occasionally merge in this chapter. *Transactions of the Royal Historical Society* 8, no. 2 (1998): 91–115.

8. David Eastwood, "Robert Southey and the Meanings of Patriotism," *Journal of British Studies* 31 (July 1992): 282.

9. Robert Southey, *The Life of Nelson* (London: Cassell, 1909), 16. Text references are to page numbers of this edition.

10. Tim Fulford explores the metonymy between British oaks, ships, and sailors in "Romanticizing the Empire." Laura Brown's work on Alexander Pope's *Windsor Forest* points to a longer tradition of such representational practice, reading the British oak, transformed into merchant and naval ships, as the linchpin between domestic spaces and imperial practices. *Ends of Empire: Women and Ideology in Early Eighteenth-Century English Literature* (Ithaca: Cornell University Press, 1993), chapter 4, "Capitalizing on Women: Dress, Aesthetics, and Alexander Pope," 103–34.

11. Hudson Bay, the site of the mutiny that took place in 1611, gave its name to one of the largest trade monopolies in England in the nineteenth century, the Hudson's Bay Company. The HBC, in turn, supported and sponsored Britain's Arctic exploration, although in an uneasy relationship with the Admiralty. See Robert David's *The Arctic in the British Imagination 1818–1914* for a more complete account of this relationship.

12. The "brave and loyal carpenter" who chose to stay with Hudson although he could have been granted safe passage back to England became an icon of self-sacrifice in the nineteenth century, evidenced by his use as an example in Samuel Smiles's mid-century *Duty* (Chicago: Belford, Clark and Co., 1881), 116.

13. While Nelson sailed on Captain Lutwidge's *Carcass*, Olaudah Equiano accompanied John Constantine Phipps on the *Race Horse*. In service to the ship's doctor, Equiano worked on water desalination and distilling, and writes of the difficulty of a black servant finding quarters on an Arctic expedition ship stuffed with provisions. He describes the

sensation of being caught in the ice pack for almost three weeks as one of "constant apprehension" of "perishing in the ice" (133). He also documents their escape from the pack by alternately towing and dragging their ships along the edge of the ice toward open water; Southey has the young Nelson play an important role in this rescue. *The Interesting Narrative of the Life of Olaudah Equiano* (New York: Bedford Books of St. Martin's Press, 2001), 131–34.

14. Joseph Rouse discusses the relationship between scientific sites and discursive practice in *Knowledge and Power: Toward a Political Philosophy of Science* (Ithaca: Cornell University Press, 1987). See also Mary-Louise Pratt, *Imperial Eyes* and Fulford, Lee, and Kitson, *Literature, Science, and Exploration.*

15. Southey lifts his descriptions of the Arctic almost word for word from Phipps.

16. See Eric Wilson's discussion of ice and optics in *The Spiritual History of Ice*, pages 15 and following. For discussions of particular ways in which Arctic geography and climate made demands on British explorers, see Francis Spufford, *I May Be Sometime: Ice and the English Imagination*, chapters 2 and 7. See also Christy Collis, "Vertical Body/Horizontal World: Sir John Franklin and Fictions of Arctic Space," in *The Body in the Library*, ed. Leigh Dale and Simon Ryan (Atlanta: Rodopi, 1998): 225–36. Trevor Levere, *Science and the Canadian Arctic. A Century of Exploration 1818–1918*; John Moss, *Patterns of Isolation in English Canadian Fiction* (Toronto: University of Toronto Press, 1974); and Ian MacLaren, "Exploration/Travel Literature and the Evolution of the Author," *International Journal of Canadian Studies* 5 (1992): 39–68.

17. See Chauncey C. Loomis, "The Arctic Sublime" in *Nature and the Victorian Imagination*, ed. U. C. Knoepflmacher and G. B. Tennyson (Berkeley: University of California Press, 1977): 95–114. See also Francis Spufford, *I May Be Sometime*, 30–36.

18. Edward Trelawney, a friend of Byron and the author of the autobiographical *Adventures of a Younger Son* (London: T. Fisher Unwin, 1823), critiqued just such a model of patriarchal discipline when he described a privateer captain as one who "became [his] friend in its true sense, and ever after treated [him] as such, so that if fathers followed his example, we should have less of that eternal and mawkish cant about filial disobedience, dull as it is false, spawned on society by dry and drawling priests, and incubated by the barren sect of mouldy, soddened blues" (116).

19. The same skills and qualities that define British heroic masculinity establish its central paradox: while "heroism" is the constellation of certain identifiable qualities around an exemplary public self, obedience and "duty" demand selflessness.

20. So effective was Southey's model of naval and national disciplinary patriarchy, that it continued its influence through the century, evidenced when Queen Victoria, having read Southey's *Life*, used the young Nelson as an example when she instituted a prize for "marine boys" that recognized the disciplinary component of naval life by rewarding "cheerful submission to superiors, self-respect and independence of character, kindness and protection to the weak, readiness to forgive offence, a desire to conciliate the differences of others, and, above all, fearless devotion to duty and unflinching truthfulness." Queen Victoria, quoted in Smiles, *Duty*, 116.

21. As reported by Southey at least (218). In 1881, Samuel Smiles recorded Nelson's last words in his bestselling *Duty* as, "I have done my duty: I praise God for it!" (158).

22. In chapter 10 of *Imperial Leather*, Anne McClintock reveals how the logic of the fetish structures nationalism.

23. See Paul Youngquist's discussion of patriotic bodies and missing limbs, 161–90 in *Monstrosities: Bodies and British Romanticism* (Minneapolis: University of Minnesota Press, 2003). See also Alan Bewell on colonial military disease narratives in *Romanticism and Colonial Disease*, 66–130.

24. Franklin was one of only seven on his ship not wounded or killed in the battle that followed.

25. Letter quoted in L. P. Kirwan, *A History of Arctic Exploration*, 160.

26. Not only did Franklin's journey take place on land in the Canadian north, but he was searching for a navigable Northwest Passage, whereas the object of the Phipps expedition was a North*east* Passage along the coast of Russia. It is Phipps's voyage that underlies the fictional narrative of Walton in Mary Shelley's *Frankenstein*.

27. Quoted in Edwards, *The Story of the Voyage*, 49. This was a long-standing jibe aimed at producers of travel narrative; Swift famously mocked Defoe on the same grounds, while in *Gulliver's Travels* he satirized the genre.

28. Neil Smith and Cindi Katz, "Grounding Metaphor: Towards a Spatialized Politics," in *Space and the Politics of Identity*, ed. Michael Keith and Steve Pile (London: Routledge, 1993), p. 69.

29. John Franklin, *Narrative of a Journey to the Shores of the Polar Sea in The Years 1819, 20, 21, and 22* (Rutland, VT: Charles E. Tuttle, 1970), 39. Text references that follow are to page numbers of this edition.

30. Quoted in Maggie Kilgour, *The Rise of the Gothic Novel* (New York: Routledge, 1995), 30. Frances Ferguson's *Solitude and the Sublime: Romanticism and the Aesthetics of Individuation* (New York: Routledge, 1992) contains a chapter on travel writing and its deployment of the picturesque in which she discusses various strategies for "supplying" the "middle distance" necessary to picturesque travel (139). For Ferguson's Gilpin-carrying tourist, the picturesque located the viewer by making him or her the framing mechanism. For Franklin, the Arctic sublime locates him uncomfortably and precariously in the foreground.

31. The precarious position of the explorer was not limited to Arctic explorers. See Nigel Leask's "'Wandering through Eblis'; Absorption and Containment in Romantic Exoticism" in *Romanticism and Colonialism, Writing and Empire, 1780–1830*, ed. Tim Fulford and Peter J. Kitson, 165–88, for an account of other strategies for resisting the absorptive pull of the "oriental."

32. Precisely because cannibalism is often used to determine and pathologize cultural difference, a veritable "cannibal industry" developed in academe in the 1990s. For William Arens in his early anthropological work on cannibalism, *The Man-Eating Myth* (New York: Oxford University Press, 1979), the discourse of cannibalism necessarily casts the cannibal into another time—that of the "civilized" culture's past. Peter Hulme, "Introduction: The Cannibal Scene," in *Cannibalism and the Colonial World*, ed. Francis Barker, Peter Hulme, and Margaret Iverson (New York: Cambridge University Press, 1998), describes the "role of the cannibal as a means of boundary definition in the construction of modern Western identity." Hulme shows how the "newly defined cannibal served both as a foil for the emerging modern subject, and, conveniently, as a legitimization of cultural appropriation. . . . While serving thus as a mirror to the European subject, the cannibal threatened to swallow it, both literally, and also through representing the danger of Conquest was thus justified by the law of the jungle: eat or be eaten" (242–43). That the process of cannibalizing the cannibal necessarily implicates "civilized" culture in the economy of cannibalism is not lost on Arens, Hulme, or Maggie Kilgour. Kilgour, in *From Communion to Cannibalism: Metaphors of Incorporation* (Princeton: Princeton University Press, 1990, 1998), identifies the threatening nature of cannibalism in its

literalization of the mechanics of empire: by reducing humans to "mere" matter, cannibalism erases the very difference it hopes to demarcate. Chapter 5 discusses more completely the relation of cannibalism, the Arctic, and national identity.

33. Indeed, his status as a popular hero made some see him as overqualified, including Rugby headmaster and famed molder of men Thomas Arnold, who wrote to congratulate him, "I am not sure, however, how far this appointment may be a subject of congratulation to yourself, as I am sure that it is to the settlement and to the public service." G. F. Lamb, *Franklin, Happy Voyager* (London: Ernest Benn, Limited, 1956), 187.

34. Franklin's mishaps were many. To begin with, Captain Alexander Maconochie, Franklin's first secretary, wrote and posted an inflammatory account of the penitentiary that read in the press like an indictment of Franklin's governance on the colony. Then, John Montague, an assistant to the governor, perpetrated rumors about Franklin's incompetence—including the "overinfluence" of his wife, Lady Jane—in the press and in the Colonial Office on a lengthy visit to England. Montague was eventually dismissed, but not before gaining popular support of his views. See Lamb, *Franklin*, 187–204.

35. Jane Cracroft Franklin was Franklin's second wife. His first, the Romantic poet Eleanor Anne Porden, died of consumption just days after Franklin embarked on his second Arctic exploration mission. Lady Jane was the aunt of Tennyson's wife.

36. Lady Jane, quoted in Kirwan, *History of Arctic Exploration*, 246.

CHAPTER THREE. A PROPITIOUS HARD FROST

1. See Charles E. Robinson, *The Frankenstein Notebooks* (New York: Garland Publishing, 1996), xxv–xxvi. See also Jessica Richard, "'A Paradise of My Own Creation': *Frankenstein* and the Improbable Romance of Polar Exploration," *Nineteenth-Century Contexts* 25, no. 4 (2003): n. 6, 309.

2. The Records Office of the Derbyshire County Council house many of Eleanor Porden's manuscripts and journals, as well as documentation of her life with John Franklin.

3. Gary Kelly, *Women, Writing, and Revolution*, 177. See also Anne Mellor, *Mothers of the Nation: Women's Political Writing in England,*

1780–1830 (Bloomington: University of Indiana Press, 2000). Tricia Lootens documents women's poetry and nation in "Hemans and Her American Heirs: Nineteenth-Century Women's Poetry and National Identity," in *Women's Poetry, Late Romantic to Late Victorian: Gender and Genre. 1830–1900*, ed. Isobel Armstrong and Virginia Blain (New York: Macmillan-St Martin's, 1999), 243–60.

4. Patricia Meyer Spacks, "Reflecting Women," *Yale Review* 63 (Autumn 1973): 27–30. Many critics have since complicated Spacks's argument. See, for example, Stuart Curran, "Mothers and Daughters: Poetic Generation(s) in the Eighteenth and Nineteenth Centuries," in *Forging Connections:Women's Poetry from the Renaissance to Romanticism*, ed. Anne Mellor, Felicity Nussbaum, Jonathan Post (San Marino, CA: Huntington Library, 2002), 147–62.

5. George Levine, *The Realistic Imagination* (Chicago: University of Chicago Press, 1981), 25.

6. This substitution augments rather than replaces Levine's assertions about realism, as critics who link the rise of realism to the rise of nation suggest.

7. Work on the Arctic frame of the novel includes Jessica Richard's careful and insightful historicization of the Arctic frame of the novel, "'A Paradise of My Own Creation': *Frankenstein* and the Improbable Romance of Polar Exploration," 295–314. See also Andrew Griffin's discussion of heat and cold in *Frankenstein's* poetics in "Fire and Ice," in *The Endurance of Frankenstein*, ed. George Levine and U. C. Knopflmacher (Berkeley: University of California Press, 1979), 49–73, as well as Francis Spufford, *I May Be Sometime: Ice and the English Imagination*, 58–62.

8. Peter Brooks, "'God-like Science/Unhallowed Arts': Language, Nature, and Monstrosity in *Frankenstein*" in *The Endurance of Frankenstein*, 219–20.

9. John Barrow, *A chronological history of voyages into the Arctic regions [microform]: undertaken chiefly for the purpose of discovering a north-east, north-west, or polar passage between the Atlantic and Pacific* (London: John Murray, 1818), 364.

10. Jessica Richard points out that it is "difficult to read Walton sympathetically" when we understand him as also a participant in the very scientific projects that Shelley critiques, and further links Walton's exploration to "perils" that Shelley sees "in other arts of creation" ("Paradise," 296). For discussions of Romantic enthusiasm and science, see also Anne Mellor's influential argument about masculinist science in the

text, "A Feminist Critique of Science," in *One Culture: Essays in Science and Literature*, ed. George Levine (Madison: University of Wisconsin Press, 1987), 287–312; Alan Rauch, *Useful Knowledge* (Durham: Duke University Press, 2001), 96–128.

11. For further discussion of this impulse, see *Romanticism and Colonialism, Writing and Empire, 1780–1830*, and in particular Nigel Leask's "'Wandering through Eblis." See Saree Makdisi's introduction to *Romantic Imperialism: Universal Empire and the Culture of Modernity* (Cambridge: Cambridge University Press, 1998).

12. Mary Shelley, *Frankenstein*, 26.

13. Paul McInerney, *Time and Experience* (Philadelphia: Temple University Press, 1991). As McInerney understands it, "Walton's passion to discover a scene for original exploration is outweighed and predicted by his frustrated search for authorial ability and a scene of writing" (461). McInerney is one of few critics to pay close attention to Walton and understands Walton's purpose in the novel as being an essential part of Shelley's thematization of writing as a creative act.

14. Fred Randel, in "The Political Geography of Horror in Mary Shelley's *Frankenstein*," *ELH* 70 (2003): 465–91, maps the novel's engagement with the geopolitical and particularly with racial and colonial domination in its engagement with Ireland; see 482–85. See also Anne Mellor, "*Frankenstein*, Racial Science, and the Yellow Peril," *Nineteenth-Century Contexts* 23 (2001): 1–28.

15. Eric Daffron and James Holt McGavran both document male friendship, homosociality, and male desire in the novel. Eric Daffron, "Male Bonding: Sympathy and Shelley's *Frankenstein*," *Nineteenth-Century Contexts* 21, no. 3 (1999): 415–35. James Holt McGavran, "'Insurmountable Barriers to Our Union': Homosocial Male Bonding, Homosexual Panic, and Death on the Ice in *Frankenstein*," *European Romantic Review* 11, no. 1 (Winter 2000): 46–67.

16. For more on Promethean science, see George Levine, "The Ambiguous Heritage of *Frankenstein*," in *The Endurance of Frankenstein*. See also Francis Spufford, *I May Be Sometime: Ice and the English Imagination*, 59–60.

17. See Anca Vlasopolos, "*Frankenstein's* Hidden Skeleton: The Psycho-Politics of Oppression," *Science-Fiction Studies* 10, no. 2 (1983): 126, 40.

18. Fred Randel reads the English sections of the novel as Shelley's rumination on English political history. See "Political Geography," 476–80.

19. For larger discussion of women's participation in the public sphere via writing and political engagement, see the work of Anne Mellor, including *Mothers of the Nation, Romanticism and Gender*. See also Devoney Looser *British Women Writers and the Writing of History* (Baltimore: Johns Hopkins University Press, 2000); Linkin Harriet Kramer and Stephen C. Behrendt, eds., *Romanticism and Women Poets* (Lexington: The University Press of Kentucky, 1999). Gender relations in the nineteenth century took the form of what Sylvia Walby terms "private patriarchy" (243). *Theorizing Patriarchy* (Oxford: B. Blackwell, 1990). "That is, although some women certainly had public roles, the majority still answered to male authority, labored for their husbands or fathers, and were excluded from the public domain." See Walby's "Woman and Nation," in *Mapping the Nation*, ed. Gopal Balakrishnan (New York: Verso, 1996); Nira Yuvel-Davis and Floya Anthias, *Woman-Nation-State* (New York: St. Martin's Press, 1989). Yuval-Davis and Anthias identify five ways in which women have been implicated in nationalism. In addition to the three above, women may reproduce boundaries of national groups through marital restrictions, or may actively participate in national struggles.

20. See Johanna Smith, *Mary Shelley* (New York: Twayne, 1996), 178–79; Kate Ferguson Ellis, *The Contested Castle: Gothic Novels and the Subversion of Domestic Ideology* (Urbana: University of Illinois Press, 1989), 123–26.

21. While suttee was not banned in the colonial Bengal Code, there exist numerous petitions and addresses on the practice of suttee dated between 1818 and 1831. The creature's death as suttee has been noted by Jaqueline Labbe in "A Monstrous Fiction: *Frankenstein* and the Wifely Ideal," *Women's Writing* 6, no. 3 (1999): 345–63, and by Elizabeth Bohls in *Women Travel Writers and the Language of Aesthetics, 1716–1818* (Cambridge: Cambridge University Press, 1995). For a critical history of the practice, see Mani Lata's "Contentious Traditions: The Debate on Sati in Colonial India." *Cultural Critique* 7 (1987): 119–56.

22. Gayatri Spivak, "Can the Subaltern Speak?" in *Marxism and the Interpretation of Culture*, ed. Cary Nelson and Lawrence Grossberg (Urbana: University of Illinois Press, 1988), 297.

23. From the preface dated March 31, 1818: "The following lines were prompted by a visit to His Majesty's ships the Alexander and Isabella, lying at Deptford, on Monday the 30th instant. The objects of the expeditions of which these vessels form a part, the dangers they may have to encounter, and their prospects of success, have been made so

familiar to every one by the very able and delightful article in the last Quarterly Review, and the disquisitions to which it has given rise, that any details are unnecessary. The prayers of science and humanity will attend the voyagers on their way, and whatever may be their success, the historian and the bard will find pleasure in recording it. Should this short and hasty effusion (not originally intended for the public eye) meet with the indulgence shewn to a former work, it is possible that I may then resume the theme."

24. Eleanor Anne Porden, *The Arctic Expeditions: a poem* (London: John Murray, 1818), ll. 1–5. Text references are to line and page numbers of this edition.

25. Pope also used the Arctic in his 1715 *Temple of Fame.*

26. Porden may have been disingenuous when she claimed the loss of the veil a "trifling incident." The mock-medieval setting of the poem may reveal her familiarity with the early modern trope of the lost or torn-away veil as the search for or encounter with knowledge.

27. Eleanor Anne Porden, *The Veils; or The Triumph of Constancy* (London: John Murray, 1815), Book I, ll. 893–94. Text references are to page numbers of this edition.

28. Porden, *The Veils*, Book IV, l. 5, n. page 152.

29. See Laura Brown, *Ends of Empire*, chapter 4, "Capitalizing on Women: Dress, Aesthetics, and Alexander Pope," 103–34.

30. On the idea of a polar vortex, see Fulford, Lee, and Kitson, *Literature, Science, and Exploration*, 160–61. See also Victoria Nelson, *The Secret Life of Puppets* (Cambridge: Harvard University Press, 2002), chapter 6; Francis Spufford *I May Be Sometime*, 67–70.

31. E. M. Gell's biography of Porden, *John Franklin's Bride: Eleanor Anne Porden* (London: John Murray, 1930), reprints a selection of Porden's unpublished letters and uncollected poetry. Text references to Porden's correspondence are to page numbers of this edition. Porden's daughter with Franklin, also named Eleanor, married Philip Gell. E. M. Gell was the wife of their son or Eleanor Porden's granddaughter-in-law.

32. She recognizes that her independence of spirit is at least in part due to her financial independence in the concluding paragraph of her letter. "For some months I have endeavoured that you should see my character, good or bad, as unreservedly as possible. If you have liked what I really am, if a sincere attachment to yourself, and an earnest wish to render towards you the attention and the duty of an affectionate wife, be sufficient to make you happy, I am willing to be yours. But you must not

expect me to change my nature. I am seven and twenty, an age after which woman alters little, and I, who have been almost uncontrolled mistress of a family for half that period, am even older than my years. If on the contrary you find that your imagination has sketched a false portrait of me, that your feelings are changed, or, no matter what the cause, that you have taken a rash and inconsiderate step, do not hesitate to tell me so" (111–12).

33. Mary Poovey, *The Proper Lady and the Woman Writer* (Chicago: University of Chicago Press, 1984), 35.

34. Public interest in the Arctic was avid following Franklin's return from his 1819 mission. Porden wrote Franklin on May 22, 1822: "Mr. Bullock has been exhibiting for some months a family of Laplanders, and a herd of reindeer, fed on Lapland moss, from Bagshot Heath. They have been unlucky in their visit, for like the Greenlander who wintered at Copenhagen, they could find no reasonable degree of cold. When I went to see them in February, the heat was almost suffocating." She continues, "The Panorama of Spitzbergen has been converted into the Bay of Naples—and your portrait, which you were so proud of, is swallowed up in Mount Vesuvius" (Gell, *John Franklin's Bride*, 57).

35. Of course any representation of a place necessarily cannot be "wholly original." As Karen Lawrence observes in *Penelope Voyages: Women and Travel in the British Literary Tradition* (Ithaca: Cornell University Press, 1994), there is never "a place from which the sound of echoing footsteps is entirely absent or a scene of writing that doesn't acknowledge a previous scene" (24).

36. In a reading that focuses on "metaphors of polarity," rather than the politics of polar geography, Fulford, Lee, and Kitson read Porden's representation of the pole "as either affirming the self in a masculine, phallic, self-centeredness, or alternatively as destructive, with a feminine chasm, holding the ship in an everlasting magnetic suspension" (169).

CHAPTER FOUR. A PALE BLANK OF MIST AND CLOUD

1. Karen Chase, "Jane Eyre's Interior Design," in *New Casebooks: Jane Eyre*, ed. Heather Glen (New York: St. Martin's Press, 1997), 52.

2. Charlotte Brontë, *Jane Eyre* (New York: Penguin, 1985), 39. Text references are to page numbers of this edition.

3. Indeed, *Jane Eyre* has been for many *the* literary text with which to make arguments about Victorian colonialism and imperialism. Argu-

ments that the novel is complicit in imperialism include Gayatri Spivak's "Three Women's Texts and a Critique of Imperialism," *Critical Inquiry* 12 (1985): 243–61, Firdous Azim's *The Colonial Rise of the Novel* (London: Routledge, 1993), as well as Suvendrini Perera's *Reaches of Empire: The English Novel from Edgeworth to Dickens* (New York: Columbia University Press, 1991). My argument here aligns more fully with those of Deirdre David, Philip Rogers, and Jenny Sharpe, who examine contemporary colonial discourse in their arguments. David is interested in women's position in empire (*Rule Britannia: Women, Empire, and Victorian Writing* [Ithaca: Cornell University Press, 1995]), and Sharpe assesses Brontë's depiction of women's agency and writing (*Allegories of Empire: The Figure of Woman in the Colonial Text*). Philip Rogers's "'My Word Is Error:' Jane Eyre and Colonial Exculpation," *Dickens Studies Annual* 34 (2004): 329–50, convincingly reads the novel's engagement with colonial affairs as "distancing mid-century Britain from its baneful inheritance—the crime of slavery" (329) in a carefully historicized examination of representations of Jamaica, colonial citizens, and Madeira in the novel. I view my argument about Arctic space as supplementing Rogers's very fine arguments about the novel as a "reaffirm[ation of] Britain as a moral nation" in reaction to a colonial "taint," in addition to enlarging the novel's models for women's agency and subjectivity examined by David and Sharpe.

4. For representative readings, see David Lodge, "Fire and Eyre: Charlotte Brontë's War of Earthly Elements," in *Language of Fiction* (London: Routledge, 2001), and Andrew Griffin, "Fire and Ice in *Frankenstein*," 51–55. I believe these approaches to be more appropriate to Brontë's work in *Villette*, as well as Emily Brontë's use of cold and the rough Yorkshire landscape in *Wuthering Heights*.

5. See Francis Spufford, *I May Be Sometime*, 103. Spufford argues that the identification enabled by this similarity made women more interested in Arctic exploration accounts than in other accounts of colonial expansion.

6. Quoted in Susan Meyer, *Imperialism at Home: Race and Victorian Women's Fiction* (Ithaca: Cornell University Press, 1996), 47.

7. In Gaskell's autobiography of Brontë, quoted by Spufford, *I May Be Sometme*, 106.

8. The strong presence of Ross, Parry, Bonaparte, and Wellington is felt in the Brontë juvenilia. See *An Edition of the early Writings of Charlotte Brontë*, ed. Christine Alexander, 3 vols. (Oxford: Basil Blackwell, 1987–91), Juliet Barker, *The Brontës: A Life in Letters* (Woodstock, NY:

Overlook Press, 1998), and Rebecca Fraser, *The Brontës: Charlotte and Her Family* (New York: Ballantine, 1990). Philip Rogers, in "Tory Brontë: *Shirley* and the 'Man'," *Nineteenth-Century Literature* 58, no. 2 (2003): 141–75, documents the centrality of Wellington to Charlotte's mature political imagination. Susan Meyer notes in her work on the young Brontë's African stories in *Imperialism at Home*, that the territories of Charlotte's imaginary "Wellington" included "Upper Canada" (34).

9. James Thomson, *The Seasons [microform]* (Dublin: John Enslow, 1770), 178, ll. 862–70.

10. Ibid., 246, ll. 921–35.

11. Jane at Lowood is suddenly living *Gulliver's Travels*, a book she reads as "a narrative of facts," that asserts the reality of elves and fairies until her illness in the red room, whereupon she sees it as "eerie and dreary; the giants were gaunt goblins, the pigmies malevolent and fearful imps, Gulliver a most desolate wanderer in most dread and dangerous regions" (53).

12. The death of Helen Burns in Jane's embrace while, yes, the standard fare of melodrama, is also eerily evocative of a moment in John Franklin's *Journey to the Polar Sea*, in which Franklin climbs into bed with one of his men in an effort to keep him alive.

13. See Susan Meyer, *Imperialism at Home*, 171–72. For Meyer, the novel's obsession with housecleaning is an attempt to get rid of the colonial scourge and restore normal, "clean" social relations among the middle class of England. Philip Rogers develops the notion of "colonial taint" further, reading Jane as vehicle for Rochester's redemption from colonial entanglements. See "'My Word Is Error'," passim.

14. Elsie Michie illuminates Rochester's racialized "Irishness" in her chapter "'The Yahoo, Not the Demon': Heathcliff, Rochester, and the Simianization of the Irish," in *Outside the Pale : Cultural Exclusion, Gender Difference, and the Victorian Woman Writer* (Ithaca: Cornell University Press, 1993).

15. Later nineteenth century narratives cast the colonies as the proving ground of masculinity, but Brontë sees them as eroding British masculinity. See Philip Rogers, "'My Word Is Error'," for historical documentation of colonial discourse on sexual profligacy and miscegenation in Jamaica.

16. Again, there are peculiar, persistent Arctic exploration echoes here. In Franklin's *Voyage to the Polar Seas*, the expedition loses a voyageur when a canoe caroms down some rapids. In addition, the passage's echo of the native woman's suicide in Felicia Hemans's poem,

"Indian Woman's Death-Song" here solidifies the connection between distant geographies and domesticity.

17. Karen Chase, "*Jane Eyre*'s Interior Design," 63.

18. Sandra Gilbert and Susan Gubar. *Madwoman in the Attic: The Woman Writer and the Nineteenth-Century Literary Imagination* (New Haven: Yale University Press, 1979), 367.

19. In this I follow Philip Rogers's argument in "My Word Is Error."

20. George Back was the expedition artist on Franklin's first voyage. Quoted in Leslie Neatby, *The Search for Franklin* (New York: Walker and Company, 1970), 80.

21. Alan Bewell bases a similar conclusion on his reading of disease, Irishness, and colonialization in the novel: "*Jane Eyre* would seem to suggest that England, in colonizing the world, had succeeded in transforming itself into a colonial environment, as much in need of curing as any other region of the world" (802). "*Jane Eyre* and Victorian Medical Geography," *ELH* 63, no. 3 (Fall 1996): 773–808.

22. Jenny Sharpe, "The Rise of Women in an Age of Progress: *Jane Eyre*" in *Allegories of Empire*, 27–56.

23. Spivak, "Three Women's Texts," 246–47.

CHAPTER FIVE. ARCTIC HIGHLANDS AND ENGLISHMEN

1. Cited by Richard Altick in his study of popular reading and Victorian print culture, *The English Common Reader* (Chicago: University of Chicago Press, 1957), 220.

2. Anonymous. "Modern Light Literature—Travellers' Tales," *Blackwood's Edinburgh Review* 78 (November 1855), 589. In addition to theorizing about the great ages in travel literature, the reviewer admired Burton's *Travels In Arabia* and, interesting in terms of this chapter, favorably reviewed Wilkie Collins's travel book about Cornwall, *Rambles beyond Railways.* "For we cannot all travel in Africa or the east; and when the Rhine becomes a bore, and even Switzerland savours of vulgarity, where are we to spend our holiday?" The answer the reviewer arrives at, having read Collins, is the "foreign" landscape of rural Britain.

3. Benedict Anderson, *Imagined Communities*, 7, 26.

4. Robert Louis Brannan, *Under The Management of Mr. Charles Dickens: His Production of "The Frozen Deep"* (Ithaca: Cornell University

Press, 1966). Lillian Nayder further documents and analyzes the collaboration in *Unequal Partners: Charles Dickens, Wilkie Collins, and Victorian Authorship* (Ithaca: Cornell University Press, 2002), 71–99.

5. Deborah Vlock, *Dickens, Novel Reading, and the Victorian Popular Theatre* (Cambridge: Cambridge University Press, 1998), 18.

6. The indebtedness of the sensation genre to melodrama is generally acknowledged and perhaps as a result underexamined.

7. *The Times*, quoting John Rae (24 October 1854).

8. Close examination of physical evidence—literally under the microscope—had long been a part of determining Franklin's fate; in 1850, several issues of *The Times* carried a lengthy discussion of whether a scrap of wood, a length of rope, and a piece of canvas found by Arctic searchers were from the Franklin expedition.

9. John Rae, *The Times* (7 November 1854).

10. Quoted in Harry Stone, *The Night Side of Dickens: Cannibalism, Passion, Necessity* (Columbus: University of Ohio Press, 1994), 3.

11. Charles Dickens, "The Noble Savage," in *Household Words* 7 (11 June 1853), 337.

12. Dickens quoted in Anne Lohrli, ed., *Household Words* (Toronto: University of Toronto Press, 1973), 25.

13. Lohrli, *Household Words*, 25.

14. Jenny Bourne Taylor quoted in Lohrli, *Household Words*, 25.

15. Dickens quoted in Lohrli, *Household Words*, 8. On Dickens and class, Mrs. Oliphant wrote in *Blackwood's Magazine* (April 1855), "[W]e cannot but express our conviction that it is to the fact that he represents a class that he owes his speedy elevation to the top of the wave of popular favour. . . . [H]e is, perhaps more distinctly than any other author of the time, a *class* writer . . . it is the air and the breath of middle class respectability which fills the books of Mr. Dickens." She continues, describing him as "the historian of a class—the literary interpreter of those intelligent, sensible, warm-hearted households, which are the strength of our country" (lxxvii, 456).

16. "The Lost Arctic Voyagers," 368. "The Lost Arctic Voyagers" was the title of a three-part series that appeared in *Household Words* 10 on December 2, December 9, and December 23, 1854. Dickens authored the first two installations; the third is listed as co-authored by Dickens and Rae, although it is primarily Rae's rebuttal. The magazine then ran "Dr. Rae's Report" on December 30, which was an edited version of Rae's report to the Admiralty. Text references to follow are to page numbers in this volume.

17. Maggie Kilgour, *From Communion to Cannibalism*, 239. Kilgour identifies the threatening nature of cannibalism as its literalization of the mechanics of empire: by reducing humans to "mere" matter, cannibalism erases the very difference it hopes to demarcate.

18. Recent scholarly attention to these debates in addition to Harry Stone's *The Night Side of Dickens* include Ian R. Stone, "'The Contents of the Kettles': Charles Dickens, John Rae, and Cannibalism on the 1845 Franklin Expedition," *The Dickensian* 83 (Spring 1987): 7–16; James Marlow, "English Cannibalism: Dickens After 1859," *Studies in English Literature* 23 (Autumn 1983): 647–66; "Sir John Franklin, Mr. Charles Dickens, and the Solitary Monster," *Dickens Studies Newsletter* 12 (December 1981): 97–103. Winona Howe and Lillian Nayder also discuss this exchange in their work on *The Frozen Deep*. Winona Howe, "Charles Dickens and The 'Last Resource': Arctic Cannibalism and *The Frozen Deep*," *Cahiers Victoriens et Edouardiens* 44 (1996): 61–83; Lillian Nayder, *Unequal Partners*, 65–69.

19. Claude Levi-Strauss, *The Raw and the Cooked* (New York: Harper and Row, 1969). Francis Spufford documents nineteenth-century popular and scholarly ethnography in his chapter "Imagining Eskimos," in *I May Be Sometime*, 184–235. He also notes the importance of cooking to the Dickens/Rae debate, 199–200.

20. Rae, *The Times* (7 November 1854).

21. This is the sort of blame-the-victim approach that Patrick Brantlinger in *Rule of Darkness* identifies as being typical of imperial writing. Francis Spufford comments on Inuit cultural perceptions of cannibalism as follows: "Cannibalism was abhorred among the northern peoples because in times of extreme dearth it might well be resorted to. It was horrible, but it was within the compass of things that happened, rather than standing for an ultimate reversal of moral standards" (*I May Be Sometime*, 124).

22. In Henry Morley's "Our Phantom Ship among The Ice" (*Household Words* 3 [1851]: 66–72) the Inuit are "loving children of the north" "for ever happy in their lot," "hungry or full" (70–71). In "Unspotted Snow," Morley describes them as "an amiable race; on amiable terms with visitors whose manners are invariably kind" (241).

23. Linda Colley, *Britons*; Keith Robbins, *Nineteenth-Century Britain: England, Scotland, and Wales The Making of a Nation* (Oxford: Oxford University Press, 1988).

24. Thomas Carlyle took the savage/cannibal link farther in his *Reminiscenses of My Irish Journey* of 1849, describing those who had

survived the Famine as *"eating* the slain." (quoted in H. L. Malchow, *Gothic Images of Race in Nineteenth-Century Britain* [Stanford: Stanford University Press, 1996], 71). Swift's *Modest Proposal* is a famous early Irish cannibal account. The cannibal barber Sweeney Todd was Irish; Sawney Beane was his Scottish counterpart. Francis Spufford also discusses this cultural nuance of cannibalism; see chapter 4 of *I May Be Sometime*.

25. Quoted in Malchow, *Gothic Images*, 71. For further discussion of Scots as savage and cannibalistic, see Lillian Nayder, "The Cannibal, The Nurse, and The Cook: Variants of *The Frozen Deep*," in *Unequal Partners: Charles Dickens, Wilkie Collins, and Victorian Authorship* (Ithaca: Cornell University Press, 2002), 69–70. She cites another Dickens article, "The North Against the South" in *Household Words*, where Walter Scott was "grouped with 'the man of the polar regions' as having 'a pastoral and hunting life' . . . render[ing] him nomadic and barbarous" (quoted in Nayder, 70).

26. H. M. Daleski documents Dickens's complicated use of analogy in his fiction in *Dickens and the Art of Analogy* (New York: Schocken Books, 1970).

27. "Dr. Rae's Report," *Household Words* 10, 458.

28. While the closing lines of the first of Dickens's "Lost Arctic Voyagers" series invoked Richardson and Franklin's earlier experience as part of the "mass of experience" indicating the impossibility of English cannibalism, no matter how bad the circumstance, the connection between the Arctic and the cannibal infiltrated even the most innocent sources. For instance, Richard Horne's poem "Arctic Heroes," which appeared in *Household Words* in April 1850, reads in part:

> We, to the last,
> With firmness, order, and considerate care
> Will act as though our deathbeds were at home,
> Grey heads with honour sinking to the tomb;
> So future times shall record bear that we,
> Imprisoned in these frozen horrors, held
> Our sense of duty, both to man and God. (April 27, 109)

Horne's poem presages Dickens's argument in its emphasis on "firmness" and "order" in the face of death. While ostensibly narrated by a soon-to-die sailor, the poem's collective "we" includes first the other sailors, but also eventually the readers. "Home," for Horne is something carried with the explorer, with "firmness, order, and considerate care."

The explorers die of natural causes, peacefully, as they would at home, but with the grey hair of old age (which the explorers will never see) replaced by the grey of hoarfrost. "Honour" and "duty," so long the bywords of Arctic endeavor, remain certainties in the last hours of the men. But that same introduction of "honour" and "duty" seem, as it does in Dickens's work five years later, to call their stability and certainty into question. What, after all, is an explorer's "duty, both to man and God"? Horne's readers could speculate that one of the few commandments left to a starving, lost Arctic explorer is "Thou shalt not kill," and since the only people left to kill in the lonely Arctic scenario imagined by Horne are fellow sailors, one of the reasons to do so would be cannibalism.

29. Malchow, *Gothic Images*, 109.

30. Caleb Crane, "Lovers of Human Flesh: Homosexuality and Cannibalism in Melville's Novels," *American Literature* 66, no. 1 (March 1994): 25–53.

31. Paul Lyons, "From Man-Eaters to Spam-Eaters: Literary Tourism and the Discourse of Cannibalism from Herman Melville to Paul Theroux," *Arizona Quarterly* 52, no. 2 (1995): 33–62. Lyons goes on to say that the "severity of the charge proves the basis for the suspicion; we would not experience awe if they were not awful" (57).

32. See D. A. Miller, *The Novel and The Police* (Berkeley: University of California Press, 1988).

33. "The Wreck of the 'Golden Mary'," *Household Words* (6 December 1856), Extra Christmas Number: 1–36. Text references that follow are to pages in the text. Like *The Frozen Deep*, "The Wreck of the 'Golden Mary'" was a collaborative affair, with the opening, wreck, ordeal and linking passages by Dickens; the continuing ordeal and rescue by Collins (see Stone, *Night Side*, 545; Nayder, *Unequal Partners*, 35–59).

34. Lillian Nayder illuminates the cannibal subtext in her reading of *The Frozen Deep* as using conjectures about the Franklin expedition to examine class tensions in Great Britain: the "savage" and cannibalizing male Inuit rewritten into the character of the Scottish nurse, "whose otherness obscures the class tensions," and "in so doing contrasts civilized Englishmen with uncivilized Scots, complacent male workers with resentful female servants, fathers who nurture with mothers who devour." "The Cannibal, The Nurse, and The Cook," 3.

35. Wilkie Collins, *The Frozen Deep*, in *Under the Management*, ed. Robert Brannan. Text references are to page numbers of this edition.

36. Peter Brooks, in *The Melodramatic Imagination: Balzac, Henry James, Melodrama, and the Mode of Excess* (New Haven: Yale University

Press, 1976), links melodrama to a healthy or managed body politic, 21. Simon Shepherd cautions against viewing the power of these moments, which he labels pauses of mutual agitation," as hegemonic, since audiences who are used to melodrama anticipate such moments and experience them on different levels. See his essay of the same name in *Melodrama: Stage, Picture, Screen*, ed. Jacky Bratton, Jim Cook, Christine Gledhill (London: British Film Institute, 1994), 25–49.

37. Charles Dickens about *The Frozen Deep* in a letter to W. F. De Cerjat, Jan. 17, 1857.

38. Joseph Roach, "Vicarious: Theater and the Rise of Synthetic Experience," in *Theorizing Practice: Redefining Theatre History*, ed. W. B. Worthen with Peter Holland (New York: Palgrave Macmillan 2003), 121.

39. Carol Hanbery MacKay, ed. *Dramatic Dickens*. New York: St. Martin's, 1989. Jean Ferguson Carr discusses Dickens's use of theatrical metaphors in "Dickens's Theatre of Self-Knowledge," 27–44. Michael R. Booth's contribution contextualizes Dickens's middle-class readership with theatre-going middle and lower classes, discussing portrayals of class relations in popular stage melodramas. "Melodrama and the Working Class," 98–109. Judith L. Fisher sees Dion Boucault's "sensation scenes" on the stage as being indebted to sensation scenes in Dickens's novels. "The 'Sensation Scene' in Charles Dickens and Dion Boucicault," 152–167. Paul Schlicke argues that Dickens desire "to entertain . . . motivates all his fiction" (35). *Dickens and Popular Entertainment* (London: Allen and Unwin, 1985). Claims such as Edwin Eigner's that Dickens "appropriates" the pantomime, "not to give each of the genres equal weight so that they might cancel one another out but clearly to privilege the concluding vision . . . in order to create the anarchy necessary to facilitate the ultimate shift and to effect a change of heart in the reader" (45), seem clearly linked to Raymond Williams's reading of Dickens as the voice of popular culture (Eigner, *The Dickens Pantomime* [Berkeley: University of California Press, 1989]; Williams, *Culture and Society 1780–1950* [New York: Columbia University Press, 1958]). Joseph Litvak claims Dickens's work "repeatedly emphasizes the *normalization* of theatricality, its subtle diffusion throughout the culture that would appear to have repudiated it . . . [and shows] how, if theatrical structures and techniques underlie or enable various coercive cultural mechanisms, the same structures and techniques can threaten those mechanisms' smooth functioning" (*Caught in the Act: Theatricality in the Nineteenth-Century English Novel*. [Berkeley: University of California

Press, 1992], x–xi). See also Joseph Roach, *The Player's Passion* (Ann Arbor: University of Michigan Press, 1993), passim. Martin Meisel addresses the cross-fertilization between genres in Dickens in chapters 4 and 5 of *Realizations* (Princeton: Princeton University Press, 1983). Recent work on the relation of the novel to theatrical culture more broadly includes J. Jeffrey Franklin. *Serious Play: The Cultural Form of the Nineteenth-Century Realist Novel.* (Philadelphia: University of Pennsylvania Press, 1999); Emily Allen, *Theater Figures: The Production of the Nineteenth-Century British Novel* (Columbus: The Ohio State University Press, 2003).

40. Joseph Roach, *Player's Passion*, x.

41. From "The Uncommercial Traveller" ("Two Views of Cheap Theatre"), in *All The Year Round*, vol. 2 (25 February 1860), 416–21. Quoted in Schlicke, *Dickens and Popular Entertainment*, 193. Schlicke sees Dickens as wanting the theatre to "teach discrimination and improve taste" (204) and offering in "The Amusements of the People" an "explicit proposal" of government surveillance through sponsored amusements, the effect of which is a "real, responsible educational trust" (208).

42. See Peter Bailey, *Popular Culture and Performance in the Victorian City* (Cambridge: Cambridge University Press, 1998), 157.

43. Quoted in Schlicke, *Dickens and Popular Entertainment*, 197.

44. Michael Booth, *Victorian Spectacular Theatre* (Boston: Routledge and Kegan Paul, 1981), 151.

45. Robert Brannan's work on the manuscript of the play identifies Dickens as responsible for this.

46. Michael Booth, *Victorian Spectacular Theatre*, 155.

47. Homi Bhabha, *Nation and Narration* (New York: Routledge, 1990), 294. For Bhabha, the pedagogic narrates an event of fragment from the everyday into a causal chain whose telos is the inevitability of nation.

48. Booth, *Victorian Spectacular Theatre*, 167.

49. Brooks, *The Melodramatic Imagination*, 22.

50. Nadine Holdsworth, "Haven't I Seen You Somewhere Before? Melodrama, Postmodernism, and Victorian Culture," in *Varieties of Victorianism: The Uses of a Past*, ed. Gary Day (New York: St. Martin's Press, 1998), 195.

51. It is tempting to read the nurse's accusation at the end of Act I as an attempt to implicate Clara in the cannibal economy, too: Act I ends with the nurse proclaiming: "Doos the Sight show me Frank? Aye! And

anither beside Frank. I see the lamb I' the grasp o' the lion. I see your bonnie bird alone wi' the hawk. I see you and all around you crying bluid! The stain is on you ... the stain o' that bluid is on *you!*" (116) After all, while Clara claims that Wardour misunderstood her affections, her dismissal of him provokes the rage that fuels his cannibal appetite.

52. Susan Stewart, "Scandals of the Ballad," *Representations* 32 (1990): 134–54.

53. For Nadine Holdsworth, the privileging of feeling over reason is a defining characteristic of melodrama. "This revelling in bodily thrills, once again, points to the duality of the melodramatic mode. The spectator experiences the juxtaposition of a narrative which encourages clear cognitive appreciation of motives and action, with the irrational physicality of sensation whereby the precarious, unconscious body takes precedence over and defies reason" ("Haven't I Seen You," 198).

54. Quoted in Crosby, *Ends of History*, 69.

55. Ibid., 69. A reviewer for the *Leader* noted the play's "power over the laughter, the tears and the interest of the audience" (69). One need only look at the ending of Collins's rather turgid rewrite of *The Frozen Deep* as a novel to see the effectiveness of affective dynamics in the stage production. "The loss is ours. The gain is his. He has won the greatest of all conquests—the conquest of himself. And he has died in the moment of victory. Not one of us here but may live to envy *his* glorious death" (*The Frozen Deep and Other Stories* [London: Richard Bentley and Son, 1874], I: 219).

56. Quoted in S. J. Fitz-gerald, *Dickens and Drama, Being an Account of Charles Dickens' Connection with the Stage and the Stage's Connection with Him* (London: Chapman and Hall, 1910), 64.

57. Wilkie Collins, *Nonesuch* 2, 834.

58. Brannan, *Under the Management*, 1.

59. 9 January 1857, quoted in Stone, *Night Side*, 278. Later, he came back again to the image of writing publicly while performing in *The Frozen Deep*: "It enables me, as it were, to write a book in company instead of in my own solitary room, and to feel its effect coming freshly back upon me from the reader" (8 July 1857, ibid., 278).

60. This was not the first time Dickens had mentioned inhabiting Wardour in his correspondence. In September 1857, Collins and Dickens went hiking in the north of England. Collins sprained his ankle while descending a waterfall. Dickens's account: "How I enacted Wardour over again in carrying him down, and what a business it was to get

him down . . . now I carry him to bed, and into and out of carriages, exactly like Wardour in private life"(*Nonesuch* 2, 891).

61. *Blackwood's Magazine* 102 (September 1857): 257–80. 257.

62. Martin Meisel, *Realizations*, 65.

63. Wilkie Collins, *Basil* (New York: Harper, 1893), 63.

64. Schmitt, *Alien Nation*, 118.

65. Oliphant, "Sensation Novels," 565.

66. Collins, *The Moonstone* (Garden City, NY: Penguin, 1946), 365, 368.

67. John Ruskin, *Fiction, Fair and Foul* (New York: John W. Lovell Company, 1890), 14.

68. *The Spectator*, September 28, 1889, quoted in Catherine Peters, *Wilkie Collins*, 251. The novel has been dismissed as a strange footnote of sensation/medical drama. Nicholas Rance, in *Wilkie Collins and Other Sensation Novelists: Walking the Moral Hospital* (Rutherford, NJ: Fairleigh Dickinson University Press, 1991), wrote of *Poor Miss Finch* that its "fantastic plot" "suggests a temporary revulsion against accepting society as constituted in the 1870s as fact" (143).

69. Collins, *Poor Miss Finch* (Oxford: Oxford World Classics, 1995), 33. Text references are to page numbers in this edition.

70. Quoted in Peters, *Wilkie Collins*, 191.

71. John Ruskin, *Fiction, Fair and Foul*, 14.

CHAPTER SIX. ENDS OF THE EARTH, ENDS OF THE EMPIRE

1. Graham Dawson, *Soldier Heroes: British Adventure, Empire and the Imagining of Masculinities* (New York: Routledge, 1994), 54.

2. Joseph Bristow, *Empire Boys: Adventures in a Man's World*, 2.

3. Andrea White closely documents the connection between nineteenth-century travel writing, boys' adventure novels, and imperial subjectivity in the first two chapters of *Joseph Conrad and the Adventure Tradition: Constructing and Deconstructing the Imperial Subject*, and argues that its resemblance to travel writing lent "special status" to adventure fiction in that it retained an authority associated with non-fiction accounts (40).

4. Quoted in Patrick Brantlinger, *Rule of Darkness*, 239. Unlike Ballantyne, whose *Giant of the North* departs in its fantastic plotting from his other novels, Haggard embraced fantasy. His contribution to

(quasi)Arctic adventure was the ice-age adventure-romance, *Allan and the Ice Gods.*

5. For thorough documentation of the Race for the Poles, see Beau Riffenburgh, *The Myth of the Explorer* (London: Wiley, 1993) and Lisa Bloom, *Gender on Ice*, passim.

6. Andrea White has argued that the subversion of the adventure genre that she and others attribute to Joseph Conrad can be seen earlier in H. Rider Haggard's Quartermain novels, in which the adventurer is either reluctant or refuses to return to England. *Joseph Conrad*, 93–99.

7. Ballantyne, *Hudson Bay or Everyday Life in the Wilds of North America* (Edinburgh: Blackwood's, 1848), 39. Text references are to page numbers of this edition.

8. See Eric Quayle, *Ballantyne the Brave* (London: Rupert Hart-Davis, 1967), 14–18.

9. One promised success of empire was its ability to produce men such as Ballantyne, young men who had to leave Great Britain in order to have the opportunity to prove themselves, make their fortunes, in order to return as enfranchised males. Thus, the imperial masculinity that Ballantyne's adventure novels are so concerned with is also intertwined with national masculinity, echoing the logic present in the Arctic narratives of the early century, in which qualities of British manhood made legible or discovered at empire's margins are essential not only to the successful extension of the empire but in the domestic imaginary as well.

10. Joseph Bristow's chapter "Island Stories" more fully documents the tropes of the tradition he calls "The Robinsonade." Bristow, *Empire Boys*, 104–26.

11. Graham Dawson offers a history and overview of adventure in "The Adventure Quest and Its Cultural Imaginaries," chapter three of *Soldier Heroes*. Michael Nerlich argues that adventure is a historical construct closely tied to bourgeois ideas of capitalism, in which adventure justifies upper-class privilege in *The Ideology of Adventure* (Minneapolis: University of Minnesota Press, 1987). Martin Green, in *Dreams of Adventure, Deeds of Empire* (New York: Basic Books, 1979) reveals how the adventure novel is related to the history of colonial expansion, with particular attention to class and caste dynamics. Richard Phillips examines the relation between geography, masculinity, and adventure in *Mapping Men and Empire: A Geography of Adventure* (New York: Routledge, 1997).

12. Green, *Dream of Adventure*, 37.

13. Bristow, *Empire Boys*, 21.

14. This logic echoes the logic of bourgeois capitalism, a link documented by Michael Nerlich in *The Ideology of Adventure*.

15. Joseph Bristow in his discussion of island adventure stories argues that each island story invokes a previous and therefore claims "every right to be told because it has happened time and again." *Empire Boys*, 94.

16. Ballantyne, *Giant of the North* (New York: Thomas Nelson and Sons, 1881), 70–72. Text references are to page numbers of this edition.

17. While a possible Northwest Passage had been confirmed in the 1851 meeting of the crews of the Franklin search ships *Investigator* and *Resolute*, each ship had started their navigation at opposite coasts. The *Investigator* was abandoned to the icepack, so no ship actually navigated the full passage until much later.

18. *Snowflakes and Sunbeams; or, The Young Fur Traders* (London: T. Nelson, 1856), appeared in 1856, but while it documents life in the Canadian Northwest, it does not extend its geography outside of the spaces covered in *Hudson Bay*.

19. Native women do appear in most exploration accounts and in most of Ballantyne's fictions, but they are not extended the qualities of British womanhood. In his Arctic novels, descriptions of native women are often used as moments in which to document difference of culture and appearance, with Ballantyne reserving agency (limited though it may be) for male natives.

20. Ballantyne, *Ungava* (London: T. Nelson, 1858), 208. Text references are to page numbers of this edition.

21. Ballantyne, *The Coral Island* (London: J. M. Dent, 1928), 15–16. Text references are to page numbers of this edition.

22. I don't mean to suggest that after Ballantyne the genre was somehow "finished." As the popularity of the genre and the successful careers of H. Rider Haggard and George Henty and others attest, the imperial narratives that fueled boys' adventure had staying power.

23. Ballantyne, *The World of Ice* (London: T. Nelson and Sons, 1904), 113. Text references are to page numbers of this edition

24. Andrea White, *Joseph Conrad*, 23.

25. See Abdul JanMohamed, "The Economy of the Manichean Allegory: The Function of Racial Difference in Colonialist Literature," in *Critical Inquiry* 12, no. 1 (1985): 63. See also Patrick Brantlinger, *Rule of Darkness*, for an overview of racial difference in Victorian fiction. For

more extensive treatment of race in adventure fiction, see Andrea White, *Joseph Conrad*, chapter 3.

26. Bristow, *Empire Boys*, 225.

27. Andrea White, *Joseph Conrad*, 108.

BIBLIOGRAPHY

Alexander, Christine, ed. *An Edition of the Early Writings of Charlotte Brontë.* Oxford: Basil Blackwell, 1987–91.

Allen, Emily. *Theater Figures: The Production of the Nineteenth-Century British Novel.* Columbus: The Ohio State University Press, 2003.

Altick, Richard. *The English Common Reader.* Chicago: University of Chicago Press, 1957.

Anderson, Benedict. *Imagined Communities: Reflections on the Origin and Spread of Nationalism.* New York: Verso, 1991.

Anonymous or Unknown. "Modern Light Literature—Travellers' Tales." *Blackwood's Edinburgh Magazine* 78, no. 481 (November 1855): 586–99.

Appadurai, Arjun. "Sovereignty without Territoriality: Notes for a Post-national Geography." In *The Geography of Identity,* ed. Patricia Yaeger, 40–58. Ann Arbor: University of Michigan Press, 1996.

Arens, William. *The Man-Eating Myth: Anthropology and Anthropophagy.* New York: Oxford University Press, 1979.

Ashcroft, Bill. "Constructing the Postcolonial Male Body." In *The Body in the Library,* ed. Leigh Dale, 207–23. Amsterdam: Ropodi, 1998.

Ashcroft, Bill, Gareth Griffiths, and Helen Tiffin, eds. *The Empire Writes Back: Theory and Practice in Post-Colonial Literatures.* London: Routledge: 1989.

———. *The Post-Colonial Studies Reader.* London: Routledge, 1995.

Auerbach, Nina. *Private Theatricals.* Cambridge: Harvard University Press, 1990.

Azim, Firdous. *The Colonial Rise of the Novel*. London: Routledge, 1993.

Bailey, Peter. *Popular Culture and Performance in the Victorian City*. Cambridge: Cambridge University Press, 1998.

Balibar, Etienne, and Immanuel Wallerstein. *Race, Nation, Class. Ambiguous Identities*. New York: Verso, 1991. Repr. from Balibar, Etienne. "The National Forum: History and Ideology." Trans. Chris Turner. *Review. Fernand Braudel Center* 13, no. 3 (Summer 1990): 329–61.

Ballantyne, R. M. *The Coral Island*. London: J. M. Dent, 1928.

———. *Giant of the North*. New York: Thomas Nelson and Sons, 1881.

———. *Hudson Bay or Everyday Life in the Wilds of North America*. Edinburgh: Blackwood's, 1848.

———. *Snowflakes and Sunbeams: or, The Young Fur Traders, a Tale of the Far North*. London: T. Nelson, 1856

———. *Ungava*. London: T. Nelson, 1858.

———. *The World of Ice*. London: T. Nelson and Sons, 1904.

Barker, Francis, Peter Hulme, and Margaret Iversen, eds. *Cannibalism and the Colonial World*. Cambridge: Cambridge University Press, 1998.

Barker, Juliet. *The Brontës: A Life in Letters*. Woodstock, NY: Overlook Press, 1998.

Barnes, Trevor J., and James S. Duncan, eds. *Writing Worlds: Discourse, Text, and Metaphor in the Representation of Landscape*. London: Routledge, 1992.

Barrow, John. *A chronological history of voyages into the Arctic regions [microform]: undertaken chiefly for the purpose of discovering a north-east, north-west, or polar passage between the Atlantic and Pacific*. London: John Murray, 1818.

Baucom, Ian. *Out of Place*. Princeton: Princeton University Press, 1999.

Beer, Gillian. *Darwin's Plots: Evolutionary Narrative in Darwin, George Eliot, and Nineteenth-Century Fiction*. Boston: Routledge and Kegan Paul, 1983.

Behrisch, Erika. "Voices of Silence, Texts of Truth: Imperial Discourse and Cultural Negotiations in Nineteenth-Century British Arctic Exploration Narrative." PhD diss. Queen's University, 2002.

Benedict, Barbara M. *Framing Feeling: Sentiment and Style in English Prose Fiction, 1745–1800*. New York: AMS Press, 1994.

———. *Making the Modern Reader: Cultural Mediation in Early Modern Literary Anthologies*. Princeton: Princeton University Press, 1996.

Ben-Merre, Diana. "Conrad's Marlow and Britain's Franklin: Redoubling the Narrative in *Heart of Darkness.*" *Conradiana* 34, no. 3 (Fall 2002): 211–26.

Berlant, Lauren. *The Anatomy of National Fantasy: Hawthorne, Utopia, and Everyday Life.* Chicago: University of Chicago Press, 1991.

Bewell, Alan. "*Jane Eyre* and Victorian Medical Geography." *ELH* 63, no. 3 (Fall 1996): 773–808.

———. *Wordsworth and the Enlightenment : Nature, Man, and Society in the Experimental Poetry.* New Haven: Yale University Press, 1989.

———. *Romanticism and Colonial Disease.* Baltimore: Johns Hopkins University Press, 2000.

Bhabha, Homi, ed. *Nation and Narration.* London: Routledge, 1990.

Bloom, Lisa. *Gender on Ice.* Minneapolis: University of Minnesota Press, 1993.

Blunt, Alison, and Gillian Rose, eds. *Writing Women and Space: Colonial and Postcolonial Geographies.* New York: Guilford Press, 1994.

Bohls, Elizabeth. *Women Travel Writers and the Language of Aesthetics, 1716–1818.* Cambridge: Cambridge University Press, 1995.

Booth, Michael R. *English Plays of the Nineteenth Century.* Vol. I–IV. Oxford: Clarendon Press, 1969–76.

———. "Melodrama and the Working Class." In *Dramatic Dickens*, ed. Carol Hanbery McKay. 98–109. New York: St. Martin's 1989.

———. *Prefaces to English Nineteenth-Century Theatre.* Manchester: Manchester University Press, 1980.

———. "Soldiers of the Queen: Drury Lane Imperialism." In *Melodrama: The Cultural Emergence of a Genre*, ed. Michael Hays and Anastasia Nikolopoulou, 3–20. New York: St. Martin's Press, 1996.

———. *Theatre in the Victorian Age.* New York: Cambridge University Press, 1991.

———. *Victorian Spectacular Theatre.* Boston: Routlege and Kegan Paul, 1981.

Boyle, Thomas. *Black Swine in the Sewers of Hampstead: Beneath the Surface of Victorian Sensationalism.* New York: Viking, 1989.

Brannan, Robert Louis. *Under The Management of Mr. Charles Dickens: His Production of "The Frozen Deep."* Ithaca: Cornell University Press, 1966.

Brant, Clare. "Climates of Gender." In *Romantic Geographies: Discourses of Travel 1775–1844*, ed. Amanda Gilroy, 129–49. Manchester: Manchester University Press, 2000.

Brantlinger, Patrick. "What Is Sensational about the 'Sensation Novel'?" *Nineteenth Century Fiction* 37 (June 1982): 1–28.

———. *The Reading Lesson: The Threat of Mass Literacy in the Nineteenth-Century British Fiction.* Bloomington: Indiana University Press, 1998.

———. *Rule of Darkness: British Literature and Imperialism, 1830–1914.* Ithaca: Cornell University Press, 1988.

Bratton, Jacky, Jim Cook, and Christine Gledhill, eds. *Melodrama: Stage, Picture, Screen.* London: British Film Institute, 1994.

Brinks, Ellen. *Gothic Masculinity: Effeminacy and the Supernatural in English and German Romanticism.* Lewisburg, PA: Bucknell University Press, 2003.

Bristow, Joseph. *Empire Boys: Adventures in a Man's World.* London: HarperCollinsAcademic, 1991.

Brontë, Charlotte. *Jane Eyre.* New York: Penguin, 1985.

Brooks, Peter. "'Godlike Science/Unhallowed Arts': Language, Nature, and Monstrosity." In *The Endurance of Frankenstein,* ed. George Levine and U. C. Knopflmacher, 205–20. Berkeley: University of California Press, 1979.

———. "Melodrama, Body, Revolution." In *Melodrama: Stage Picture Screen,* ed. Jacky Bratton, Jim Cook, and Christine Gledhill, 11–24. London: British Film Institute, 1994.

———. *The Melodramatic Imagination: Balzac, Henry James, Melodrama, and the Mode of Excess.* New Haven: Yale University Press, 1976.

Brown, Laura. *Ends of Empire: Women and Ideology in Early Eighteenth-Century English Literature.* Ithaca: Cornell University Press, 1993.

Browne, R. Review of *Yachting in the Arctic Seas,* by James Lamont. *Appleton's Journal of Literature, Science, and Art* 15 (1876): 385.

Carr, Jean Ferguson. "Dickens's Theatre of Self-Knowledge." In *Dramatic Dickens,* ed. Carol Hanbery McKay, 27–44. New York: St. Martin's, 1989.

Castle, Terry. *Masquerade and Civilization: The Carnivalesque in Eighteenth-Century English Culture and Fiction.* Stanford: Stanford University Press, 1986.

Chase, Karen. "Jane Eyre's Interior Design." In *New Casebooks: Jane Eyre,* ed. Heather Glen, 52–67. New York: St. Martin's Press, 1997.

Cheek, Pamela. *Sexual Antipodes: Enlightenment Globalization and the Placing of Sex.* Stanford: Stanford University Press, 2003.

Cheyfitz, Eric. *The Poetics of Imperialism: Translation and Colonization from the Tempest to Tarzan.* New York: Oxford University Press, 1991.

Colley, Linda. *Britons: Forging the Nation, 1707–1837.* New Haven: Yale University Press, 1992.

———. "Britishness and Otherness: An Argument." *Journal of British Studies* 31 (1992): 309–29.

Collins, Wilkie. *Basil, A Novel.* New York: Harper, 1893.

———. *The Frozen Deep: A Drama in Three Acts.* London: Printed by C. Whiting, 1866.

———. *The Frozen Deep and Other Stories.* 2 vols. London: Richard Bentley and Son, 1874. I:2–220.

———. *The Moonstone.* Garden City, NY: Penguin, 1946.

———. *Poor Miss Finch.* ed. Catherine Peters. Oxford: Oxford World Classics, 1993.

Collis, Christy. "The Voyage of the Episteme: Narrating the North." *Essays in Canadian Writing* 59 (1996): 26–45.

———. "Vertical Body/Horizontal World: Sir John Franklin and Fictions of Arctic Space." In *The Body in the Library*, ed. Leigh Dale and Simon Ryan, 225–36. Atlanta: Rodopi, 1998.

Conrad, Joseph. *Heart of Darkness.* ed. Cedric Watts. Oxford: Oxford Classics, 2002.

———. *Last Essays.* Toronto: J. M. Dent and Sons, 1926.

Cooper, Frederick, and Ann Laura Stoler. "Between Metropole and Colony. Rethinking a Research Agenda." In *Tensions of Empire: Colonial Cultures in a Bourgeois World*, ed. Frederick Cooper and Ann Laura Stoler, 1–56. Berkeley: University of California Press, 1997.

———. *Tensions of Empire. Colonial Cultures in a Bourgeois World.* Berkeley: University of California Press, 1997.

Cox, Jeffrey. "The Ideological Tack of Nautical Drama." In *Melodrama: The Cultural Emergence of a Genre*, ed. Michael Hays and Anastasia Nikolopoulou, 167–190. New York: St. Martin's, 1996.

Crane, Caleb. "Lovers of Human Flesh: Homosexuality and Cannibalism in Melville's Novels." *American Literature* 66, no. 1 (March 1994): 25–53.

Croker, John Wilson. "Article V: Frankenstein, or the Modern Prometheus." *Quarterly Review* 28, no. 36 (May 1818): 379–85.

Crosby, Christina. *The Ends of History.* New York: Routledge, 1991.

Cunningham, Hugh. "The Language of Patriotism, 1850–1914." *History Workshop Journal* 13 (1981): 9–13.

Curran, Stuart. *Poetic Form and British Romanticism.* New York: Oxford University Press, 1986.

————. "Mothers and Daughters: Poetic Generation(s) in the Eighteenth and Nineteenth Centuries." In *Forging Connections: Women's Poetry from the Renaissance to Romanticism*, ed. A. K. Mellor, F. Nussbaum, and J. F. S. Post, 147–62. San Marino, CA: Huntington Library, 2002.

Cvetkovitch, Ann. *Mixed Feelings: Feminism, Mass Culture, and Victorian Sensationalism*. New Brunswick: Rutgers University Press, 1992.

Daffron, Eric. "Male Bonding: Sympathy and Shelley's *Frankenstein*." *Nineteenth-Century Contexts* 21 (1999): 415–35.

Daleski, H. M. *Dickens and the Art of Analogy*. New York: Schocken Books, 1970.

Dann, Otto, and John R. Dinwiddy, eds. *Nationalism in the Age of the French Revolution*. London: Hambledon Press, 1988.

David, Deirdre. *Rule Britannia: Women, Empire, and Victorian Writing*. Ithaca: Cornell University Press, 1995.

David, Robert G. *The Arctic in the British Imagination 1818–1914*. Manchester: Manchester University Press, 2000.

Davidoff, Leonore, and Catherine Hall. *Family Fortunes: Men and Women of the English Middle Class, 1780–1850*. Chicago: University of Chicago Press, 1987.

Davidson, Cathy N., and Jessamyn Hatcher, eds. *No More Separate Spheres!* Durham: Duke University Press, 2002.

Davies, R. C. "Thrice-Told Tales: The Exploration Writing of John Franklin." In *The Canadian North: Essays in Culture and Literature*, ed. J. Carlsen and B. Streijffert, 15–26. Lund, Sweden: The Nordic Association for Canadian Studies, 1989.

Davis, Jim, and Victor Emeljanow. *Reflecting the Audience: London Theatregoing, 1840–1880*. Iowa City: University of Iowa Press, 2001.

Dawson, Graham. *Soldier Heroes: British Adventure, Empire, and the Imagining of Masculinities*. New York: Routledge, 1994.

de Groot, J. "'Sex' and 'Race': The Construction of Language and Image in the Nineteenth Century." In *Sexuality and Subordination: Interdisciplinary Studies of Gender in the Nineteenth Century*, ed. Susan Mendus and Jane Rendall, 89–130. New York: Routledge, 1989.

Deleuze, Gilles, and Félix Guattari. *A Thousand Plateaus: Capitalism and Schizophrenia*, Vol. II. Translated by Brian Massumi. London: Atholone, 1988.

Dickens, Charles. "The Noble Savage." *Household Words* 7 (11 June 1853): 337–39.

————. "'The Lost Arctic Voyagers [i]." *Household Words* 10 (2 December 1854): 361–65.

————. "The Lost Arctic Voyagers [ii]." *Household Words* 10 (9 December 1854): 385–408.

Dickens, Charles, ed. *The Amusements of the People: and Other Papers: Reports, Essays, and Reviews, 1834–51*. Columbus: The Ohio State University Press, 1968.

Donaldson, Laura E. *Decolonizing Feminisms: Race, Gender, and Empire Building*. Chapel Hill: University of North Carolina Press, 1992.

Donelan, Charles. *Romanticism and Male Fantasy in Byron's Don Juan*. New York: St. Martin's Press, 2000.

Driver, Felix. *Geography Militant: Cultures of Exploration and Empire*. Oxford: Blackwell, 2001.

————. "Geography Triumphant? Joseph Conrad and the Imperial Adventure." *The Conradian* 18, no. 2 (1994): 103–11.

Dudink, Stefan, Karen Hagemann, and John Tosh, eds. *Masculinities in Politics and War: Gendering Modern History*. Manchester: Manchester University Press, 2004.

Easthope, Antony. *Englishness and National Culture*. New York: Routledge, 1999.

Eastwood, David. "The Age of Uncertainty: Britain in the Early-Nineteenth Century." *Transactions of the Royal Historical Society* 8, no. 2 (1998): 91–115.

————. "Patriotism Personified: Southey's Life of Nelson Reconsidered." *Mariner's Mirror* 77 (1991): 143–49.

————. "Robert Southey and the Meanings of Patriotism." *Journal of British Studies* 31 (1992): 265–87.

Edwards, Philip. *The Story of the Voyage*. New York: Cambridge University Press, 1994.

Eger, Elizabeth, C. Grant et al., eds. *Women, Writing, and the Public Sphere 1700–1830*. Cambridge: Cambridge University Press, 2001.

Eigner, Edwin. *The Dickens Pantomime*. Berkeley: University of California Press, 1989.

Eley, Geoff, and Ronald G. Suny, eds. *Becoming National: A Reader*. New York: Oxford University Press, 1996.

Ellis, Kate Ferguson. *The Contested Castle: Gothic Novels and the Subversion of Domestic Ideology*. Urbana: University of Illinois Press, 1989.

Ellis, Sarah Stickney. *The Women of England: Their Social Duties and Domestic Habits*. In *The Select Works of Mrs. Ellis*. New York: Langley, 1854.

Ellison, Julie K. *Delicate Subjects: Romanticism, Gender, and the Ethics of Understanding.* Ithaca: Cornell University Press, 1990.

Elshtain, Jean B. *Public Man, Private Woman: Women in Social and Political Thought.* Amherst: University of Massachusetts Press, 1982.

Equiano, Olaudah. *The Interesting Narrative of Olaudah Equiano.* New York: Bedford Books of St. Martin's Press, 1995.

Fabian, Johannes. *Time and the Other.* New York: Columbia University Press, 1983.

Fay, Elizabeth A. *Eminent Rhetoric: Language, Gender, and Cultural Tropes.* Westport, CT: Bergin and Garvey, 1994.

———. *A Feminist Introduction to Romanticism.* Malden, MA: Blackwell, 1998.

Ferguson, Frances. *Solitude and the Sublime: Romanticism and the Aesthetics of Individuation.* New York: Routledge, 1992.

Ferres, Kay. "Gender, Biography, and the Public Sphere." In *Mapping Lives: the Uses of Biography*, ed. Peter France and William St. Clair, 303–20. New York: Oxford University Press, 2001.

Fisch, Audrey A., Anne K. Mellor et al., eds. *The Other Mary Shelley: Beyond Frankenstein.* New York: Oxford University Press, 1993.

Fisher, Judith L. "The 'Sensation Scene' in Charles Dickens and Dion Boucicault." In *Dramatic Dickens*, ed. Carol Hanbery McKay. 152–67. New York: St. Martin's, 1989.

Fitz-gerald, S. J. A. *Dickens and Drama, Being an Account of Charles Dickens' Connection with the Stage and the Stage's Connection with Him.* London: Chapman and Hall, 1910.

Fitzgerald, Percy H. *Memories of Charles Dickens with an Account of "Household Words" and "All The Year Round" and of the Contributors Thereto.* Bristol, UK: J. W. Arrowsmith, 1913.

Fitzpatrick, Kathleen. *Sir John Franklin in Tasmania 1837–1843.* Melbourne: Melbourne University Press, 1949.

Flint, Kate. *Dickens.* Brighton, Sussex: Harvester Press, 1986.

———. *The Woman Reader, 1837–1914.* Oxford New York: Oxford University Press, 1993.

Foucault, Michel. *Discipline and Punish.* Translated by Alan Sheridan. New York: Pantheon, 1978.

Franklin, J. Jeffrey. *Serious Play: The Cultural Form of the Nineteenth-Century Realist Novel.* Philadelphia: University of Pennsylvania Press, 1999.

Franklin, John. *Narrative of a Journey to the Shores of The Polar Sea in The Years 1819, 20, 21, and 22.* Rutland, VT: Charles E. Tuttle, 1970.

Frantz, Ray W. *The English Traveller and the Movement of Ideas, 1660–1732*. New York: Octagon Books, 1968.

Fraser, Rebecca. *The Brontës: Charlotte and Her Family*. New York: Ballantine, 1990.

Fulford, Tim. "Romanticizing the Empire: The Naval Heroes of Southey, Coleridge, Austen, and Marryat." *Modern Language Quarterly* 60, no. 2 (1999): 161–96.

———. "Romanticism and Colonialism: Races, Places, Peoples, 1800–30." In *Romanticism and Colonialism, Writing and Empire, 1780–1830*, ed. Tim Fulford and Peter J. Kitson, 35–48. New York: Cambridge University Press, 1998.

———. *Romanticism and Masculinity : Gender, Politics, and Poetics in the Writings of Burke, Coleridge, Cobbett, Wordsworth, De Quincey, and Hazlitt*. New York: St. Martin's Press, 1999.

Fulford, Tim, and Peter J. Kitson, eds. *Romanticism and Colonialism, Writing and Empire, 1780–1830*. New York: Cambridge University Press, 1998.

Fulford, Tim, Debbie Lee, and Peter J Kitson. *Literature, Science, and Exploration in the Romantic Era*. Cambridge: Cambridge University Press, 2004

Gallagher, Catherine. *Nobody's Story: The Vanishing Acts of Women Writers in the Marketplace, 1670–1820*. Berkeley: University of California Press, 1994.

———, and Stephen Greenblatt. *Practicing New Historicism*. Chicago: University of Chicago Press, 2000.

Garis, Robert. *The Dickens Theatre*. Oxford: Clarendon Press, 1965.

Gell, E. M. *John Franklin's Bride: Eleanor Anne Porden*. London: John Murray, 1930.

Gibbon, Luke. "'Subtilized into Savages': Edmund Burke, Progress, and Primitivism." *The South Atlantic Quarterly* 100, no. 1 (2001): 83–109.

Giddings, Robert, ed. *Literature and Imperialism*. New York: St. Martin's, 1991.

Gikandi, Simon. *Maps of Englishness: Writing Identity in the Culture of Colonialism*. New York: Columbia University Press, 1996.

Gilbert, Pamela K. *Disease, Desire, and the Body in Victorian Women's Popular Novels*. Cambridge: Cambridge University Press, 1997.

Gilbert, Sandra, and Susan Gubar. *The Madwoman in the Attic: The Woman Writer and the Nineteenth-Century Literary Imagination*. New Haven: Yale University Press, 1979.

Gilroy, Amanda, "Introduction." In *Romantic Geographies: Discourses of Travel, 1775–1844*, ed. Amanda Gilroy, 1–18. Manchester: Manchester University Press, 2000.

Gilroy, Amanda, ed. *Romantic Geographies: Discourses of Travel, 1775–1844.* Manchester: Manchester University Press, 2000.

Gittings, C. E. *Imperialism and Gender: Constructions of Masculinity.* New Lambton, N.S.W.: Dangaroo Press, 1996.

Glavin, John. *After Dickens: Reading Adaptation and Performance.* Cambridge: Cambridge University Press, 1999.

Glissant, Edouard. *Poetics of Relation.* Translated by Betsy Wing. Ann Arbor: University of Michigan Press, 1997.

Godlewska, Anna, and Neil Smith, eds. *Geography and Empire.* New York: Oxford University Press, 1994.

Green, Martin. *Dreams of Adventure, Deeds of Empire.* New York: Basic Books, 1979.

Greenblatt, Stephen. *Renaissance Self-Fashioning: From More to Shakespeare.* Chicago: University of Chicago Press, 1980.

Grewal, Inderpal. *Home and Harem: Nation, Gender, Empire, and the Cultures of Travel.* Durham: Duke University Press, 1996.

Griffin, Andrew. "Fire and Ice in *Frankenstein*." In *The Endurance of Frankenstein*, ed. George Levine and U. C. Knoepflmacher, 49–73. Berkeley: University of California Press, 1979.

Griffin, Dustin. *Patriotism and Poetry in Eighteenth-Century Britain.* Cambridge: Cambridge University Press, 2002.

Guillory, John. *Cultural Capital.* Chicago: University of Chicago Press, 1993.

Habermas, Jurgen. *The Structural Transformation of the Public Sphere: An Inquiry into a Category of Bourgeois Society.* Cambridge: MIT Press, 1989.

Hadley, Elaine. *Melodramatic Tactics: Theatricalized Dissent in the English Marketplace, 1800–1885.* Stanford: Stanford University Press, 1995.

Hall, Catherine. *Civilising Subjects: Metropole and Colony in the English Imagination, 1830–1867.* Cambridge: Cambridge University Press, 2002.

———. "Of Gender and Empire: Reflections on the Nineteenth Century." In *Gender and Empire*, ed. Philippa Levine, 46–76. Oxford: Oxford University Press, 2004.

———. "Thinking the Postcolonial, Thinking the Empire." In *Cultures of Empire. A Reader. Colonizers in Britain and the Empire in the*

Nineteenth and the Twentieth Centuries, ed. Catherine Hall, 16–20. Manchester: Manchester University Press, 2000.

Harley, J. B. "Deconstructing the Map." In *Writing Worlds: Discourse, Text, and Metaphor in the Representation of Landscape,* ed. Trevor J. Barnes and James S. Duncan, 231–47. New York: Routledge, 1992.

Harvey, David. *Justice, Nature, and the Geography of Difference.* Cambridge, MA: Blackwell, 1996.

Hayward, Jennifer. *Consuming Pleasures: Active Audiences and Serial Fictions from Dickens to Soap Opera.* Lexington: University Press of Kentucky, 1997.

Hechter, Michael. *Internal Colonialism: The Celtic Fringe in British National Development, 1536–1966.* Berkeley: University of California Press, 1975.

Helgerson, Richard. *Forms of Nationhood.* Chicago: University of Chicago Press, 1992.

Helms, Mary W. *Ulysses' Sail: An Ethnographic Odyssey of Power, Knowledge, and Geographical Distance.* Princeton: Princeton University Press, 1988.

Helsinger, Elizabeth K. *Rural Scenes and National Representation: Britain, 1815–1850.* Princeton: Princeton University Press, 1997.

Helsinger, Elizabeth K., R. L. Sheets, and W. Veeder, eds. *The Woman Question: Social Issues, 1837–1883.* 3 vols. Manchester: Manchester University Press, 1983.

Hemans, Felicia. *Felicia Hemans: Selected Poems, Prose and Letters.* Ed. Gary Kelly, Peterborough, ON: Broadview Press, 2002.

Henighan, T. *Natural Space in Literature: Imagination and Environment in Nineteenth and Twentieth Century Fiction and Poetry.* Ottawa: Golden Dog Press, 1982.

Hertz, Neil. *The End of the Line.* New York: Columbia University Press, 1985.

Hewitt, Douglas. "'Heart of Darkness' and Some 'Old Unpleasant Reports.'" *The Review of English Studies* new series 38, no. 151 (1987): 374–76.

Hobsbawm, Eric J. *Nations and Nationalism since 1780.* New York: Cambridge University Press, 1990.

Hodgson, M. "The Exploration Journal as Literature." *The Beaver* 298 (1967): 4–12.

Holdsworth, Nadine. "Haven't I Seen You Somewhere Before? Melodrama, Postmodernism, and Victorian Culture." In *Varieties of*

Victorianism: The Uses of a Past, ed. Gary Day. New York: St. Martin's Press, 1998.

Howe, Winona. "Charles Dickens and The 'Last Resource': Arctic Cannibalism and *The Frozen Deep.*" *Cahiers Victoriens et Edouardiens* 44 (1996): 61–83.

Hughes, Winifred. *Maniac in the Cellar: Sensation Novels of the 1860s.* Princeton: Princeton University Press, 1980.

Hulme, Peter. "Introduction: The Cannibal Scene." In *Cannibalism and the Colonial World*, ed. Francis Barker, Peter Hulme, and Margaret Iversen, 1–38. New York: Cambridge University Press, 1998.

Hume, R. D. "Gothic versus Romantic: A Reevaluation of the Gothic Novel." *PMLA* 84 (1969): 282–90.

Hyam, Ronald. *Empire and Sexuality: The British Experience.* Manchester: Manchester University Press, 1990.

Ivy, Marilyn. *Discourses of the Vanishing.* Chicago: University of Chicago Press, 1995.

JanMohamed, Abdul. "The Economy of the Manichean Allegory: The Function of Racial Difference in Colonialist Literature." *Critical Inquiry* 12, no. 1 (1985): 59–87.

Jones, Frederick L., ed. *Mary Shelley's Journal.* Norman: University of Oklahoma Press, 1957.

Jordan, G., and N. Rogers. "Admirals as Heroes: Patriotism and Liberty in Hanoverian England." *Journal of British Studies* 28 (1989): 201–24.

Kaplan, Fred. *Dickens: A Biography.* New York: Avon Books, 1988.

Keith, Michael, and Steve Pile, eds. *Place and the Politics of Identity.* New York: Routledge, 1993.

Kelly, Gary. *Women, Writing, and Revolution, 1790–1827.* Oxford: Clarendon Press, 1993.

———. *Bluestocking Feminism: Writings of the Bluestocking Circle, 1738–1785.* London: Pickering and Chatto, 1999.

Kilgour, Maggie. *From Communion to Cannibalism: Metaphors of Incorporation.* Princeton: Princeton University Press, 1990.

———. *The Rise of the Gothic Novel.* New York: Routledge, 1995.

Kirwan, L. P. *A History of Arctic Exploration.* New York: W. W. Norton, 1960.

Kitson, Peter J., ed. *Travels, Explorations, and Empires: Writings from the Era of Imperial Expansion, 1770–1835.* Vol. 3, *North and South Poles.* London: Pickering and Chatto, 2003.

Klein, L. E. "Gender and the Public/Private Distinction in the Eighteenth Century: Some Questions about Evidence and Analytic Procedure." *Eighteenth-Century Studies* 29, no. 1 (1995): 97–109.

Knox, T. Wallace. *Adventures of Two Youths in the Open Polar Sea. The Voyage of the "Vivian" to the North Pole and Beyond*. New York: Harper and Brothers, 1885.

Koven, Seth. "From Rough Lads to Hooligans: Boy Life, National Culture, and Social Reform." In *Nationalisms and Sexualities*, ed. A. Parker, M. Russo, D. Sommer, and P. Yaeger, 365–94. New York: Routledge, 1992.

Kramer, Linkin Harriet, and Stephen C. Behrendt, eds. *Romanticism and Women Poets*. Lexington: The University Press of Kentucky, 1999.

Kruger, Loren. *The National Stage*, Chicago: University of Chicago Press, 1992.

Kumar, Krishan. *The Making of English National Identity*. Cambridge: Cambridge University Press, 2003.

Labbe, Jaqueline M. "A Monstrous Fiction: Frankenstein and the wifely ideal." *Women's Writing* 6, no. 3 (1999): 345–62.

Lamb, Geoffrey F. *Franklin, Happy Voyager*. London: Ernest Benn, Limited, 1956.

Langland, Elizabeth. *Nobody's Angels: Middle-class Women and Domestic Ideology in Victorian Culture*. Ithaca: Cornell University Press, 1995.

Lata, Mani. "Contentious Traditions: The Debate on Sati in Colonial India." *Cultural Critique* 7, no. 2 (1987): 119–56.

Lawrence, Karen. *Penelope Voyages: Women and Travel in the British Literary Tradition*. Ithaca: Cornell University Press, 1994.

Leask, Nigel. *British Romantic Writers and the East: Anxieties of Empire*. Cambridge: Cambridge University Press, 1992.

———. *Curiosity and the Aesthetics of Travel Writing, 1770–1840: "From an Antique Land."* Oxford: Oxford University Press, 2002.

———. "Wandering through Eblis: Absorption and Containment in Romantic Exoticism." In *Romanticism and Colonialism, Writing and Empire, 1780–1830*, ed. Tim Fulford and Peter J. Kitson, 165–88. New York: Cambridge University Press, 1998.

Levere, Trevor. *Science and the Canadian Arctic. A Century of Exploration 1818–1918*. Cambridge: Cambridge University Press, 1993.

Levine, George. "The Ambiguous Heritage of Frankenstein." In *The Endurance of Frankenstein*, ed. George Levine and U. C.

Knoepflmacher, 3–30. Berkeley: University of California Press, 1981.

———. *The Realistic Imagination*. Chicago: University of Chicago Press, 1981.

Levine, G., and U. C. Knoeplflmacher, eds. *The Endurance of Frankenstein: Essays on Mary Shelley's Novel*. Berkeley: University of California Press, 1979.

Levine, Philippa, ed. *Gender and Empire*. Oxford: Oxford University Press, 2004.

Levi-Strauss, Claude. *The Raw and the Cooked*. New York: Harper and Row, 1969.

Lewis, Martin W., and Kären E. Wigen. *The Myth of Continents*. Berkeley: University of California Press, 1997.

Linkin, Harriet, and Stephen Behrendt. "Introduction: Recovering Romanticism and Women Poets." In *Romanticism and Women Poets: Opening the Doors of Reception*, ed. Harriet Linkin and Stephen Behrendt, 1–14. Lexington: The University Press of Kentucky, 1999.

———, eds. *Romanticism and Women Poets: Opening the Doors of Reception*. Lexington: University Press of Kentucky, 1999.

Litvack, Joseph. *Caught in the Act: Theatricality in the Nineteenth-Century English Novel*. Berkeley: University of California Press, 1992.

Locy, Sharon. "Travel and Space in Charlotte Brontë's *Jane Eyre*." *Pacific Coast Philology* 37 (2002): 105–21.

Lodge, David. *Language of Fiction*. London: Routledge, 2001.

Loesburg, Jonathan. "The Ideology of Narrative Form in Sensation Fiction." *Representations* 13 (Winter 1986): 115–38.

Lohrli, Anne, ed. *Household Words*. Toronto: University of Toronto Press, 1973.

Loomis, Chauncey C. "The Arctic Sublime." In *Nature and the Victorian Imagination*, ed. U. C. Knoepflmacher and G. B. Tennyson, 95–114. Berkeley: University of California Press, 1977.

———. *Weird and Tragic Shores: The Story of Charles Francis Hall, Explorer*. Lincoln: University of Nebraska Press, 1991.

Looser, Devoney. *British Women Writers and the Writing of History*. Baltimore: Johns Hopkins University Press, 2000.

Lootens, Tricia. "Hemans and Her American Heirs: Nineteenth-Century Women's Poetry and National Identity." In *Women's Poetry, Late Romantic to Late Victorian: Gender and Genre. 1830–1900*, ed.

Isobel Armstrong and Virginia Blain, 243–60. New York: Macmillan–St. Martin's, 1999.

———. "Hemans and Home: Victorianism, Feminine 'Internal Enemies', and the Domestication of National Identity." *PMLA* 109, no. 2 (1994): 238–53.

———. "Receiving the Legend, Rethinking the Writer." In *Romanticism and Women Poets: Opening the Doors of Reception*, ed. Harriet Linkin and Stephen Behrendt, 242–59. Lexington: University Press of Kentucky, 1999.

Lyons, Paul. "From Man-Eaters to Spam-Eaters: Literary Tourism and the Discourse of Cannibalism from Herman Melville to Paul Theroux." *Arizona Quarterly* 52, no. 2 (1995): 33–62.

MacCannell, Dean. *The Tourist: A New Theory of the Leisure Class.* New York, Schocken Books, 1976.

MacDonald, R. *The Language of Empire: Myths and Metaphors of Imperialism, 1880–1918.* New York, Manchester University Press, 1994.

MacKay, Carol Hanbery, ed. *Dramatic Dickens.* New York: St. Martin's Press, 1989.

MacLaren, Ian. "Exploration/Travel Literature and the Evolution of the Author." *International Journal of Canadian Studies* 5 (1992): 39–68.

———. "Tracing One Discontinuous Line through the Poetry of the Northwest Passage." *Canadian Poetry* 39 (1995): 7–48.

Makdisi, Saree. *Romantic Imperialism: Universal Empire and the Culture of Modernity.* Cambridge: Cambridge University Press, 1998.

Malchow, H. L. *Gothic Images of Race in Nineteenth-Century Britain.* Stanford: Stanford University Press, 1996.

Marcus, S. "Frankenstein: Myths of Scientific and Medical Knowledge and Stories of Human Relations." *Southern Review* 38, no. 1 (2002): 188–201.

Markham, Clements R. *Franklin's Footsteps; A Sketch of Greenland, along the Shores of Which His Expedition Passed, and of the Parry Isles, Where the Last Traces of It Were Found.* London: Chapman and Hall, 1853.

Marlow, J. E. "English Cannibalism: Dickens after 1859." *Studies in English Literature* 23 (1983): 647–66.

———. "The Fate of Sir John Franklin: Three Phases of Response in Victorian Periodicals." *Victorian Periodicals Review* 15 (1982): 3–11.

———. "Sir John Franklin, Mr. Charles Dickens, and the Solitary Monster." *Dickens Studies Newsletter* 12 (December 1981): 97–103.

Massey, Doreen. *Space, Place, and Gender*. Minneapolis: University of Minnesota Press, 1994.

Matless, D. *Landscape and Englishness*. London: Reaktion Books, 1998.

Mayer, T. *Gender Ironies of Nationalism : Sexing the Nation*. London: Routledge, 2000.

McClintock, Anne. *Imperial Leather: Race, Gender, and Sexuality in the Colonial Contest*. New York: Routledge, 1995.

McDayter, Gislaine, Guinn Batten, and Barry Milligan eds. *Romantic Generations: Essays in Honor of Robert F. Gleckner*. Lewisburg, PA: Bucknell University Press, 2001.

McGavran, James H. "'Insurmountable Barriers to Our Union': Homosocial Male Bonding, Homosexual Panic, and Death on the Ice in *Frankenstein*." *European Romantic Review* 11, no. 1 (2000): 46–67.

McInerney, Peter K. *Time and Experience*. Philadelphia: Temple University Press, 1991.

McWilliam, Rohan. *Popular Politics in Nineteenth-Century England*. New York: Routledge, 1998.

Meisel, Martin. *Realizations: Narrative, Pictorial, and Theatrical Arts in Nineteenth-Century England*. Princeton: Princeton University Press, 1983.

Mellor, Anne K. "The Female Poet and the Poetess: Two Traditions of Women's Poetry, 1780–1830." *Studies in Romanticism* 36 (1997): 261–76.

———. "A Feminist Critique of Science." In *One Culture: Essays in Science and Literature*, ed. George Levine. Madison: University of Wisconsin Press, 1987.

———. "*Frankenstein*, Racial Science, and the Yellow Peril." *Nineteenth-Century Contexts* 23 (2001): 1–28.

———. *Mary Shelley: Her Life, Her Fiction, Her Monsters*. New York: Methuen, 1988.

———. *Mothers of the Nation: Women's Political Writing in England, 1780–1830*. Bloomington: Indiana University Press, 2000.

———. *Romanticism and Gender*. New York: Routledge, 1993.

Meyer, Susan. *Imperialism at Home: Race and Victorian Women's Fiction*. Ithaca: Cornell University Press, 1996.

Michie, Elsie B. *Outside the Pale: Cultural Exclusion, Gender Difference, and the Victorian Woman Writer*. Ithaca, NY: Cornell University Press, 1993.

———, ed. *Charlotte Brontë's Jane Eyre: A Casebook*. Oxford: Oxford University Press, 2006.

Midgley, Claire. *Gender and Imperialism*. Manchester: Manchester University Press, 1998.

Mighall, Robert. *A Geography of Victorian Gothic Fiction*. Oxford: Oxford University Press, 1999.

Miller, D. A. *The Novel and the Police*. Berkeley: University of California Press, 1988.

Morgan, Susan. *Place Matters: Gendered Geography in Victorian Women's Travel Books about Southeast Asia*. New Brunswick: Rutgers University Press, 1996.

Morley, Henry. "Official Patriotism." *Household Words* 15 (1857): 385–91.

———. "Our Phantom Ship Among The Ice." *Household Words* 3 (1851): 66–72.

———. "Unspotted Snow." *Household Words* 8 (1853): 241–46.

Moss, John. *Patterns of Isolation in English Canadian Fiction*. Toronto: University of Toronto Press, 1974.

Nayder, Lillian. "The Cannibal, The Nurse, and The Cook in Dickens's *The Frozen Deep*." *Victorian Literature and Culture* 19 (1991): 1–24.

———. *Unequal Partners: Charles Dickens, Wilkie Collins, and Victorian Authorship*. Ithaca: Cornell University Press, 2002.

Neatby, Leslie H. *The Search for Franklin*. New York: Walker, 1970.

Nelson, Victoria. *The Secret Life of Puppets*. Cambridge: Harvard University Press, 2001.

Nerlich, Michael. *The Ideology of Adventure: Studies in Modern Consciousness 1100–1750*. Translated by Ruth Crowley. Minneapolis: University of Minnesota Press, 1987.

Newman, Gerald. *The Rise of English Nationalism: A Cultural History, 1740–1830*. New York: St. Martin's Press, 1997.

Newman, Peter C. *Company of Adventurers*. London: Penguin Books, vols 1–3, 1985, 1987, 1991).

Nussbaum, Felicity. *Torrid Zones: Maternity, Sexuality, and Empire in Eighteenth-Century English Narratives*. Baltimore: Johns Hopkins University Press, 1995.

Oliphant, Margaret. "Sensation Novels." *Blackwood's Magazine* 91 (1862): 565–72.

Palmer, William J. *Dickens and New Historicism*. New York: St. Martin's Press, 1997.

Parker, Andres, M. Russo et al., eds. *Nationalisms and Sexualities*. New York: Routledge, 1992.

Parker, Christopher. "Race and Empire in the Stories of R. M. Ballantyne." In *Literature and Imperialism*, ed. Robert Giddings, 44–63. New York: St. Martin's Press, 1991.

————, ed. *Gender Roles and Sexuality in Victorian Literature*. Brookfield, VT: Ashgate Publishing Company, 1995.

Parry, Benita. *Conrad and Imperialism: Ideological Boundaries and Visionary Frontiers*. London: Macmillan, 1989.

Peck, John. *Maritime Fiction: Sailors and the Sea in British and American Novels*. New York: Palgrave, 2001.

Perera, Suvendrini. *Reaches of Empire: The English Novel from Edgeworth to Dickens*. New York: Columbia University Press, 1991.

Peters, Catherine. *The King of Inventors A Life of Wilkie Collins*. Princeton: Princeton University Press, 1991.

Phegley, Jennifer. *Educating the Proper Woman Reader: Victorian Family Literary Magazines and the Cultural Health of the Nation*. Columbus: The Ohio State University Press, 2004).

Phillips, Richard. *Mapping Men and Empire: a Geography of Adventure*. New York: Routledge, 1997.

Phillips, R. S. "The Language of Images in Geography." *Progress in Human Geography* 17, no. 2 (1993): 180–94.

Phillipson, N. T. "Nationalism and Ideology." In *Government and Nationalism in Scotland*, ed. J. N. Wolfe, 167–88. Edinburgh: Edinburgh University Press, 1968.

Poovey, Mary. *Making a Social Body: British Cultural Formation, 1830–1864*. Chicago: University of Chicago Press, 1995.

————. *The Proper Lady and the Woman Writer*. Chicago: University of Chicago Press, 1984.

————. *Uneven Developments: The Ideological Work of Gender in Mid-Victorian England*. Chicago: University of Chicago Press, 1988.

Porden, Eleanor Anne. *The Arctic Expeditions, a poem*. London: John Murray, 1818.

————. *The Veils; or the Triumph of Constancy*. London, John Murray, 1815.

Porter, Roy and Mikulás Teich. *Romanticism in National Context*. Cambridge: Cambridge University Press, 1988.

Postans, R. B. "Red Rockets." *Household Words* (1856): 534–35.

Pratt, Mary-Louise. *Imperial Eyes: Travel Writing and Transculturation*. New York: Routledge, 1992.

Pykett, Lyn, ed. *Wilkie Collins*. New York: St. Martin's Press, 1998.

————. *The "Improper" Feminine: The Woman's Sensation Novel and the New Woman's Writing*. London: Routledge, 1992.

————. *The Sensation Novel from The Woman in White to The Moonstone*. Plymouth: Northcote, 1994.

Quayle, Eric. *Ballantyne the Brave: A Victorian Writer and His Family*. London: Rupert Hart-Davis, 1967.

———. *R. M. Ballantyne: A Bibliography of First Editions*. London: Rupert Hart-Davis, 1968.

Rae, John. "Report to the Secretary of the Admiralty." *The Times*, 23 October 1854: 7.

———. "The Fate of Sir John Franklin." *London Times*, 7 November 1854: 8.

———. "Dr. Rae's Report." *Household Words* 10 (23 December 1854): 457–59.

———. "Sir John Franklin and His Crews." *Household Words* 11 (3 February 1855): 12–20.

Rahill, Frank. *The World of Melodrama*. University Park,: University of Pennsylvania Press, 1967.

Rance, Nicholas. *Wilkie Collins and Other Sensation Novelists*. Rutherford, NJ: Fairleigh Dickinson University Press, 1991.

Randel, F. V. "The Political Geography of Horror in Mary Shelley's *Frankenstein*." *ELH* 7 (2003): 465–91.

Ranford, B. "Bones of Contention." *Equinox* 74 (1994): 69–87.

Rauch, Alan. *Useful Knowledge: The Victorians, Morality, and the March of Intellect*. Durham: Duke University Press, 2001.

Renan, Ernst. "Qu'est-ce qu'une nation?" Translated by Martin Thom. In *Nation and Narration*, ed. Homi Bhabha, 8–22. London: Routledge, 1990.

Reynolds, Mark. *The Realms of Verse, 1830–1870: English Poetry in a Time of Nation-Building*. New York: Oxford University Press, 2001.

Rich, E. E., ed. *John Rae's Correspondence with the Hudson's Bay Company on Arctic Exploration, 1844–1855*. London: The Hudson's Bay Record Society, 1953.

Richard, Jessica. "'A Paradise of My Own Creation': *Frankenstein* and the Improbable Romance of Polar Exploration." *Nineteenth-Century Contexts* 25, no. 4 (2003): 295–314.

Richards, Thomas. *The Imperial Archive: Knowledge and the Fantasy of Empire*. New York: Verso, 1993.

Ricou, Laurence R. *Vertical Man, Horizontal World; Man and Landscape in Canadian Prairie Fiction*. Vancouver, BC: University of British Columbia Press, 1973.

Riffenburgh, Beau. *The Myth of the Explorer*. London: Wiley, 1993.

Roach, Joseph. *The Player's Passion*. Ann Arbor: University of Michigan Press, 1993.

————. "Vicarious: Theater and the Rise of Synthetic Experience." In *Theorizing Practice: Redefining Theatre History*, ed. W. B. Worthen with Peter Holland, 120–35. New York: Palgrave Macmillan, 2003.

Robbins, Keith. *Nineteenth-Century Britain: England, Scotland, and Wales; The Making of a Nation*. Oxford: Oxford University Press, 1988.

Robinson, Charles E. *The Frankenstein Notebooks*. New York: Garland, 1996.

Rogers, Philip. "My Word Is Error: Jane Eyre and Colonial Exculpation." *Dickens Studies Annual* 34 (2004): 329–50.

————. "Tory Brontë: *Shirley* and the 'Man.'" *Nineteenth-Century Literature* 58, no. 2 (2003): 141–75.

Roper, Michael, and John Tosh, eds. *Manful Assertions Masculinities in Britain since 1800*. New York: Routledge, 1991.

Rosenberg, Rosalind. *Beyond Separate Spheres: Intellectual Roots of Modern Feminism*. New Haven: Yale University Press, 1982.

Ross, Marlon. *The Contours of Masculine Desire: Romanticism and the Rise of Women's Poetry*. New York: Oxford University Press, 1989.

Rouse, Joseph. *Knowledge and Power: Toward a Political Philosophy of Science*. Ithaca: Cornell University Press, 1987.

Rowell, George. *The Victorian Theatre 1792–1914, A Survey*. Cambridge: Cambridge University Press, 1978.

Ruskin, John. *Fiction, Fair and Foul*. New York: John W. Lovell Company, 1890.

Said, Edward. *Culture and Imperialism*. New York: Alfred A. Knopf, 1993.

————. *Orientalism*. New York: Vintage Books, 1979.

Samuel, Raphael, ed. *Patriotism: The Making and Unmaking of British National Identity*. London: Routledge, 1989.

Sanday, Peggy Reeves. *Divine Hunger: Cannibalism as a Cultural System*. Cambridge: Cambridge University Press, 1986.

Saul, John. "Enduring Themes? John Moss, the Arctic and the Crisis in Representation." *Studies in Canadian Literature* 24, no. 1 (1999): 93–108.

Schlicke, Paul. *Dickens and Popular Entertainment*. London: Allen and Unwin, 1985.

Schmitt, Cannon. *Alien Nation: Nineteenth-Century Gothic Fictions and English Nationality*. Philadelphia: University of Pennsylvania Press, 1997.

Scott, Joan Wallach. *Gender and the Politics of History*. New York: Columbia University Press, 1999.

Segwick, Eve Kosofsky. *Between Men: English Literature and Male Homosocial Desire*. New York: Columbia University Press, 1985.

Selby, J. "Ballantyne and the Fur Traders." *Canadian Literature* 18 (1963): 40–46.

Seltzer, Mark. *Bodies and Machines*. New York: Routledge, 1982.

Seward, Anna. *The Poetical Works of Anna Seward*. Edinburgh: James Ballantyne, 1810.

Sharpe, Jenny. *Allegories of Empire: The Figure of Woman in the Colonial Text*. Minneapolis: University of Minnesota Press, 1993.

Shelley, Mary *Collected Tales and Stories*. Baltimore: Johns Hopkins Press, 1976.

———. *Frankenstein*. ed. Johanna M. Smith. Boston: Bedford Books of St. Martin's Press, 1992.

Shepherd, Simon. "Pauses of Mutual Agitation." In *Melodrama: Stage, Picture, Screen*, ed. Jacky Bratton, Jim Cook, Christine Gledhill. London: British Film Institute, 1994.

Shields, Rob. *Places on the Margin: Alternative Geographies of Modernity*. New York: Routledge, 1991.

Shohat, Elaine. "Imagining Terra Incognita: The Disciplinary gaze of Empire." *Public Culture* 3, no. 2 (1991): 41–70.

Simmonds, P. L. *The Arctic Regions, and Polar Discoveries During the Nineteenth Century: with the Discoveries Made by Captain McClintock as to the Fate of the Franklin Expedition*. London: Routledge, Warne, and Routledge, 1860.

Sinha, Mrinilini. "Nations in an Imperial Crucible." In *Gender and Empire*, ed. Philippa Levine, 181–202. Oxford: Oxford University Press, 2004.

Smiles, Samuel. *Duty*. Chicago: Belford, Clarke and Co., 1881.

Smith, Johanna. *Mary Shelley*. New York: Twayne, 1996.

Smith, Neil. "Geography, Empire, and Social Theory." *Progress in Human Geography* 18, no. 4 (1994): 491–500.

Spacks, Patricia Meyer. "Reflecting Women." *Yale Review* 63 (Autumn 1973): 27–30.

Spivak, Gayatri Chakravorty. "Can the Subaltern Speak?" In *Marxism and the Interpretation of Culture*, ed. Cary Nelson and Lawrence Grossberg, 271–313. Urbana: University of Illinois Press, 1988.

———. *In Other Worlds: Essays in Cultural Politics*. New York: Methuen, 1987.

———. *Outside in the Teaching Machine*. New York: Routledge, 1990.

————. "Three Women's Texts and a Critique of Imperialism." *Critical Inquiry* 12 (1985): 243–61.

Spufford, Francis. *I May Be Sometime: Ice and the English Imagination.* London: Faber and Faber, 1996.

Spurr, David. *The Rhetoric of Empire: Colonial Discourse in Journalism, Travel Writing, and Imperial Administration.* Durham: Duke University Press, 1993.

Southey, Robert. *The Life of Nelson.* London: Cassell, 1909.

Sterrenberg, Lee. "Psycholanalysis and the Iconography of Revolution." *Victorian Studies* 19 (December 1975): 241–64.

Stewart, Susan. *On Longing: Narratives of the Miniature, the Gigantic, the Souvenir, the Collection.* Durham, NC: Duke University Press, 1993.

————. "Scandals of the Ballad." *Representations* 32 (1990): 134–56.

Stitt, Megan Perigoe. *Metaphors of Change: The Language of Nineteenth-Century Fiction.* Oxford: Clarendon Press, 1998.

Stoler, Ann Laura. *Carnal Knowledge and Imperial Power: Race and the Intimate in Colonial Rule.* Berkeley: University of California Press, 2002.

————. *Race and the Education of Desire: Foucault's History of Sexuality and the Colonial Order of Things.* Durham: Duke University Press, 1995.

Stone, Harry. *The Night Side of Dickens: Cannibalism, Passion, Necessity.* Columbus: The University of Ohio Press, 1994.

————, ed. *The Uncollected Writings of Charles Dickens: 'Household Words', 1850–1859.* Bloomington: Indiana University Press, 1968.

Stone, Ian R. "'The Contents of the Kettles': Charles Dickens, John Rae, and Cannibalism on the 1845 Franklin Expedition." *Dickensian* 83, no. 1 (1987): 7–15.

Taussig, Michael T. *Mimesis and Alterity: A Particular History of the Senses.* New York: Routledge, 1993.

Taylor, George. *Players and Performance in the Victorian Theatre.* Manchester: Manchester University Press, 1989.

Taylor, Jenny Bourne. *In the Secret Theatre of Home: Wilkie Collins, Sensation Narrative, and Nineteenth-Century Psychology.* New York: Routledge, 1988.

Thompson, Andrew. *Imperial Britain. The Empire in British Politics, c. 1880–1932.* New York: Longman, 2000.

Tierney, John. "Explornography." *New York Times Magazine:* July 26, 1998.

Thompson, James. *The Seasons* [microform]. Dublin: John Enslow, 1770.

Tillotson, John. *Adventures in the Ice*. London: James Hogg and Son, 1869.

Todd, Anthea. "Collaborating in Open Boats: Dickens, Collins, Franklin, and Bligh." *Victorian Studies* 42, no. 2 (2000): 201–25.

Togovnick, Marlene. *Gone Primitive: Savage Intellects, Modern Lives*. Chicago: University of Chicago Press, 1990.

Tompkins, Jane P. *Sensational Designs: The Cultural Work of American Fiction, 1790–1860*. New York: Oxford University Press, 1986.

Tosh, John. "The Old Adam and the New Man: Emerging Themes in the History of English Masculinities, 1750–1850." In *Manliness and Masculinities in Nineteenth-Century Britain*, ed. Michael Roper and John Tosh, 61–82. New York: Routledge, 2005.

———. "Hegemonic Masculinity and the History of Gender." In *Masculinities in Politics and War: Gendering Modern History*, ed. Stefan Dudink, Karen Hagemann, and John Tosh, 41–58. Manchester: Manchester University Press, 2004.

Trelawney, Edward J. *Adventures of a Younger Son*. London: T. Fisher Unwin, 1890.

Tromp, Marlene. *The Private Rod: Marital Violence, Sensation, and the Law in Victorian Britain*. Charlottesville: University Press of Virginia, 2000.

Van Den Abeele, Georges. *Travel as Metaphor*. Minneapolis: University of Minnesota Press, 1992.

Vaughan, Richard. *The Arctic: A History*. Dover, NH: A. Sutton, 1994.

Vicinus, Martha, ed. *Suffer and Be Still: Women in the Victorian Age*. Bloomington: University of Indiana Press, 1972.

Vlasopolos, Anca. "*Frankenstein's* Hidden Skeleton: The Psycho-Politics of Oppression." *Science-Fiction Studies* 10, no. 2 (1983): 125–36.

Vlock, Deborah. *Dickens, Novel Reading, and Victorian Popular Theatre*. Cambridge: Cambridge University Press, 1998.

Walby, Sylvia. *Theorizing Patriarchy*. Oxford: B. Blackwell, 1990.

———. *Gender Transformations*. London: Routledge, 1997.

———. "Woman and Nation." In *Mapping the Nation*, ed. Gopal Balakrishnan, 235–54. New York: Verso, 1996.

Watson, Francis. *The Year of the Wombat, England: 1857*. New York: Harper and Row, 1974.

Watt, Ian. *Conrad in the Nineteenth Century*. Berkeley: University of California Press, 1979.

———. "Oral Dickens." *Dickens Studies Annual* 3 (1974): 165–81.

Weiskel, Thomas. *The Romantic Sublime: Studies in the Structure and Psychology of Transcendence.* Baltimore: Johns Hopkins University Press, 1976.

White, Andrea. *Joseph Conrad and the Adventure Tradition: Constructing and Deconstructing the Imperial Subject.* New York: Cambridge University Press, 1993.

Wiley, Michael. *Romantic Geography: Wordsworth and Anglo-European Spaces.* New York: St. Martin's Press, 1998.

Williams, Raymond. *Culture and Society 1780–1950.* New York: Columbia University Press, 1958.

———. *The Country and the City.* Oxford: Oxford University Press, 1973.

Wilson, Eric G. *The Spiritual History of Ice: Romanticism, Science, and the Imagination.* New York: Palgrave Macmillan, 2003.

Young, E. R. *Winter Adventures of Three Boys in the Great Lone Land.* London: Robert Cullen, 1899.

Young, Robert J. C. *Colonial Desire: Hybridity in Theory, Culture, and Race.* London: Routledge, 1995.

———. *Postcolonialism: An Historical Introduction.* Oxford: Blackwell Publishers, 2001.

———. *White Mythologies: Writing History and the West.* London: Routledge, 1990.

Youngquist, Paul. *Monstrosities: Bodies and British Romanticism.* Minneapolis: University of Minnesota Press, 2003.

Yuval-Davis, Nira. *Gender and Nation.* London: Sage Publications, 1997.

———, and Floya Anthias, eds. *Woman—Nation—State.* New York: St. Martin's Press, 1989.

Zantop, Susanne. *Colonial Fantasies: Conquest, Family, and Nation in Pre-Colonial Germany, 1770–1870.* Durham: Duke University Press, 1997.

INDEX